D1798225

ENGLISH WITS

Edited by Leonard Russell

THE SATURDAY BOOK
Volumes 1, 2 and 3: 12*s*. 6*d*. net each

PARODY PARTY
New and cheaper edition: 5s. net

PRESS GANG!
CRAZY WORLD CHRONICLE
New and cheaper edition: 5s. net

ENGLISH WITS

Edited by LEONARD RUSSELL with
contributions by

JAMES AGATE
CAMPBELL DIXON
JOHN GORE
W. W. HADLEY
HAROLD HOBSON
GERARD HOPKINS
RONALD A. KNOX
D. B. WYNDHAM LEWIS
ROBERT LYND
DESMOND MACCARTHY
ERNEST NEWMAN
DILYS POWELL
A. J. A. SYMONS
OLGA VENN

HUTCHINSON & CO. (Publishers) LTD.
LONDON :: NEW YORK :: MELBOURNE

To DILYS

First Impression .	*November 1940*
Second Impression	*December 1940*
Third Impression	*January 1941*

PRINTED IN
GREAT BRITAIN,
AT THE ANCHOR
PRESS, TIPTREE,
:: ESSEX ::

INTRODUCTORY NOTE

EDITOR: You have heard of the man who couldn't see a butterfly without thinking of the wheel?

FRIEND: No.

EDITOR: Oh! Well, I was about to identify him as that inferior writer who has discussed wit, humour and so on under not a few different names. Sometimes you will find him inquiring into the nature of laughter, and that, of course, is no laughing matter. Sometimes he will treat of his subject on a system, but too often it resembles the system of a gambler at the tables—it has to be kept secret. Even from his readers. Occasionally he will define wit and cite examples: this is obscurity illustrated by obscurity.

FRIEND: May I ask why he is mentioned at all?

EDITOR: To draw your attention to the superior understanding of the authors of *English Wits*, who know quite well that these problems have taxed many great intelligences from Aristotle downwards.

FRIEND: I see. Then they have not attempted to enclose wit within a theory or a definition?

EDITOR: No. That, they said, is a job for the editor.

FRIEND: Remarkable unanimity!

EDITOR: Not present, unhappily, throughout all our traffic. There is no passion in human nature, I have discovered, as the passion to deny wit to another's favourite wit.

FRIEND: Myself, I may claim to enjoy wit in its many shapes and appearances as I enjoy a fine morning. No one wants to subtilize a fine morning.

EDITOR: Exactly! Because you enjoy, shall we say, Wilde you wouldn't wish to exclude from the company of English wits somebody utterly different—say, Lamb.

FRIEND: Oh, but I should! Lamb was a humorist, not a wit.

EDITOR: The strength of the passion! No, I won't try to define wit—I would as soon try to define a fine morning. What I will do is recall briefly one or two of the more celebrated discourses on it. To Locke wit lay mostly in a quick association of ideas directed to showing resemblances in things, this producing pleasant pictures and agreeable visions in the fancy. To Dryden it was merely a propriety of thoughts and words. Hazlitt said it illustrated and heightened the absurdities of life by finding some sudden and unexpected likeness or opposition of one thing to another. Sydney Smith thought it arose from the discovery of similarity in two things in which no similarity was suspected. Oh yes, and there are the lexicographers, who look at stopped watches and tell us the time as it used to be.

FRIEND: You mean?

EDITOR: They give us some very happy definitions of the antiquated forms of the word. But I forget Chesterton, who——

FRIEND: Wait! I am trying to elucidate all those elucidations.

EDITOR: Sorry. But Chesterton—I think it is Chesterton—is easier. Wit, he said, is reason on its judgment seat; offenders are sentenced but the judge is untouched. Whereas humour always has in it some idea of the humorist himself being entangled in the difficulties and contradictions of human life.

FRIEND: Then it is as I say with Lamb. He is a humorist because he is very much of this imperfect world. Surely we never find Lamb wearing the ermine?

EDITOR: The simple truth is that he is both wit and humorist. To confound the two is, of course, a vulgar error, but it is not easy to understand why wit and humour are always placed in opposition. Most wit—most English wit—is irrigated by humour: a trickle or a conduit-pipe. Not the humour of the thump on the back, of course, but something nearer humour of the mind. The trouble with Lamb, although this isn't strictly to the point, is that he is undervalued today because the gentle Elia nonsense with which he has been surrounded obscures his true personality. Judge for yourself on the evidence of this book.

FRIEND: All right. But those definitions convey no sense of that brilliant and sharp quality one associates with wit.

EDITOR: Of wit as a shining sword? In an old meaning the word signified intellectual excellence. Nowadays it seems to be applied almost exclusively to what is called *repartee.* Let us say that the major wits wield the sword for truth's sake and the minor merely to dazzle the passers-by. Or, with Hazlitt, that verbal and accidental strokes are not the best and most lasting.

FRIEND: What does verbal and accidental mean?

EDITOR: Listen to the story of the Prince Regent and one Jack Towers. While out walking in Portsmouth the Regent saw Towers across the way, and called out, "Hullo, Towers! I hear you are the greatest blackguard in the place." Towers answered, bowing, "I hope your Royal Highness has not come here to take away my reputation." Clever, sharp, unanswerable—but really not worth repeating. Yet so narrow is the current acceptance of wit that the style and form of the remark would pass pretty generally as the style and form for all wit—in reality, as I say, *repartee.*

FRIEND: You overstate, I think.

EDITOR: Perhaps. All the same, you mustn't expect the subjects of this book to be for ever on the bubble, like soda-water.

FRIEND: No, no; I am aware, as I said just now, that wit has many shapes and appearances.

EDITOR: So much so that the diversity of this book defeats synthesis. Pope and Johnson have intellectual excellence and a supreme gift of epigrammatic style. Wilde and Whistler are what Arthur Symons calls artists in attitudes. Sydney Smith works to a method. Hook, Lamb, and Sheridan wear a wonderfully unpremeditated air. Wilkes-and-Liberty and Labouchere are audaciously amusing. No need for me to pigeonhole Max Beerbohm, Shaw, "Saki", Mary Russell Mitford. Or to distribute first and second classes by arranging the entire group in order of merit. But I will say that first-class spoken wit is a greater achievement than first-class literary wit. Even supposing that your famous talker prepares his remarks, as Swift did, by lying abed till eleven and thinking of wit for the day, they will be savourless unless artfully delivered. So to the talker's gift of thoughts and words is added a talent for acting—a very enviable talent. You know how it is when you or I say a good thing at table. Somebody murmurs, "Sorry," and passes the salt.

FRIEND: Really? Then I shan't come to you for wit in a couple of easy lessons. By the way, why have you left out Congreve, and Chesterfield, and Disraeli, and Foote, and Hood, and Brummell?

EDITOR: Some Continental critic once complained that literary history has treated Congreve in a very stepmotherly fashion, and the neglect unfortunately continues. Never mind, we will get him into the second volume of *English Wits*, with Chesterfield, the dandies, and others. But Foote? Fond as I am of that uproarious rascal, I rather think he wielded not a sword but a cudgel. All the same, with the possible exception of Hook, there has been no one quite like him for setting the table on a roar. Do you know the story of his meeting with a country gentleman who had just buried a relative, an attorney? "Why, do you bury your attorneys here?" says Foote. "Yes, to be sure. How else?" "Oh, we never do that in London." "But how do you manage, then?" "Why, when the patient happens to die, we lay him out overnight in a room by himself, lock the door, throw open the sash, and in the morning he is entirely off." "Indeed, what becomes of him?" "Why, that we cannot exactly tell. All we know is, there's a strong smell of brimstone in the room next morning!" But on the whole Foote's acted wit died with its context—yet for that matter so did Hook's. We must consider Foote next time.

FRIEND: And Hood?

EDITOR: So far no Hood. People tell me that he was one of the better minor wits, but whenever I come across him I discover nothing but this sort of grievousness: "I wonder none of the quack doctors have got up a nostrum against sea-sickness. It would be sure, one would think, of a sail. . . . Passenger: 'Well, Doctor, I have tried your sea-sick remedy.' Doctor: 'Well, and how did it turn out?' " No, not Hood. The knitting-needle is his weapon.

FRIEND: Anything else?

EDITOR: Merely that these studies of English wits are not cut to a pattern. Sometimes the emphasis falls on biography, sometimes on works. Oh yes, and death to any old meticulous who quarrels with the word English in the title or refuses to acknowledge that Whistler was English by adoption!

FRIEND: Well, it *is* a fine morning.

EDITOR: You must be off to enjoy it. Good-bye.

LEONARD RUSSELL.

September 1940.

I have to thank MR. VYVYAN HOLLAND, JOHN LANE THE BODLEY HEAD LTD., *and* WILLIAM HEINEMANN LTD., *for permission to quote from the works of Oscar Wilde, "Saki", and Sir Max Beerbohm respectively.*

L. R.

CONTENTS

PAGE

ALEXANDER POPE
Dilys Powell 9

DR. JOHNSON
Ronald A. Knox 20

OSCAR WILDE
Desmond MacCarthy 29

WHISTLER
D. B. Wyndham Lewis 39

SYDNEY SMITH
Ernest Newman 51

THEODORE HOOK
A. J. A. Symons 61

CHARLES LAMB
Robert Lynd 73

SHERIDAN
Campbell Dixon 81

JOHN WILKES
Olga Venn 93

HENRY LABOUCHERE
W. W. Hadley 111

MAX BEERBOHM
Gerard Hopkins 120

GEORGE BERNARD SHAW
Harold Hobson 129

"SAKI"
John Gore 141

MARY RUSSELL MITFORD
James Agate 150

ALEXANDER POPE

DILYS POWELL

IN HIS RETREAT THE DYING MAN AWAITS THE END WITH COMPOSURE AND dignity. "I am so certain of the soul's being immortal," says the musical voice, "that I seem to feel it within me as it were by intuition." The long disease is over. Three days before the last he asks to be brought to the table where his friends are sitting at dinner; immortality, they can see, already shrouds him, and: "Lord, have mercy upon us, this is quite an Egyptian feast!" one of them exclaims, shocked into a macabre witticism. For a few weeks now his words have held a kind of gay serenity. When the doctor assures him of the improvement in his breathing, the strength of his pulse: "Here am I," he says, "dying of a hundred good symptoms!" In farewell he sends round copies of his Ethic Epistles: "Here am I, like Socrates, distributing my morality among my friends, just as I am dying." The trivialities of the material recede. "What's that?" he asks a friend, pointing, his large melancholy eyes gazing steadily into the air; then softly, smiling, "'Twas a vision." Life dwindles and fades; the lingerer murmurs of vanity, innocent love, virtue, friendship. At last he is asked if a priest shall be fetched. "I do not suppose that is essential," he replies, "but it will look right; and I heartily thank you for putting me in mind of it." In the sad assembly of friends the churchman and the man of the world, the deist, mourn together. "I never in my life knew a man that had so tender a heart for his particular friends, or a more general friendship for mankind. . . . I have known him these thirty years: and value myself more for that man's love, than ——" The deist is overcome, and Bolingbroke—for it is he—bursts into tears.

It is the model Christian deathbed of the eighteenth century; how different from the rakish end of Wycherley, marrying on his deathbed "to plague his damned nephew", how infinitely more respectable this readiness to die than the reluctance of Kneller, who, when assured that he would go to a better place, retorts: "Ah, my good friend, I wish God would let me stay at Whitton!" Who then is the hero, who is this mild and exemplary moralist? It is Alexander Pope: Pope "the wicked wasp of Twickenham"; the "hunchback'd Toad", the "squab, short gentleman" whose form, "tho' it should be that of downright Monkey", could not differ so much from human shape "as his immaterial unthinking part does from human Understanding"; in short, the "malignant and ungenerous heart. . . base enough to assume the mask of a moralist, in order to decry human nature, and to give a decent vent to his hatred of man and womankind." The calm of the death-room is impermanent. "The life of a Wit," said Pope, "is a warfare upon earth." The warfare outlasts the life. Soon Bolingbroke dries his tears and accuses his dead friend of treachery; and Bishop Warburton, bounding to the defence, is called the most Impudent Man living for his pains. The warfare grumbles on through the second half of the eighteenth century, then bursts out with a bellow at the beginning of the nineteenth. Bowles, pupil of the Wartons, denigrates Pope, Byron reaffirms that Pope is "the great moral poet of all times, of all climes, of all feelings, of all stages of existence". The argument begins to flounder in the tricky ground of sexual morality, and Bowles is censorious of Pope's relations with his life-long friend Martha Blount; though, he adds dejectedly, "whatever there might be of criminality in the connexion, it did not take place till the 'hey-day' of youth was over". Campbell, Gilchrist, Isaac Disraeli join battle; in the shindy the combatants are infected with Dunciad manners, and Gilchrist, rebutting Bowles, speaks of "the pruriency with which his nose is laid to the ground"; while Hazlitt takes a smack at Byron's *pribble-prabble*. A few years more, and Macaulay is snarling and roaring in his fine detestable prose: "A distorted and diseased body, tenanted by a yet more distorted and diseased mind; spite and envy thinly disguised by sentiments as benevolent and noble as those which Sir Peter Teazle admired in Mr. Joseph Surface: a feeble, sickly licentiousness; an odious love of filthy and noisome images"—Lord Hervey, Lady Mary Wortley Montagu, Dennis himself could not have bettered the indictment. And still it goes on; still the writer whose Iliad, said Johnson, "tuned the English tongue" (or, according to Coleridge, was "the main source of our *pseudo*-poetic diction"), must be defended not only for his poetry but also for his life. The Dreyfus case of English literature proceeds.

2

But why this controversy over a writer who claimed no innovations, why this concentration of censure on a man whose life was, after all, no more maleficent than that of a hundred other public figures? The mind of sad Cowper was as diseased; Macaulay himself was as spiteful; Shakespeare as licentious; and the Bible far filthier. The fact is that Pope had committed the sin against the English Ghost of being a wit. The English fear, not emotion, but reason; they mistrust, not poetry, but intellect; Nature they love, and to Hell with Art. Mr. Tillotson* says that the Romantics "seem to have preferred any accidental assemblage of 'natural objects'—even if the result of what the insurance companies would call an 'act of God'—to the art of man". Much Pater has run under the bridge since the Romantics. But the aversion from art, the fear of the intellect, persist; in England the word 'intellectual' is still a term of abuse; and since wit is a by-product of the intellect, to be witty is to be subversive, dangerous, almost an enemy alien.

For once, however, a great wit was born into an era when, as the result of a complex train of social, political and religious causes, the intellect was not suspect, and the exercise of the critical reason was as much applauded as today the eye of a Bradman or the punch of a Louis. Pope, born in 1688 and dying in 1744, complained of perpetual warfare. But the warfare was after his own heart. Indeed, he was fortunate in decorating an age whose temper so aptly matched the mingled melancholy and violence of his own mind; an age, moreover, when the man of letters overtopped the demagogue, and the translator of the Iliad moved in a blaze of celebrity scarcely outshone by the victor of Blenheim.

* "On the Poetry of Pope." (Clarendon Press.)

Macaulay remarks that at the time when Addison entered the Commons the cessation of the Press censorship combined with the lack of Parliamentary reports to put writers in a superior position. Speakers were heard by only a few, writers could be read by many; for a space the writer became more important to his political party than the orator. Even for a non-political writer the conditions were favourable. The competition for the attention of the public was not formidable; once that attention had been caught it was not distracted, certainly not from the elegant salacities and the exquisitely-turned insults of Popes' mature genius. The contemporary, the eternal taste for personal abuse was satisfied in his work; and at the same time another taste now lost, forgotten, was satisfied: the taste for fine verse. To be stung by the wasp of Twickenham was the certain way to notoriety: far more certain than, today, the most expensive methods of publicity. An optimistic Alderman, indeed, hinted that he might give four or five thousand pounds for a favourable mention; the poet, however, intimated that he accepted no advertisements. To be lampooned by Pope had all the inconvenience (without, of course, the improbability) of being lampooned by the B.B.C.

The age, then, suited him as well as any age could suit a spirit so irascible. It must be remembered, too, that his warfare was largely private, or, in so far as it was public, it brought him into conflict only with the general faults of mankind, not with the political or religious constitution of his time and country. There was nothing of the revolutionary about Pope; his attitude to the great questions of belief was the conventional attitude of the cultivated society of the day; and when the Essay on Man was accused of heterodoxy he was distressed as well as frightened. He could not bear even that his associates should be suspected of irreligion. One day he overheard Warburton and Hooke discussing Bolingbroke's disbelief of the moral attributes of God. Shocked, he confronted his friend with the charge, which was denied. "I told you," said Pope triumphantly to the others, "I was sure you must be mistaken." The contrast with the great doubting, destructive intelligence of Voltaire is singular. It would be a mistake to suppose that because Pope's moral satire is concentrated in form it is therefore the work of a miniaturist. But his criticism of humanity is local; it has not the universal irony of the Frenchman. The idea of attacking powerful institutions, of undermining respectable beliefs, would have been profoundly alarming to Pope, whose blows, when they were not directed at individual Dunces, were reserved for a highly particularized Dulness. It is true that Voltaire expressed admiration for the Essay on Man. But he was soon to revolt against the complacency of its principles. To its optimism he opposes the irony of "Candide"; against Pope's WHATEVER IS, IS RIGHT he sets the imbecile consolations of Pangloss amid the Lisbon earthquake: ". . . tout ceci est ce qu'il y a de mieux; car, s'il y a un volcan à Lisbonne, il ne pouvait être ailleurs; car il est impossible que les choses ne soient pas où elles sont; car tout est bien." The gulf between the conventional religion of the one and the mischievous contempt for forms of the other is illustrated by the story of Voltaire's affiliation with the Capucins. In 1770 it became necessary to appoint a new temporal father of the order of Capucins for the district of Gex; Voltaire applied for the post, secured it, and found an urchin pleasure in writing letters to his enemy the Bishop of Annecy signed with a cross and his name: "✠ Voltaire, Capucin indigne". "It will look right," said Pope on his deathbed, sending for a priest. To Voltaire also it looked right; but from a very different angle.

But audacious as was Voltaire's assault on so dangerous an opponent as the Church, it was no more audacious than Pope's assault on society. The English aristocracy of the eighteenth century had at least this to their credit, that they took less advantage of their privileges than the aristocracies of the Continental Powers. Voltaire in France was first caned, then imprisoned, for a pert answer; Lytton Strachey points out that in France Pope would hardly have escaped whipping. In England, his only beating was as a child at the hands of a schoolmaster whom he had lampooned. Materially his life passed smoothly enough, in spite of two heavy disabilities: he was a Catholic, a member of a persecuted Church, and so disqualified for public office; and he was crippled by a tubercular infection which resulted in spinal curvature. After the middle of life, says Johnson, he was "so weak as to stand in perpetual need of female attendance; extremely sensible of cold, so that he wore a kind of fur doublet, under a shirt of a very coarse warm linen with fine sleeves. When he rose, he was invested in bodice made of stiff canvas, being scarce able to hold himself erect till they were laced, and he then put on a flannel waistcoat. One side was contracted." There was, according to his Victorian biographers, a third handicap hardly inferior to the others: want of a public-school education. "He knew nothing," says Courthope, "of that manly conflict between equals which does so much to strengthen and correct the character of boys in an English public school." Instead he suffered a desultory education from Catholic priests and Catholic seminaries; and the years which might have been spent in manly conflict between equals were squandered in reading English poetry. At one of the seminaries the child put together a play from Ogilby's Iliad to be acted by his schoolfellows and the gardener, who played Ajax. When he was twelve he wrote part of an epic poem about Deucalion, which "opened under water with a description of the Court of Neptune". "Igad," said an observer, "that young fellow will either be a madman or make a very great poet."

Already as a boy living in Windsor Forest with his parents, a simple loving mother and an indulgent, well-to-do father, a retired linen-draper, he had chosen his way of life. Unguided, he had decided to be a poet; and nothing was to entice him from that way, nothing. All his years he would devote himself to his calling, harnessing his industry, his wit, his sensitiveness, his very vanity and vindictiveness, to the single purpose of excelling as a poet. He might quarrel with his friends, lie, deceive; he never quarrelled with poetry, and his life still conserved its central truth, the artist's truth. At seventeen he began to pay for his single-mindedness. He fell ill from constant study: in a puff of the theatrical melancholy which was characteristic of him he "resolved to give way to his distemper; and sat down calmly, in a full expectation of death in a short time". But such a display of Roman resignation must not pass unhonoured. He wrote to his friends to acquaint them with his resolution. One of them had the sense to consult a doctor, who advised less work and more riding. The expiring boy lived to be fifty-six.

No doubt the intellectual concentration in which his boyhood was spent affected his health and hastened his deformity. But his precocity put him into touch with men for the time being useful to him: Walsh, who told him to be a *correct* poet; Henry Cromwell, a rakish dilettante of whom Johnson learned "nothing particular but that he used to ride a hunting in a tye-wig"; and Wycherley, decaying but still scribbling. The amiable old libertine had long lost his memory; he would, according to Pope, repeat the same thought in the compass of ten lines; when it was pointed out: "Gads-so, so it is!" he would say. "I thank you very much—pray blot it out." In a moment, perhaps, of condescension he entrusted some of his poems for revision to the enthusiastic boy who followed him about with such gratifying respect. The boy, disregarding his father's warning against making enemies, was suitably flattered. But now his enthusiasm took a different and less obliging form. He had been invited to revise; very well, he would revise. He set to work. By the time he had finished with the poems there was very little Wycherley left, but a great deal of Pope. "Wycherley," he said afterwards with aggrieved surprise, "was really angry with me for correcting his verses so much. I was extremely plagued, up and down, for almost two years with them." The episode is valuable as illustrating not only Pope's diamond honesty, his absolute refusal of compromise, where the writing of verse was concerned, but also his dishonesty about the face he presented to the world. Professor Sherburn reminds us that it was usual in the eighteenth century to revise letters for publication. Pope's ideas of revision, however, in correspondence as well as in poetry, were individual, to say the least of it. When he published his letters it appeared from those to Wycherley that the fading old celebrity had offered extravagant flattery to the brilliant young newcomer, and that the brilliant young newcomer had modestly rejected it. The truth was the other way round. Pope it was who had flattered, Wycherley who had protested: and the modest letter published as having been addressed to Wycherley was worked up from one written to a different person altogether, to John Caryll.

In 1709 the Pastorals, "which had been for some time handed about among poets and criticks", were published, and two years later the Essay on Criticism. The application of the early years was rewarded; the Pastorals were praised, the Essay on Criticism was referred to in the *Spectator* as a masterpiece. Pope, by now much in London and a frequenter of literary society, was still only twenty-three. By the end of 1713 Windsor Forest and the first version of The Rape of the Lock had appeared; he had met Gay and Swift, had been invited by Addison to write the Prologue to "Cato"; and the subscription had been opened for his translation of the Iliad, an undertaking which, though at the outset it brought him only apprehension and dreams of failure ("I wished any body would hang me, a hundred times"), was to give him when completed an overwhelming eminence in letters. He was, in fact, well on the road to being the great Mr. Pope.

But something else beside success was happening to him, something from our point of view much more important. The grit had been dropped into the oyster's shell. Pope had encountered Dennis.

3

The Essay on Criticism is, when we consider its author, oddly blameless of personalities. But it contained three lines more dangerous than they look:

> But Appius reddens at each word you speak,
> And stares, tremendous, with a threat'ning eye,
> Like some fierce Tyrant in old tapestry.

Dennis, the belligerent, middle-aged author of "Appius and Virginia", noted the reference to himself and replied in a pamphlet slashing at the poet's matter, style, and person. The passages of physical abuse were abominable even for the savage manners of the eighteenth century, and Pope, naturally sensitive about his miserable crooked body, never forgot them. "When I heard, for the first time, that Dennis had written against me, it gave me some pain; but it was quite over as soon as I came to look into his book, and found he was in such a passion." But it was useless for Pope to feign indifference, then and always; as useless for him to be lofty over Dennis's as it was to smile later over Cibber's pamphlet: "These things are my diversion." For the Richardsons* "sat by him while he perused it, and saw his features writhen with anguish; and young Richardson said to his father, when they returned, that he hoped to be preserved from such diversion as had been that day the lot of Pope". His writing, quick, nervous, touchy, gives the lie to the pretence of indifference. After The Rape of the Lock all that is best in his work, whatever is most truly Pope, takes fire from friction with hostile tempers or alien views. The warfare it was which made him a great wit.

With Pope, however, it was not a case of isolated battles, however prolonged; it was a general campaign of peculiar complexity in which an engagement in one quarter had wildfire effects on every other theatre of war. He struck at Dennis *via* Addison; Addison offended him, and all the Whigs at Button's must tremble; to avenge a snigger from Cibber, Theobald was dethroned and the ranks of the Dunces were re-formed. Ambrose ("Namby-Pamby") Philips was the first to suffer. His Pastorals had been published in the same Miscellany with Pope's; he was one of Addison's group, and a series of papers duly appeared in Steele and Addison's *Guardian*, ignoring Pope but putting Philips in the class of Theocritus, Virgil and Spenser. With a deplorable lack of public school spirit Pope concocted an anonymous supplementary paper for the *Guardian*, ostensibly extolling his rival but actually making mincemeat of him. "Those artful repetitions of the epithets!" he wrote, quoting a couplet of exceptional fatuity: "I defy the most common reader to repeat them without feeling some motions of compassion!" The irony went undetected, the paper was published, and a crack appeared in the relations between Pope and the Addisonians. A few months later Dennis made an attack on Addison's "Cato". Delighted, Pope rushed to counter-attack with a pamphlet all horseplay and boisterous personal ridicule; but Addision, odiously priggish, wrote to his enemy's printer dissociating

* To Jonathan Richardson the elder is attributed the portrait of Pope in the National Portrait Gallery.

himself from the assault. The crack widened. The final rift came when simultaneously with the first volume of Pope's Iliad in 1715 there appeared the first book of Tickell's Iliad. Tickell, like Philips, was one of Addison's men. Pope, who felt that his whole career depended on the success of his translation, suspected a plot to undo him by competition; soon he had convinced himself that not Tickell but Addison was the translator. No matter that his own Iliad won the day, gave him financial independence (£9000 to be exact) and made him the most celebrated English writer of the day. There was Addison, scheming to ruin him. The oyster closed furiously over the speck of grit and set to work to make a pearl of it. Years later the pearl was set into the Epistle to Dr. Arbuthnot:

Should such a man, too fond to rule alone,
Bear, like the Turk, no brother near the throne,
View him with scornful, yet with jealous eyes,
And hate for arts that caus'd himself to rise;
Damn with faint praise, assent with civil leer,
And without sneering, teach the rest to sneer;
Willing to wound, and yet afraid to strike,
Just hint a fault, and hesitate dislike;
Alike reserv'd to blame, or to commend,
A tim'rous foe, and a suspicious friend;
Dreading ev'n fools, by Flatterers besieg'd,
And so obliging, that he ne'er oblig'd;
Like *Cato*, give his little Senate laws,
And sit attentive to his own applause;

—there, in the antithetical style and the devastating psychological marksmanship is the essence of Pope's wit.

Damn with faint praise, assent with civil leer—the words are picked out with a kind of sensual pleasure. Pope must have liked to run his thumb along the edge of a phrase before he used it. We are told that he was not witty in talk; only one retort is recorded, and that, says Johnson wryly, against a dictionary-maker: "He would," he said, "allow the publisher of a Dictionary to know the meaning of a single word, but not of two words put together." But in verse he is all point. His wit is not risible; literary wits never laugh in their writing. Even The Rape of the Lock, a work so flawless that to quote *from* it is like plucking one petal from a rose, has no laughter in it, only an exquisitely civilized mockery. This lovely poem has a wit distinct from the wit of all the later works, from the Moral Essays, the Satires and The Dunciad; for it is composed with a detachment which a writer as irritable as Pope could not hope to preserve. Life, the impact of society and his own temperament drove him to satire, satire which, however general it might appear to be, was in reality sharply personal. Here is his great achievement; and here also the devilish ingenuity with which he builds up the figure he is out to destroy, the terrible accuracy of his mocking, afford a delight less violent but sharper than laughter. The incongruity of the exquisite manner and the libel expressed is in itself a kind of wit. And how he hits off a character! The erratic:

Drunk at a Borough, civil at a Ball;
Friendly at Hackney, faithless at Whitehall

—the coquette:

"Odious! in woollen! 'twould a Saint provoke,"
(Were the last words that poor Narcissa spoke)
"No, let a charming Chintz, and Brussels lace
Wrap my cold limbs, and shade my lifeless face:
One would not, sure, be frightful when one's dead—
And—Betty—give this Cheek a little Red"

—the "pretender to taste", Lord Halifax, and his sycophants:

Much they extoll'd his pictures, much his seat,
And flatter'd ev'ry day, and some days eat:
Till grown more frugal in his riper days,
He paid some bards with port, and some with praise;
To some a dry rehearsal was assign'd,
And others (harder still) he paid in kind.
Dryden alone (what wonder?) came not nigh,
Dryden alone escap'd this judging eye:
But still the *Great* have kindness in reserve,
He help'd to bury whom he help'd to starve

—every couplet is electric. The reference to Dryden is interesting. "Mr. Dryden," says the author's note, "after having liv'd in exigencies, had a magnificent Funeral bestowed upon him by the contribution of several persons of quality." Time and topicality have failed to kill the verse.

The number and variety of Pope's enemies supply a fantastic flow of references to Grub Street authors, scholars, women of fashion. Nothing escapes him, no scandal, no scribble, no name, not even the straits of Settle's old age, when, after being in turns an anti-Popish pamphleteer and a King James's man, he played in "St. George for England" "in a Dragon of green leather of his own invention":

Tho' long my Party built on me their hopes,
For writing Pamphlets, and for roasting Popes;
Yet lo! in me what authors have to brag on!
Reduc'd at last to hiss in my own dragon.

As Pope's fame increased the warfare increased. Soon the bookseller Curll was in the opposition; once more the spirit of fair play was lamentably absent; Pope in a froth of revenge gave him an emetic and wrote a pamphlet describing the consequences. Cibber, Lady Mary Wortley Montagu, Lord Hervey—the list of enemies takes in stage as well as society, the notorious as well as the fashionable. Whether the quarrel with Lady Mary was due to the return dirty of a pair of borrowed sheets or, as Bowles puts it, to Pope's advances "a step farther than decorum would allow", it is impossible to know for certain. What is certain is that from the start no quarter was given:

Slander or Poison dread from Delia's rage,
Hard words or hanging, if your Judge be Page.
From furious Sappho scarce a milder fate,
Pox'd by her love, or libell'd by her hate.

Violent, yes; but the eighteenth century, the polite Augustan era, was a violent age. Pope used the contemporary weapons; it was only that he used them more effectively than the rest. He could, of course, have handled Curll without the disgusting episode of the emetic; but now and then a street-urchin devilry burst out. As for the implications of the Sappho couplet, well, the type of insult was not rare; and Cibber used it when he described Pope's visit to "a house of carnal recreation" and his own rescue of the "Tom Tit" from "a diseased bawd".

4

The battle, then, rages without mercy: Mr. Pope against society, against the world. He has, of course, his friends: Gay; Bolingbroke; warm Arbuthnot, who "was so neglectful of his writings, that his children tore his manuscripts, and made paper-kites of them"; Swift, who, though his own bitterness against society doubtless influenced Pope, had the sense when the young man (he was twenty-five at the time) complained of "a glut of the world" to tell him that he "had not yet either acted or suffered enough in the world to have become weary of it". (Most of them were Tories; some were movers with him in the Martin Scriblerus Club.) He has, too, his adored mother; after the death of his father at the Popes' house in Chiswick he took her with him to Twickenham, where she remained until her death in 1733; and his letter to the artist Richardson, begging him to come and sketch her dead face, gives touching proof that he has the heart of a poet as well as a wit: "I am sure if there be no very prevalent obstacle, you will leave any common business to do this, and I shall hope to see you this evening as late as you will, or tomorrow morning as early, before this winter flower is faded." He has, then, his refuges. But he suffers; from criticism, from calumny, from the whole brunt of the world he suffers. He insists that he wants peace. "I did not care," he says, explaining why he failed to write something he had planned, "for living always in boiling water." Part of him, no doubt, longed for calm, the soothing society of friends, the gratifying exercise of moral reflection. But something much stronger said: Attack! Attack the money-grubber and the business cheat:

> . . . some farm the Poor-box, some the Pews;
> Some keep Assemblies, and would keep the Stews;
> Some with fat Bucks on childless dotards fawn;
> Some win rich Widows by their Chine and Brawn;
> While with the silent growth of ten per cent,
> In dirt and darkness, hundreds stink content.

Attack the scribbler in his study:

> Next, o'er his Books his eyes began to roll,
> In pleasing memory of all he stole,
> How here he sipp'd, how there he plunder'd snug,
> And suck'd all o'er, like an industrious Bug.

Attack Sappho-Lady Mary; attack Atossa-Duchess of Marlborough:

> Full sixty years the World has been her Trade,
> The wisest Fool much Time has ever made.
> From loveless youth to unrespected age,
> No Passion gratify'd except her Rage.
> So much the Fury still out-ran the Wit,
> The Pleasure miss'd her, and the Scandal hit.

Attack, above all, Sporus-Lord Hervey:

Let *Sporus* tremble—A. What? that thing of silk?
Sporus, that mere white curd of Ass's milk?
Satire or sense, alas! can *Sporus* feel?
Who breaks a butterfly upon a wheel?
P. Yet let me flap this bug with gilded wings.
This painted child of dirt, that stinks and stings;
Whose buzz the witty and the fair annoys,
Yet wit ne'er tastes, and beauty ne'er enjoys:
So well-bred Spaniels civilly delight
In mumbling of the game they dare not bite.
Eternal smiles his emptiness betray,
As shallow streams run dimpling all the way.
Whether in florid impotence he speaks,
And, as the prompter breathes, the puppet squeaks;
Or at the ear of *Eve*, familiar Toad,
Half froth, half venom, spits himself abroad,
In puns, or politics, or tales, or lies,
Or spite, or smut, or rhymes, or blasphemies.
His wit all see-saw, between *that* and *this*,
Now high, now low, now master up, now miss,
And he himself one vile Antithesis.
Amphibious thing! that acting either part,
The trifling head or the corrupted heart,
Fop at the toilet, flatt'rer at the board,
Now trips a Lady, and now struts a Lord.
Eve's tempter thus the Rabbins have exprest,
A Cherub's face, a reptile all the rest;
Beauty that shocks you, parts that none will trust;
Wit that can creep, and pride that licks the dust.

Let Sporus tremble, let society tremble, let everybody tremble.

Yes, I am proud; I must be proud to see
Men not afraid of God, afraid of me:

Pope paints an impressive portrait of himself as a man called by destiny to scourge his contemporaries; enough for half the Greatest

To 'scape my Censure, not expect my Praise.

But, says Arbuthnot in his last letter to Pope, "study more to *reform* than *chastise*; though the one cannot be effected without the other." "To *reform*, and not to *chastise*," Pope replies sternly, "is impossible"; then, in a burst of confidence,

Fools rush into my head, and so I write.

They have been rushing into his head in a pretty steady stream since the day when Dennis made his first savage rejoinder. It is true that after the quarrel with Addison and the early skirmish with Curll there is a period of comparative quiet. His Homer, of course, helps to keep him out of trouble: "The Iliad took me up six years." In 1718, two years before the appearance of the last volume, he removed to Twickenham; and the next five years are among the least belligerent of his life. The world is preoccupied with such affairs as the South Sea Bubble; Pope is preoccupied with Homer, his garden and his grotto; attacks there are, yet not mortal attacks. But the pause cannot last. The Iliad is followed by a translation of the Odyssey, done in collaboration with Fenton and Broome, and an edition of Shakespeare. The Shakespeare appears in 1725; in 1726 Theobald publishes his attack on it, "Shakespeare Restored"; and in 1728 there is The Dunciad, and there is Theobald crowned King of the Dunces. Pope has sixteen years left him; he uses them in a passion of conflict. The Essay on Man apart, between 1730 and 1738 he produces the Moral Essays, the Epistle to Dr. Arbuthnot, the Imitations of Horace and the Epilogue to the Satires. In 1742 there appears the New Dunciad; and in 1743, the year before Pope's death, Theobald is deposed and Cibber takes his place in the final version. The warfare has been brought to an annihilating conclusion; Pope has every reason for triumph.

Yet occasionally there is a note of self-justification in his satire. He is, he insists in the Epistle to Dr. Arbuthnot, "more a dupe than wit", the most pacific of men, the most humble, the most generous: did he not write a Prologue for Dennis's benefit, did he not wait ten years before replying to his libellers by The Dunciad? Anxiously he considers the opinion of the world. Perhaps something can be done by adroit handling of his correspondence to convince people of the mildness and probity of his character as well as of his wit. But it would not "look right" to publish his letters unasked. His correspondence with Henry Cromwell has already been printed without his consent; now, by prodigious stratagems, he gets his correspondence with Wycherley into the hands of Curll, who of course publishes it. Pope is the most injured man in the world. His letters have been stolen; nothing remains for him but in self-defence to bring out an authoritative edition. The Swift correspondence presents a more tricky problem. Pope writes to ask for the return of all letters as a safeguard against further theft. But Swift is obtuse; he does not answer; Lord Orrery has to be sent to persuade him. At last Pope holds the correspondence in his own hands. He prints it; and has a copy sent anonymously to Swift with a brilliantly tempting note. Swift, his mind now shadowed, is deceived, thinks it, perhaps, too late to prevent publication, and sends the book to his own printer; and Pope is left in a position to reproach him with perfidy. It was said of Pope that "he hardly drank tea without a stratagem". One begins to understand that; and one remembers, too, Addison saying to Lady Mary: "Leave him as soon as you can, he will certainly play you some devilish trick else: he has an appetite to satire!"

The single mind, the double face: to the end the antithesis persists. Yet it is to be remembered that the duplicity proceeds, not from fear, but from vanity; the deceiver is not afraid that the world will censure, but anxious that it shall admire. Poor Pope could not foresee that nineteenth-century research, relentlessly nosey, would expose his tricks. But however ugly the discoveries of the scholars, in many respects his character obstinately remains admirable. No doubt has been cast on his courage. After the first edition of The Dunciad, and while he "was preparing another yet more irritating", he was often threatened; alarmed, his friends warned him against walking alone to Richmond. "He thought it better," he said, "to die, than to live in fear of such rascals"; and putting pistols in his pocket and taking his dog Bounce, he hobbled off alone to Richmond. Nor could he be persuaded to change his religion, preferring to be ineligible for office rather than give pain to his family. Calculating, yet in his fashion incorruptible, Pope "had his liberty without a coach". Certainly the warfare did not leave him unscathed; for every sally, every battle, he paid a dozen times over in humiliation, rage, the pain of the twitched nerve. But the reader is not concerned with the suffering of the Wit, only with what it produces. The continual assault on Pope's sensibilities has given English poetry its most polished and yet most ferocious invective. Richness of illustration and parody, riotousness of allusion—these are contributory to the "perpetual delight" of which Johnson speaks. But the core of enjoyment is in the spectacle of the remorseless, beautiful precision with which Pope transfixes his opponents. Inside literature he never had cause to fear an enemy, since there was none whom he could not write to a standstill. And after two centuries they are still there, the enemy, caught, preserved in his satire with the terrible lifelike freshness of a corpse in a glacier. Only Pope himself, eternally contradictory, eludes us. There he goes now: spitting murder at a critic, weeping over a passage in Homer; a raconteur in private company, tongue-tied in public; now on his high moral horse, now hurrying from his sick-bed to eat stewed lampreys; now talking in Roman fashion of leaving the world, now bouncing from the table because Lady Mary sat opposite—a mischievous, vivacious, sad little man, setting about him with the only weapon he had, genius. It is not for us to shudder if the battle is not always conducted on the highest moral lines.

DR. JOHNSON

RONALD A. KNOX

GRATITUDE, DR. JOHNSON SAID, IS A FRUIT OF GREAT CULTIVATION; YOU DO not find it among gross people. The same is surely true of wit, as that term has any meaning for literature. Wit demands a soil of civilization to grow in; it will not spring up self-sown, like the ale-house humour of a Villon. Commonly, too, wit will derive its colour and character from its own environment; and what one generation takes for granted as part of its standpoint the next generation may see as something absurd, satirizable—our great-grandfathers are a joke to us for having made a joke out of Brown, Jones, and Robinson. With this shifting of humour-values, how is it that any residuum defies the centuries? Perhaps because there is a subtle quality about the really great wits which is not of the period to which they belong. Not in the sense that they are misfits, that they are unrepresentative of their periods; Johnson could only have happened in the middle of the eighteenth century, and it is difficult enough to believe that he happened then. Rather in the sense that they overflow the common watercourses, and leave a saline deposit for after ages to admire.

It would be out of place to give biographical details here about one who, whatever else he was, must certainly be regarded as the prince of biographees. Enough to say that he was born in the year of Malplaquet, and lived to see the loss of the American colonies. He missed John

Evelyn by two years, Pepys by four; he died in the birth-year of Leigh Hunt. The eighteenth century may be pictured as a rather sluggish estuary, through which the stream of English history debouches upon the ocean of its modern achievement. Johnson bestrides it like a colossus.

To call Johnson a wit is a curiously inadequate definition of him. If anyone should study his life with the idea of cultivating the art of repartee, the effect would be disastrous. Tell us if you will, with Cibber, that Johnson knocked you down with the butt of his pistol if it failed to go off, or tell us with Garrick that "Johnson gives you a forcible hug, and shakes the laughter out of you whether you will or no"; the plain fact is that his idea of scoring a personal triumph in conversation hardly ever rose above the private-school level. When he is asked, importunately, why he went to Mrs. Abington's benefit performance, where he could neither see nor hear, he is content to reply, "Because, Sir, she is a favourite of the public, and when the public cares the thousandth part for you that it does for her, I will go to your benefit too." When somebody defends Dominicetti's vapour baths, "Well, sir, go to Dominicetti, and get thyself fumigated, but be sure that the stream be directed to thy head, for that is the peccant part." And when it is agreed that, for his own sake, a spendthrift must be induced to leave London as soon as may be, Boswell is (quite gratuitously) attacked: "Nay, Sir, we'll send you to him. If that does not drive a man out of his house, nothing will." Was Johnson subject to attacks of liver? More probably, I think—you cannot be certain, once the tones of a man's voice are silenced in death—he was one of those boisterous people who have no conception how much confusion their ill manners occasionally heap on the sensitive. But whatever the cause, it is certain that Johnson hardly ever scored a real success with a purely personal repartee. He never made Boswell look a fool *qua* Boswell, only *qua* Scot. His genius was for generalization, not for satirizing the individual.

Was Johnson, then, a wit in the sense of producing readily in conversation those flashy pieces of comment upon life which used to go by the name of epigrams, but in these last few years have been very regrettably labelled "wisecracks"? My impression is that Johnson could, because almost anybody could, but that he seldom did, because he realized almost anybody could. Take a phrase like the one he uses about Law, author of the "Serious Call", and his admiration for Jacob Behmen, "whom Law alleged to have been somewhat in the same state with St. Paul, and to have seen unutterable things. Were it even so, said Johnson, Jacob would have resembled St. Paul still more, by not attempting to utter them"—that is only smart talking, and a hundred people can do it for you in any generation. A gentleman who had been unhappy in marriage married again immediately after his wife died; Johnson said it was the triumph of hope over experience—but quickly, you feel, for fear somebody else should say it first. "In lapidary inscriptions a man is not upon oath", "I never take a nap after dinner, but when I have had a bad night, and then the nap takes me", "There is less flogging in our great schools than formerly, but then less is learned there, so that what the boys get at one end they lose at the other"—all this is well enough, but it is curiously not characteristic Johnson. Or, to speak more accurately, it is not characteristic Boswell-Johnson. All these last five quotations were "communicated" to Boswell by friends, not heard and reported by him. It is to be remembered, always, that we see Johnson refracted through a glass hardly less peculiar than himself; he may have made a lot of witty remarks, in the current fashion, which have not been preserved to us because Boswell did not happen to think them interesting. Literature is so overstocked with witty remarks in the current fashion; perhaps it is a good thing that Boswell, by accident or design, did leave that region unexplored, and concentrated on the more proper fruits of his friend's genius, the unquestionable Johnsoniana.

What is the nature of these; what is it that gives them their wholly individual flavour? Why are we quite certain that we should not dare to recommend Gibbon or Horace Walpole to a friend who wanted to read something "like" the life of Johnson? I despair of any attempt at accurate definition. What I mean to do here is to indicate a few of the qualities in which Johnson's conversation excels, and to collect a few instances under each heading to illustrate the kind of excellence I mean. Probably my choice would not be everybody's choice; but if it suffices to illustrate, I am content.

2

In the first place, the Johnsonian dictum is apt to take your breath away by its sudden penetration of thought. You may think the sentiment wholly untrue, wholly misleading, and yet the fact remains that there was a way of looking at the facts which you had never thought of, although you had had the facts under review scores of times—and Johnson seemed to read his way straight into them. "In the House of Commons there are members enough who will not vote what is grossly unjust or absurd. No, Sir, there must always be right enough, or appearance of right, to keep wrong in countenance." "The rod produces an effect which terminates in itself . . . whereas, by exciting emulation, and comparisons of superiority, you lay the foundation of lasting mischief." "Every man has a right to utter what he thinks truth, and every other man has a right to knock him down for it. Martyrdom is the test." Democratic government—corporal punishment—religious toleration—you would have thought it impossible to rough out, and on the spur of the moment, three such unhackneyed methods of approach to three such hackneyed subjects of debate. Johnson's temptation was, no doubt, to say the unpopular thing, as it was certainly his temptation in argument to take, merely for that reason, the unpopular side. But it is to be remembered that he was in revolt against cant, living in an age of dawning sentimentalism. "When a butcher tells you that his heart bleeds for his country he has, in fact, no uneasy feeling." He was in revolt against the noble savage. "Do not allow yourself, Sir, to be imposed upon by such gross absurdity; it is sad stuff, it is brutish. If a bull could speak, he might as well say, Here am I with this cow and this grass, what being can enjoy greater felicity?" And he was in revolt, by anticipation, against the modern anthropology that has superseded Rousseau: "What account of their religion can you suppose to be learnt from savages? Only consider, Sir, our own state . . . ask the first ten gross men you meet, and hear what they can tell you of their religion."

I must not, however, be thought to suggest that Johnson is by preference and by trade a paradox-monger. Considering how steadily Boswell plied the arts of the "interviewer", and how commonplace on the whole Boswell's views were, it does credit to his friend that he was not driven more frequently into eccentricities of opinion. But Johnson did not need controversy to knock out sparks from the tinder-box of his prompt mind. "People are influenced by what a man says, if his practice is suitable to it—because they are blockheads. I have all my life long been lying till noon, yet I tell all young men, and tell them with great sincerity, that nobody who does not rise early will do any good." Johnson did not merely say that; he thought it. "Music is a method of employing the mind, without the labour of thinking at all, and with some applause from a man's self." Quite unmusical himself, Johnson could look over the player's shoulder and detect the glance of self-admiration. Less cynically: "Every man thinks meanly of himself for not having been a soldier, or not having been at sea"; we shall find the generosity of the sentiment more striking when we reflect that the England of the Napoleonic wars used, and was content to use, the press-gang as its machinery of recruitment. Johnson was prepared to "debunk" false sentiment when he found it, but I do not think he had any instinct of cynicism. "Hell is paved with good intentions"—yes, but that means with good resolutions which were never kept, not with misguided efforts at philanthropy, if you consult the original context.

Sometimes it is not the thought itself, but a twist given to the expression of the thought, which takes your breath away. Especially, as became the author of a dictionary, Johnson was meticulous about the exact details of an expression. He would correct you, perhaps frivolously, when you had been over-enthusiastic; the Giant's Causeway was worth seeing, yes, but not worth going to see; no, he had not come back highly gratified from Mrs. Montagu's evening entertainment, "yet I do not recollect to have passed many evenings with fewer objections". And if, in these minor encounters of life, he reminds us too much of Professor Crookshank at Mrs. Mountstuart Jenkinson's dinner-party, "He pores over an inaccuracy of expression like a domestic hen", we are constantly made to realize the value of the instinct where graver issues are concerned. When somebody doubts, for example, whether the whole of Sennacherib's army, all those thousands, can really have been destroyed: "You are not to suppose that the angel of the Lord went about and stabbed each of them with a dagger, or knocked them on the head, man by man." And again, when Miss Seward maintains that annihilation would not, after all, be such a very dreadful thing: "The lady confounds annihilation, which is nothing, with our apprehension of it, which is dreadful." Nobody, when he liked, had better powers of showing you where you were wrong, how your tackling of the question was faulty, than Johnson had.

But the intellectual trick which is perhaps most characteristic of him is that of coining a phrase, usually with one good long word at the heart of it, to act as ballast, which sets on record for all time, marmoreally, Johnson's attitude to this or that, this person or that. It is probably a mistake to think of Johnson as specially fond of long words; certainly a mistake to think you can parody Johnson by using a lot of long words. He wrote at a period when long words were used; what is probably the best sentence in his "Journey to the Western Islands" is written, I think, entirely in monosyllables. But he had a playful love of using a long word now and again for its judicial effect; it was a kind of signature. Thus when Boswell returned from abroad, and boasted of the indiscriminate lion-hunting which had taken him to see Rousseau, there was a sudden drop in the atmosphere; good heavens, was Rousseau a bad man? Well, in a way, perhaps, but you wouldn't think of him as a bad man in the same sense as Voltaire? "Why, Sir, it is difficult to settle the proportion of iniquity between them." The long word is not quite essential; it is enough that a word should be sent spinning into circulation with a fresh shade of meaning to it. "Yes, Burke *is* an extraordinary man; his stream of mind is perpetual"—Boswell once tried to quote that, for he was fond of quoting Johnson to himself without acknowledgment, and it came out as "Burke has a constant stream of conversation". But in general the long word is preferred; "he might have ripened into an atheist" would do, but "he might have exuberated into an atheist" is the perfect form of the sentiment. So, we often say that it would be easy to do a thing if you gave up your mind to it; what a subtle sting was added to that formula when Johnson declared of "Ossian" that "a man might write such stuff for ever, if he would abandon his mind to it"!

Sometimes the effect of the polysyllable is to recall us to a judicial standpoint. "The Beggar's Opera", like the crook-film of today, was often accused of indoctrinating minds with the first notions of crime. Johnson expressed himself doubtful about this; but then, as if feeling a condemnation would be expected from him, added, "There is in it such a labefactation of all principles, as may be injurious to morality." Sometimes it does justice to the mysterious character of the subject-matter under discussion. We, with the smattering of psychological jargon we have picked up from books which know nothing about it, how ready we are to dismiss what puzzles us with chips of inadequate metaphor! Which of us does not talk gaily of "kinks" in our mental make-up; as if it were an ascertained fact that our mental make-up is a long, straight piece of wire, which can only show any variableness or shadow of turning when somebody has been tying knots in it without our knowledge? How much more adequately, because much less positively, will Johnson write of our odd tricks of thought: "Among the anfractuosities of the human mind, I know not if it may be one, that there is a superstitious reluctance to sit for a picture." The human mind, you see, is conceived as a deep bay, full of inlets and caverns; how just an estimate! Sometimes the long words will paint a picture more alluringly than their short synonyms could; witness the rousing and wholly justified comment when Thrale's brewery was sold: "We are not here to sell a parcel of boilers and vats, but the potentiality of growing rich, beyond the dreams of avarice." And sometimes the long words express what it would have been impossible to express anyhow else. No sounder reason was ever produced by a guest for habitual lateness at breakfast than when Johnson reminded Mrs. Thrale of the one occasion on which he came down too early: "Madam, I do not like to come down to vacuity." The vacuity of a country house early in the morning, who does not know it? Except those fortunate people who are always, and by instinct, late for breakfast.

It must not be thought for a moment, I repeat, that Johnson used long words because he did not know how to express himself clearly, or because he did not know how to express himself vigorously, in any other way. Imagine any modern author writing about so dull a subject as the birth-rate of Russia. Hundreds of them do; welcoming it, deploring it, terrified of it, distrustful of the statistics, and so on; but always in technical language, with a great deal about index figures and standards of living and expectation of tenure and God knows what. Curiously, the birth-rate of Russia was a subject which aroused interest in the England of Dr. Johnson's time; at least, it aroused interest in the capacious bosom of Dr. Johnson himself. And this is his comment on it: "It is not from reason and providence that people marry, but from inclination. A man is poor; he thinks, I cannot be worse, and so I'll e'en take Polly." If only our modern professors would teach us economics in such language, and with a similar regard for the concrete realities of life, one might begin to understand what the modern world is all about.

What probably won Johnson his chief fame as a conversationalist was his ready habit of providing illustration, on the spur of the moment, for the point he wanted to enforce. Occasionally it is all a little wooden; you get hints of a formula. Thus: "All power, of whatever sort, is of itself desirable. A man would not submit to learn to hem a ruffle of his wife or his wife's maid; but if a mere wish could attain it, he would rather wish to be able to hem a ruffle." Or again: "If a physician were to take to eating horseflesh, nobody would employ him, though one may eat horseflesh, and be a very skilful physician." I can conceive that on his off days there was a good deal of this sort of thing; and perhaps if Boswell had written down more of those conversations which he tearfully accuses himself of having left unrecorded, we should have been able to comprise one or two of these overworked gambits under algebraical symbols. But, even when the form of the argument is stereotyped, how rich is the fancy which supplies the illustrations! Why is it that when we are hunting about, in conversation, for an analogy which will illustrate our point, we never think of hemming ruffles or of eating horseflesh?

Here is a case where the whole phrase is imaginative: "There is not a sapling upon Parnassus more severely blown about by every wind of criticism than that poor fellow"; we are not told who the unfortunate author was, but what a picture we have of him! There is the same vigour of simile about Johnson's answer to the friend who extolled the generosity of the British sailor: "I do not call a tree generous, that sheds its fruit at every breeze." On a shy boy being sent to a public school—not a subject you would have expected to evoke his more discerning sympathy—he comments, "Placing him at a public school is forcing an owl upon day." In this connection, try as you will, you cannot avoid using one or two hackneyed examples The *congé d'élire*, for instance—Johnson had only overheard it being discussed, and there was no need to say anything on the question raised, whether it was in truth a recommendation or an out-and-out command; what he did say was, "It is such a recommendation, as if I should throw you out of a two-pair-of-stairs window, and recommend you to fall soft." And of course there is the comment on the Quaker lady's preaching, "like a dog's walking on his hinder legs. It is not done well, but you are surprised to find it done at all." There is such a lot of wisdom gathered up in that phrase, and it applies to such a lot of other things besides ladies speaking in public—if it does apply to ladies speaking in public.

Why did Johnson decry the Scots? Was the antipathy a natural one; or did he cultivate it; and if so, did he cultivate it out of perversity, or as a kind of literary asset? After all, it is no bad thing for the reputation of a humorist if there is known to be one particular subject that will "set him off", one recurring joke in his writings which appears in a hundred forms but always at the expense of the same institution. I think the quarrel with the Scots was real, though perhaps ill-defined. When it was suggested that he disliked them because they betrayed their king at the time of the Civil War, he claimed that it was a good enough reason, but did not identify it as his own. I fancy it was a temperamental want of sympathy—Lamb, it will be remembered, owns to it—exaggerated in Johnson's case by the feeling that the Scots were spreading all over the place and having everything their own way, in literature especially. It was the age of Hume, of Beattie, of Robertson, of Macpherson, of Reid, of Adam Smith. Individually, Johnson liked meeting these people, because he liked meeting nearly everybody who would consent to argue with him. But, viewed as a whole, this southward movement across the Border was an invasion of Presbyterianism and of Whiggery; "Hume, Sir, was a Tory only by chance." After as before his tour in the Hebrides, Johnson thought of the Scots as a real menace.

At the same time, the circumstance that Boswell had been the chief recorder of his conversation has no doubt exercised a profound influence on what Johnson said (as opposed to what he thought) about the Scots. What he said is probably a good deal less violent than what he thought; but it is also much cleverer, more subtly malicious. He obviously enjoyed pulling (I can find no more respectful phrase for it) Boswell's leg. This was a delicate business; for, if the humour was too broad, the honest Scottish laugh came too easily; if it was too subtle, there was the danger that Boswell would not see the joke at all. Sometimes he did not see the joke at all. They were talking one day of the respect shown to soldiers in France; Boswell was surprised that they should be so much respected where they were so numerous. "Nay, Sir," replied Johnson, "wherever a particular character or profession is high in the estimation of a people, those who are of it will be valued above other men. We value an Englishman highly in this country, and yet Englishmen are not rare in it." This was quite above Boswell's head; he records it dutifully, but without comment.

The jokes against Scotland—if your friends from beyond the Border will let us stand handkerchief in mouth for a moment or two—how good they are, even at their unfairest! The country itself, "Seeing Scotland, Madam, is seeing the flower fade away to the naked stalk"; and when Johnson loses his oak staff on the Isle of Mull, "It is not to be expected that any man in Mull who had got it will part with it. Consider, Sir, the value of such a piece of timber here." Persecuted on his native heath, Boswell must equally be persecuted in London; he tells Johnson, sycophantically to be sure, that Fleet Street is in his mind more delightful than Tempê. "Ay, Sir," returns the unpropitiated deity, "but let it be compared with Mull!" And as for the people, their learning is "like bread in a besieged city: every man gets a little, but no man gets a full meal". In a rash moment Boswell wondered whether it was not an exaggeration to describe the death of Garrick as eclipsing the gaiety of nations, in the plural. "Nations may be said," was the imperturbable reply, "if we allow the Scotch to be a nation, and to have gaiety, which they have not." But perhaps the most graphic allusion of all is when Johnson is contributing his reminiscences of Dr. John Campbell, compiler of the *Biographia Britannica*: "Campbell is a good man, a pious man. I am afraid he has not been in the inside of a church for many years, but he never passes a church without pulling off his hat, which shows that he has good principles. I used to go pretty often to Campbell's on a Sunday evening, till I began to consider that the shoals of Scotchmen who flocked about him might probably say, when anything of mine was well done, Ay, ay, he has learnt this of Cawmell."

4

Was Johnson brutal to his biographer? Most of us, I think, will be disposed to acquit him of any such charge. He was, it is to be remembered, a man of a difficult nervous constitution, never far off, I suppose, from that state which is most easily described as "wanting to scream". This will account for some of his ferocities in argument; it will account also for some of his impatience under misplaced kindness. "He sometimes could not bear being teazed with questions. I was once present when a gentleman asked so many . . . that he at last grew enraged, and said, I will not be put to the question. . . . The gentleman, who was a good deal out of countenance, said, Why, Sir, you are so good, that I venture to trouble you. JOHNSON: Sir, my being so good is no reason why you should be so ill." How often I have wished I dared to quote that! And then there was Chambers, who would hang round suggesting remedies when he was ill: "Prythee, don't teaze me. Stay till I am well, and then you shall tell me how to cure myself." We have all felt like that; and if Johnson felt it a little too keenly, at least he expressed it with admirable humour.

But with Boswell I think he was singularly gentle in his reprimands, considering what a nuisance Boswell could evidently be. When, for example, he offered to "explain" the whole of Allan Ramsay's "Gentle Shepherd" to Johnson, he surely deserved something more severe than the retort, "No, Sir, I won't learn it. You shall retain your superiority by my not knowing it." You must be on easy terms with a friend—and a Scottish friend—when you can say to him, "Boswell, lend me sixpence, not to be repaid." Boswell was importunate, and continually demanding, in his letters especially, expressions of Johnson's good will. If he had to be taught a lesson, how was he to be taught it more charmingly than this? "My regard for you is greater almost than I have words to express, but I do not choose to be always repeating it; write it down in the first leaf of your pocket-book, and never doubt of it again." Occasionally the cross-questioning became more than flesh and blood could bear. Breaking the silence of the seas among the farthest Hebrides, "I asked him if he had ever been accustomed to wear a night-cap. He said, No. I asked, if it was not best to wear one. JOHNSON: Sir, I had this custom by chance, and perhaps no man shall ever know whether it is best to sleep with or without a night-cap."

Not that Johnson resented the intrusion of the frivolous, or even the fantastic, into conversation. When Boswell asked what he would do if he were shut up in a castle, and a new-born child with him, after admitting that he would not like his company, he entered gloriously into the spirit of the thing. He would make a shed on the roof, and take it there for fresh air; he would feed it, and wash it much, and with warm water to please it. Although he was a teetotaller during most of the period when Boswell knew him, he had his own philosophy of eating: "For my part, I mind my belly very studiously and very carefully, for I look upon it, that he who does not mind his belly, will hardly mind anything else." And he said once, "This was a good dinner enough, to be sure, but it was not a dinner to ask a man to." That claret is the liquor for boys, port for men, but he who aspires to be a hero must drink brandy, is a remark which attests, at least, an interest in the cellar, though some may doubt its orthodoxy. Johnson was a man who knew how to give tongue when he was enjoying himself. "Life has not many better things than this," he said, as he drove in a fast post-chaise; and although, when Boswell quoted this remark, he objected that you were driving rapidly *from* something or *to* something, as if he were bothering about means and ends, he admitted, later, that if he had no duties and no reference to futurity he would spend his life driving briskly in a post-chaise with a pretty woman. As for London, his love of it does not need to be attested by quotation. "Why, Sir, Fleet Street has an animated appearance, but I think the full tide of human existence is at Charing Cross."

This occasional note of frivolousness—impishness, almost—suffices to mark out Johnson clearly enough from the highbrows, of his own age or another. Once, I think, the devil of laughter got the better of him; it was when he was with Boswell and Chambers, two Scots lawyers. Let Boswell tell his own story. "He now laughed immoderately, without any reason that we could perceive, at our friend's making his will; called him the *testator*, and added, I dare say he thinks he has done a mighty thing; he won't stay till he gets home to his seat in the country, to produce this wonderful deed; he'll call up the landlord of the first inn on the road, and . . . will tell him that he should not delay making his will; and here, Sir, he will say, is my will, which I have just made, with the assistance of one of the ablest lawyers in the kingdom, and he will read it to him (laughing all the time). . . . I trust you have had more conscience than to make him say, *being of sound understanding*, ha, ha, ha! I hope he has left me a legacy. I'd have his will turned into verse, like a ballad." And so on. To meet this quite irresponsible levity in the year 1773 is to me, I confess, the most surprising thing in Boswell. I am not worried, as Boswell was worried, about what Johnson found to laugh at; I think it was the faces of his companions that kept him going. But that it should, as Boswell points out, have been the author of th "Rambler". . . .

A man whose understanding had a range and a depth unexampled, certainly in his period; yet would focus the ray of his fancy to illuminate any subject, however insignificant, the history of night-caps, it would seem, alone excepted.

OSCAR WILDE

DESMOND MACCARTHY

THERE IS NO FAMOUS TALKER, JOHNSON EXCEPTED, OF WHOSE CONVERSATION—the wit and manner of it—we have more vivid records than Oscar Wilde's, and this for several reasons. His personality was imposing and he delighted to dramatize it, putting form and flourish into everything he did or uttered, thus making himself unforgettable; and in charming and amusing himself he also amused and charmed others. Even those disposed to dislike him, or those who had been put off by his appearance and behaviour, were usually disarmed by his gaiety, good nature, and abundance; though his massive bland self-confidence, the lush ostentation of his dress, gestures and diction, his heavy, white, clever face, his soft corpulence and deliberately honied utterance might confirm at first unfavourable anticipations. His pale hands were enormous and ugly, and he waved them about while talking, a cigarette between his fingers, making prelatical gestures; and though his eyes were fine, bright-grey, they were rather prominent and had a steady stare in them which contrasted disconcertingly with the dreamy word-caressing inflections of his delightful voice. Thus, at a first encounter, Oscar Wilde might have seemed all an unfriendly fancy painted, and extravagantly so, but such observers soon discovered that far from being flabby, he was vital.

It was his personality, not his achievements, that had first won the world's attention (people had flocked to see "Lady Windermere's Fan" at its opening because "Oscar" had written it), and his personality supported his eminence even more than his later writings. He was a force. Yet it was impossible to be long in his company without discovering that there was seldom a desire to dominate behind that "Oscar" pose (at least, in sympathetic company), or except in fun to play others off the stage. The impersonation was self-delighting, the actor aware of his own extravagance. He was also—this was most unexpected—capable of delicious self-mockery, and although no one could be more sentimental about whatever he took seriously, or more pontifical about it, his pronouncements were apt to be suddenly emptied of their solemnity by an afterthought in another key. These turns in his talk, quick as the twist and flash of a snipe, he enjoyed with a boyish glee most infectious. There is a more serious example of this kind of *volte face* to be found in Mr. Vincent O'Sullivan's admirable "Aspects of Oscar Wilde", which is in some ways the best account of him we have. Wilde was telling O'Sullivan about his visit to Rome from Paris after his release from prison and how he had gone to St. Peter's on a high feast day when the Pope was to show himself to the people. "And when I saw the old white Pontiff, successor of the Apostles and Father of Christendom, pass, carried high above the throng, and in passing turn and bless me where I knelt, I felt my sickness of body and soul fall from me like a worn garment and I was made whole." He paused and then added: "I wrote to Robbie Ross that I expected to see that my umbrella had blossomed." Here the emotion which reminded him of Tannhäuser was genuine—the tears, Mr. O'Sullivan says, were not far from his eyes. The after-thought was a form his wit often took: "The only way to behave to a woman if she is pretty is to make love to her—or to someone else if she is plain"; "Meredith" (he was defending Meredith's elliptic mannerisms) "is a prose Browning—and so is Browning"; "No man should have a secret from his own wife—she invariably finds it out"; "The Public is wonderfully tolerant, it forgives everything—except, of course, genius." Like some other Irish wits, he delighted in anticlimax, and this was sometimes very refreshing at the end of one of his sumptuous little fables. Here is one with such an ending which has been recorded:

"When Narcissus died, the flowers of the field hung their heads in grief, and asked the river to give them drops of water that they might weep. 'If all my drops were tears,' said the river, 'I should not have enough to mourn Narcissus, for I loved him.' 'Ah, how could you fail to love Narcissus,' sighed the flowers, 'he was so beautiful.' 'Was he beautiful?' the river asked. 'Why, who should know that better than you?' they answered. 'Every day he bent over your bank and mirrored his beauty in your waters.' Here in telling the story Oscar Wilde paused. 'If I loved him,' said the river, 'it was because, when he bent over me, I saw the reflection of my waters in his eyes.' Then, with a burst of laughter, Oscar Wilde added: '*That* story is called The Disciple'."

All reporters agree about the astonishing variety of his talk. He shone in the nonsense of irresponsible gaiety, in repartee, in pointful aphorism; as a teller of stories and inventor (this was a speciality of his) of parables. Like most distinguished talkers, he had a powerful memory, so that he had at command in conversation phrases which had occurred to him in meditation or delighted him in books he had read. The effortless finish of his diction amazed his company, while his pliancy to their mood which most masters of monologue have lacked (Coleridge, for example) enabled him to convey the impression that he was following rather than directing the conversation. It lent an air of spontaneity to the delivery of even his most carefully treasured impromptus. He was not a jealous talker, not, at least, in company intelligent enough to appreciate him.

His pleasure in others was almost as influential as his brilliance in contributing to his social success Not only could he be relied upon as a guest to banish the boredom from a country-house party marooned upon a lawn and waiting for a sail, but his hostess knew that no one would respond with more zest to anything remarkable in his company or surroundings. His flattery of persons, especially of persons of rank, was apt to be fulsome; in that he resembled Disraeli, in whom also there was something excessive, theatrical and displeasing to English good taste. But his indirect flattery in taking up some remark that had fallen from another, embellishing it and then handing it back with admiration, was very graceful. When talk became a genial little festival of ostentation, he did not forget to fan the vanity of others. He was probably the greatest self-consciously deliberate master of the Art of Conversation who has talked the English language. The qualification is important as distinguishing him from such talkers as Dr. Johnson or Sydney Smith, in whom there was nothing of the play-actor.

His mastery of that art, to which we all at times aspire, was, no doubt, present to his mind when he declared that he had only put his talent into writing but his genius into life, though he meant more than that: as his success in life ramified and towered, he came to think of himself more and more definitely as standing in a symbolic relation to his age.

In youth he had thought of himself as an Apostle of Culture, and employed his natural turn for showmanship to pass himself off as the Perfect Aesthete, the Passionate Connoisseur. It was a pose which did him a great deal of harm; not because it attracted ridicule to which his immense self-confidence made him impervious and of which he knew the advertisement value, but because it led those who understood painting and music to regard him as a charlatan. He could be witty about Art as about America: "The English have really everything in common with the Americans—except, of course, language." But wit, as Bernard Shaw has written, "is no use when you have to seize and hold the attention and interest of people who really love music and painting. Therefore, Oscar was handicapped by a false start and got a reputation for shallowness and insincerity which he never retrieved until too late. Comedy: the criticism of morals and manners *viva voce*, was his real forte. When he settled down to that he was great. But, as you found when you approached Meredith about him, his initial mistake had produced that 'rather low opinion of Wilde's capacities', that 'deep-rooted contempt for the showman in him', which persisted as a first impression and will persist until the last man who remembers his aesthetic period has perished. The world has been in some ways so unjust to him that one must be careful not to be unjust to the world."

Oscar Wilde's enthusiasm for Whistler, which succeeded without eclipsing, however, his earlier admiration of the pre-Raphaelites, did not propitiate that painter, who was exasperated by airs of authority in one whose taste, let alone his knowledge of art, was by no means reliable. "What has Oscar in common with Art?" he asked in the papers. "Except that he dines at our tables and picks from our platters the plums for the pudding he peddles in the provinces. Oscar—the amiable, irresponsible, esurient Oscar—with no more sense of a picture than of the fit of a coat, has the courage of the opinions—of others!" The last sentence was a double-edged gibe, for Oscar Wilde had already been caught by Whistler appropriating that witty definition of a disciple. He had plenty of Irish combativeness in him, but he took no pleasure in wounding. He would have been incapable of calling out, as Whistler did once on seeing Pennell enter a dining-room arm-in-arm with Mortimer Menpes, "Take care, Pennell! Remember Father Damien died."

Few of his remembered sayings are malicious, fewer perhaps than with any other wit except Sydney Smith. And it is all the greater proof of his fundamental good nature, seeing that he had a thick skin himself and a prodigious sense of his own importance. His comment on an American hostess, "She tried to start a *salon,* but only succeeded in opening a saloon"; on Bernard Shaw: "He has no enemies but he is thoroughly disliked by his friends" (not true, by the way); and the implication of his reply, "Do I know George Moore? I know him so well that I have not spoken to him in ten years"—these about exhaust the list of his wounding remarks. His comment on an actress reputed to suffer from sex propensities similar to his own, "Dear ——, she is one of Nature's gentlemen," hardly comes under the head of malice; nor does his delightful comment on "the wise youth" of the 'nineties: "The gods bestowed on Max the gift of perpetual old age." Great wits have not often been good-natured. He was extraordinarily unresentful. Henley reviewed "The Ballad of

Reading Gaol" with a brutality which, seeing that he was kicking a ruined man, left something to be desired in chivalry. But, Mr. O'Sullivan says, "as usual with Oscar, he did not seem to have much resentment against Henley." He said:

> "Henley owes me seven-and-six. The other day I read a review of his praising a novel by someone named Mary Cholmondeley. I bought the book and before I had read very far I came on this sentence: 'The birds were singing on every twig and on every little twiglet.' Now you know, when an artist comes on a sentence like that in a book it is impossible for him to go on reading it. So I consider that Henley owes me seven-and-six."

The sweetness of his temper, his serene placability, was related to his gaiety and delightful sense of fun. It is hard to select from the stories which illustrate this, but his choosing a Noah's Ark for one of his little boys is one of my favourites. After comparing the merits of several with Pateresque deliberation, and when the shopman was about to wrap up the one in which the greatest aesthetic merits had been discovered, Oscar held up his hand. "Stop! I have not yet tasted Noah's head." I like, too, the story of his stepping into a florist's and asking, "Can you take flowers out of the window?" "Certainly, sir, which do you want?" "Oh, I don't want any. I only thought some of them looked rather tired."

E. F. Benson, in his reminiscences of the 'nineties, "As We Were", gives an example of the way Oscar Wilde used to handle over-earnest people. While taking a lady down to dinner on his arm who was evidently prepared to hang upon his lips, the following conversation took place:

"What terrible weather we are having."

"Yes, but if it wasn't for this snow, how could we believe in the immortality of the soul?"

"What an interesting question, Mr. Wilde. But tell me exactly what you mean."

"I haven't the slightest idea."

Those who remember Wilde will have no difficulty in imagining the gaiety of his laugh at that moment.

He was fond of giving that turn to sententious observations in his stage dialogue:

> ALGERNON: All women become like their mothers: that is their tragedy. No man does: that's his.
>
> JACK: Is that clever?
>
> ALGERNON: It is perfectly phrased! And quite as true as any observation in civilised life should be.
>
> JACK: I am sick to death of cleverness. Everybody is clever nowadays. You can't go anywhere without meeting clever people. The thing has become a public nuisance. I wish to goodness we had a few fools left.
>
> ALGERNON: We have.

His delightful exuberant playfulness (his intellect was vigorous enough to permit him to be playful on serious topics too) and his fundamental kindliness are two of his characteristics as a wit. And there is a third: his conception of himself as a great dandy. Dandyism, as Baudelaire was so fond of expounding, is a philosophy, an attitude towards life of which dress and deportment are only symptoms. One mark of the dandy is to use frivolity, which can be "the most insolent refinement of satire", as a medium of self-expression. Oscar Wilde did so—imposingly, joyfully, but also—and it is contrary to the essence of Dandyism—good-naturedly. He was too easy-going and kind to be a real dandy, though that is how he saw himself, for he loved to be the spectator of the part he played. "He told me," Mr. O'Sullivan says, "that at an evening party in London, when he was at the height of his fame, Hubert Crackanthorpe, a young man who had just published a little book of stories, came up to him and asked: 'What do you think of my work, Mr. Wilde?' 'Your play, dear boy, your *play*,' replied Wilde. He laughed heartily as he told this, and then went on as though speaking of another. 'The great dandy who had just come in to get rid of a few minutes, and was going on to another party, saying indifferently as he was putting on his coat: 'Your play, dear boy your play.' " That anecdote reveals Oscar Wilde's delight in his conception of himself, which he so often dramatized to the exhilaration of the others, persuading them for the time that all life was malleable to the imagination.

Though Oscar Wilde was only a second-rate poet, and his plays (with the exception of "The Importance of Being Earnest" and "Salomé") were mechanical in situation and sentimental in substance, he will be remembered because, in spite of his work being in some respects artificial and imitative, he triumphed in self-expression. His "self" happened to be a full-blown specimen of recurrent type: Oscar Wilde is the Romantic with a sense of humour. Dizzy, a more complex nature, is the only other figure in nineteenth-century literature comparable to him in that respect.

It is characteristic of the Romantic to fawn upon what he seriously admires, sometimes in so excessive a manner that the reader may be made to feel positively nauseated, but the humorous Romantic is apt to conclude with a devastating quirk which leaves the reader wondering if, after all, it is not *he* who is sentimental. One condition, no doubt, of literary survival is to be unlike (in strength and weakness) other authors; a second is to bloom extravagantly after one's own manner. This is by no means the highest form of posthumous fame, but Oscar Wilde meets those conditions. And he will live thanks also to his shining wit. Scattered up and down everything he wrote are amusing and penetrating comments on life and art. Their form, which was often modish, may have ceased to amaze, as it did when it was new, but the substance of many of them cannot become insignificant.

The merit of an aphorism or proverb lies in its fixing the expression of genuine experience. You cannot ask more "truth" from it than that. Many of Oscar Wilde's aphorisms do this, though it is true that there are among them many counterfeit coins of thought which glitter for a moment and then turn dim. He had a happy gift for reversing a commonplace so as to bring out another less familiar aspect of truth: "Punctuality is the thief of Time" is an example, and "It is only shallow people who do not judge by appearances" is another. (At times this form became mechanical and tiresome.) Running over those which I have noted down from time to time, I have been astonished by their depth. No one has ever coined a truer aesthetic aphorism than "All art is at once surface and symbol." Add to this, "There are two ways of disliking art. One is to dislike it and the other is to like it rationally", and "Nothing is so dangerous as being too modern—one is apt to grow old-fashioned quite suddenly" (true, alas! to a large extent of his own works), and "It is the spectator and not life that art really mirrors"—and we have already learnt much about Art.

Then with regard to life itself, how deep the following comments go: "Experience is a question of instinct about life"; "Scandal is gossip made tedious by morality"; "Conscience makes egotists of us all"; "Don't tell me you have exhausted life. When a man says that one knows life has exhausted him." Then there are those delightful flourishes—defiant expressions of his temperament, such as "To love oneself is the beginning of a lifelong romance", or this very human confession, "I am the only person in the world I should like to know thoroughly, but I don't see any chance of it just at present", or "Enough is as good as a meal". I have been struck, too, by the way an aphorism of Oscar Wilde's will sometimes sum up a large part of the message of voluminous writers: half that of Tolstoy is contained in, "A community is infinitely more brutalized by the habitual employment of punishment than it is by the occasional occurrence of crime." Again, how much of Yeats' theory of artistic composition is expressed by saying "Man is least himself when he talks in his own person. Give him a *mask* and he will tell the truth." The essence of Samuel Butler's ethics is contained in "Conscience must be merged in instinct before we become fine"; and the upshot of Meredith's philosophy in his novels, as far as love is concerned, is recorded in "Only the senses can cure the soul, and only the soul can cure the senses." That is good, but the most illuminating of all aphorisms on physical relations in love is, I think, that of the philosopher F. H. Bradley, the author of "Appearance and Reality": "To be chaste is to have the body in the keeping of the heart. Their divorce is the one thing which makes unchastity." That is a clear word on matters which have cruelly and unnecessarily perplexed mankind.

2

Realism was Wilde's bugbear as a critic. His dialogue ("The Decay of Lying" (1889) is a whimsically extravagant pronouncement of his detestation of it. The following passage is interesting as showing what he thought of contemporary novelists from this point of view.

VIVIAN (*reading in a very clear, musical voice*). "THE DECAY OF LYING: A PROTEST.—One of the chief causes that can be assigned for the curiously commonplace character of most of the literature of our age is undoubtedly the decay of Lying as an art, a science, and a social pleasure. The ancient historians gave us delightful fiction in the form of fact; the modern novelist presents us with dull facts under the guise of fiction. The Blue-Book is rapidly becoming his ideal both for method and manner. He has his tedious *document humain*, his miserable little *coin de la création*, into which he peers with his microscope. He is to be found at the Librairie Nationale, or at the British Museum, shamelessly reading up his subject. He has not even the courage of other people's ideas, but insists on going directly to life for everything, and ultimately, between encyclopædias and personal experience, he comes to the ground, having drawn his types from the family circle or from the weekly washerwoman, and having acquired an amount of useful information from which never, even in his most meditative moments, can he thoroughly free himself.

"The loss that results to literature in general from this false ideal of our time can hardly be overestimated. People have a careless way of talking about a 'born liar', just as they talk about a 'born poet'. But in both cases they are wrong. Lying and poetry are arts—arts, as Plato saw, not unconnected with each other—and they require the most careful study, the most disinterested devotion. Indeed, they have their technique, just as the more material arts of painting and sculpture have, their subtle secrets of form and colour, their craft-mysteries, their deliberate artistic methods. As one knows the poet by his fine music, so one can recognise the liar by his rich rhythmic utterance, and in neither case will the casual inspiration of the moment suffice. Here, as elsewhere, practice must precede perfection. But in modern days while the fashion of writing poetry has become far too common, and should, if possible, be discouraged, the fashion of lying has almost fallen into disrepute. Many a young man starts in life with a natural gift for exaggeration which, if nurtured in congenial and sympathetic surroundings, or by the imitation of the best models, might grow into something really great and wonderful. But, as a rule, he comes to nothing. He either falls into careless habits of accuracy——"

CYRIL. My dear fellow!

VIVIAN. Please don't interrupt in the middle of a sentence. "He either falls into careless habits of accuracy, or takes to frequenting the society of the aged and the well-informed. Both things are equally fatal to his imagination, as indeed they would be fatal to the imagination of anybody, and in a short time he develops a morbid and unhealthy faculty of truth-telling, begins to verify all statements made in his presence, has no hesitation in contradicting people who are much younger than himself, and often ends by writing novels which are so lifelike that no one can possibly believe in their probability. This is no isolated instance that we are giving. It is simply one example out of many; and if something cannot be done to check, or at least to modify, our monstrous worship of facts, Art will become sterile, and beauty will pass away from the land.

"Even Mr. Robert Louis Stevenson, that delightful master of delicate and fanciful prose, is tainted with this modern vice, for we know positively no other name for it. There is such a thing as robbing a story of its reality by trying to make it too true, and 'The Black Arrow' is so inartistic as not to contain a single anachronism to boast of, while the transformation of Dr. Jekyll reads dangerously like an experiment out of the *Lancet*. As for Mr. Rider Haggard, who really has, or had once, the makings of a perfectly magnificent liar, he is now so afraid of being suspected of genius that when he does tell us anything marvellous, he feels bound to invent a personal reminiscence, and to put it into a footnote as a kind of cowardly corroboration. Nor are our other novelists much better. Mr. Henry James writes fiction as if it were a painful duty, and wastes upon mean motives and imperceptible 'points of view' his neat literary style, his felicitous phrases, his swift and caustic satire. Mr. Hall Caine, it is true, aims at the grandiose, but then he writes at the top of his voice. He is so loud that one cannot hear what he says. Mr. James Payn is an adept in the art of concealing what is not worth finding. He hunts down the obvious with the enthusiasm of a short-sighted detective. As one turns over the pages, the suspense of the author becomes almost unbearable. The horses of Mr. William Black's phaeton do not soar towards the sun. They merely frighten the sky at evening into violent chromolithographic effects. On seeing them approach, the peasants take refuge in dialect. Mrs. Oliphant prattles pleasantly about curates, lawn-tennis parties, domesticity, and other wearisome things. Mr. Marion Crawford has immolated himself upon the altar of local colour. He is like the lady in the French comedy who keeps talking about 'le beau ciel d'Italie'. Besides, he has fallen into the bad habit of uttering moral platitudes. He is always telling us that to be good is to be good, and that to be bad is to be wicked. At times he is almost edifying. 'Robert Elsmere' is of course a masterpiece—a masterpice of the 'genre ennuyeux', the one form of literature that the English people seems thoroughly to enjoy. A thoughtful young friend of ours once told us that it reminded him of the sort of conversation that goes on at a meat tea in the house of a serious Nonconformist family, and we can quite believe it. Indeed it is only in England that such a book could be produced. England is the home of lost ideas. As for that great and daily increasing school of novelists for whom the sun always rises in the East End, the only thing that can be said about them is that they find life crude, and leave it raw.

"In France, though nothing so deliberately tedious as 'Robert Elsmere' has been produced, things are not much better. M. Guy de Maupassant, with his keen mordant irony and his hard vivid style, strips life of the few poor rags that still cover her, and shows us foul sore and festering wound. He writes lurid little tragedies in which everybody is ridiculous; bitter comedies at which one cannot laugh for very tears. M. Zola, true to the lofty principle that he lays down in one of his pronunciamentos on literature, 'L'homme de génie n'a jamais d'esprit', is determined to show that, if he has not got genius, he can at least be dull. And how well he succeeds! He is not without power. Indeed at times, as in 'Germinal', there is something almost epic in his work. But his work is entirely wrong from beginning to end, and wrong not on the ground of morals, but on the ground of art. From any ethical standpoint it is just what it should be. The author is perfectly truthful, and describes things exactly as they happen. What more can any moralist desire? We have no sympathy at all with the moral indignation of our time against M. Zola. It is simply the indignation of Tartuffe on being exposed. But from the standpoint of art, what can be said in favour of the author of 'L'Assommoir', 'Nana' and 'Pot-Bouille'? Nothing. Mr. Ruskin once described the characters in George Eliot's novels as being like the sweepings of a Pentonville omnibus, but M. Zola's characters are much worse. They have their dreary vices, and their drearier virtues. The record of their lives is absolutely without interest. Who cares what happens to them? In literature we require distinction, charm, beauty and imaginative power. We don't want to be harrowed and disgusted with an account of the doings of the lower orders. M. Daudet is better. He has wit, a light touch and an amusing style. But he has lately committed literary suicide. Nobody can possibly care for Delobelle with his 'Il faut lutter pour l'art', or for Valmajour with his eternal refrain about the nightingale, or for the poet in 'Jack' with his 'mots cruels', now that we have learned from 'Vingt Ans de ma Vie littéraire' that these characters were taken directly from life. To us they seem to have suddenly lost all their vitality, all the few qualities they ever possessed. The only real people are the people who never existed, and if a novelist is base enough to go to life for his personages he should at least pretend that they are creations, and not boast of them as copies. The justification of a character in a novel is not that other persons are what they are, but that the author is what he is. Otherwise the novel is not a work of art. As for M. Paul Bourget, the master of the *roman psychologique*, he commits the error of imagining that the men and women of modern life are capable of being infinitely analysed for an innumerable series of chapters. In point of fact what is interesting about people in good society—and M. Bourget rarely moves out of the Faubourg St. Germain, except to come to London—is the mask that each one of them wears, not the reality that lies behind the mask. It is a humiliating confession, but we are all of us made out of the same stuff. In Falstaff there is something of Hamlet, in Hamlet there is not a little of Falstaff. The fat knight has his moods of melancholy, and the young prince his moments of coarse humour. Where we differ from each other is purely in accidentals: in dress, manner, tone of voice, religious opinions, personal appearance, tricks of habit and the like. The more one analyses people, the more all reasons for analysis disappear. Sooner or later one comes to that dreadful universal thing called human nature. Indeed, as anyone who has ever worked among the poor knows only too well, the brotherhood of man is no mere poet's dream, it is a most depressing and humiliating reality; and if a writer insists upon analysing the upper classes, he might just as well write of match-girls and costermongers at once. . . ."

At the end of this dialogue he summed up the doctrines of what he called "the new æsthetics":

"Art never expresses anything but itself. It has an independent life, just as Thought has, and develops purely on its own lines. It is not necessarily realistic in an age of realism, nor spiritual in an age of faith. So far from being the creation of its time, it is usually in direct opposition to it, and the only history that it preserves for us is the history of its own progress. Sometimes it returns upon its footsteps, and revives some antique form, as happened in the archaistic movement of late Greek Art, and in the pre-Raphaelite movement of our own day. At other times it entirely anticipates its age, and produces in one century work that it takes another century to understand, to appreciate and to enjoy. In no case does it reproduce its age. To pass from the art of a time to the time itself is the great mistake that all historians commit.

The second doctrine is this. All bad art comes from returning to Life and Nature, and elevating them into ideals. Life and Nature may sometimes be used as part of Art's rough material, but before they are of any real service to art they must be translated into artistic conventions. The moment Art surrenders its imaginative medium it surrenders everything. As a method Realism is a complete failure, and the two things that every artist should avoid are modernity of form and modernity of subject-matter. To us, who live in the nineteenth century, any century is a suitable subject for art except our own. The only beautiful things are the things that do not concern us. It is, to have the pleasure of quoting myself, exactly because Hecuba is nothing to us that her sorrows are so suitable a motive for a tragedy. Besides, it is only the modern that ever becomes old-fashioned. M. Zola sits down to give us a picture of the Second Empire. Who cares for the Second Empire now? It is out of date. Life goes faster than Realism, but Romanticism is always in front of Life.

"The third doctrine is that Life imitates Art far more than Art imitates Life. This results not merely from Life's imitative instinct, but from the fact that the self-conscious aim of Life is to find expression, and that Art offers it certain beautiful forms through which it may realise that energy. It is a theory that has never been put forward before, but it is extremely fruitful, and throws an entirely new light upon the history of Art.

"It follows, as a corollary from this, that external Nature also imitates Art. The only effects that she can show us are effects that we have already seen through poetry, or in paintings. This is the secret of Nature's charm, as well as the explanation of Nature's weakness."

3

Oscar Wilde was born in Dublin in 1854; he was the younger of the two sons of an eminent oculist who founded St. Mark's Ophthalmic Hospital in Dublin and was knighted ten years after Oscar's birth. He was of Anglo-Irish Protestant stock and he had married in 1851 a daughter of another Protestant family, Jane Francesca Elgee, known locally as a poet and a contributor to various reviews under the pseudonym "Speranza". She was a very clever, rather affected woman and an ardent Irish Nationalist. Later, in the years of her husband's professional prosperity, she became even better known as a Dublin hostess, and even in that city of conversation, as a brilliant converser. The Wildes lived with a kind of slovenly lavishness in Merrion Square, but Sir William Wilde's reputation in private life was far from good; and though in their own eyes they belonged to the Irish gentry, and were affiliated to it, it is doubtful if in Ireland, where eighteenth-century standards of social differences lingered far into the late nineteenth, that claim would have been generally recognized. Besides, the Wildes were bohemians and intellectuals. No doubt this ambiguity of status had an effect on Oscar, who was apt in after life to insist, rather unnecessarily sometimes, on special respect being paid to him as an Irish gentleman by his colleagues on the Press or by those whom he did not regard as his social equals.

The first turning-point in his life was his leaving Trinity College, Dublin, with an Oxford scholarship. Ruskin was at that time Slade Professor, but his influence, though it fired no doubt Oscar Wilde's admiration of the pre-Raphaelites, was not so profound as that of Pater, whose "Studies in the History of the Renaissance", and especially the concluding chapter, made upon Oscar Wilde an indelible impression. "It is my golden book," he used to say, "the very flower of decadence: the last trumpet should have sounded the moment it was written." From it he acquired the doctrines of Art for Art's Sake, of living for exquisite moments and of "curiously testing new opinions and courting new impressions". He became, in both senses of the word, the vulgarizer of Pater's ideas. Pater also taught him to aim at a self-conscious perfection of style. Then followed the period of his æsthetic lecturing and posturing. After visiting America, when he was approaching thirty, he went to Paris, where he developed a more mundane form of dandyism. In 1884 he married the daughter of a Q.C., Miss Constance Lloyd, and on her dowry settled at 16 Tite Street, Chelsea. He had fallen in love, and the marriage was for some time a happy one. He disliked lecturing, but as a good husband and father continued to do so and to write anonymously for the *World* and the *Pall Mall Gazette*. In 1887 he became the editor of a fashion monthly, *Woman's World*. He apparently enjoyed his journalism, but he was rather ashamed of it; and although in 1887 he wrote in addition "Lord Arthur Savile's Crime", "The Sphinx Without a Secret", and other stories, and in the next year "The Happy Prince and Other Tales", he liked to be taken for an idler. In 1889–90 "The Decay of Lying", "The Critic as an Artist", and "The Picture of Dorian Gray" appeared, and Oscar emerged before the public in the full panoply of his glittering talents. "Dorian Gray" was greeted with an indignation now difficult to understand, though there is an aroma about it capable of rousing suspicion. It also contained much praise of "sin". Then he published "The Soul of Man Under Socialism" and "Salomé". His self-confidence was at full tide and wherever he went he made a prodigious impression. In 1892 his prosperity began with the performance of "Lady Windermere's Fan". This success was followed by "A Woman of No Importance", and in January 1895 by "An Ideal Husband". Six weeks later "The Importance of Being Earnest" began to run at the St. James'. It is said that in 1894 he was making eight thousand a year. He lived extravagantly, and some observers report that he was spoilt; the earlier Oscar who took so much care to please now became confident that he must please, and spoke of himslf with an arrogance that was unrelieved by humour. This is the impression he made upon M. André Gide just before the Queensberry case (April 3, 1895), but M. Gide is not, I think, an entirely trustworthy reporter—however, there is confirmation. On April 26 he was tried at the Old Bailey for offences under the Criminal Law Amendment Act. Owing to the witnesses being blackmailers, the jury were divided on their verdict, and he was tried again. On May 25 he was sentenced by Mr. Justice Wills to two years' hard labour. There was no charge against him of corrupting youth, and Edward Marjoribanks in his life of Lord Carson, counsel for the Marquess of Queensberry, says that "had the Court of Criminal Appeal existed then, it is possible that either this conviction, owing to the circumstances of the trial and the uncorroborated evidence of his accomplices, or the sentence, which was a heavy one, would not have stood".

The only work he wrote after his release was his best poem, "The Ballad of Reading Gaol". During imprisonment he had written a long letter to Lord Alfred Douglas, parts of which were afterwards published by Robert Ross as "De Profundis", his finest piece of sustained prose.

After his release he often talked as brilliantly as ever, and his indestructible pleasure in life was never totally in abeyance, but his will was broken: he could not work. He died in Paris, and in spite of the relief he often received from his friends, in poverty, on November 30, 1900, in his forty-seventh year.

WHISTLER

D. B. WYNDHAM LEWIS

> She comes! She comes! the sable Throne behold
> Of *Night* Primæval, and of *Chaos* old!
> Before her, *Fancy's* gilded clouds decay,
> And all its varying Rain-bows die away,
> *Wit* shoots in vain his momentary fires,
> The meteor drops, and in a flash expires,
> As one by one, at dread *Medea's* strain,
> The sick'ning stars fade off th'ethereal Plain;
>
> . . . . . .
>
> Thy hand, great Anarch! lets the curtain fall;
> And Universal Darkness buries All.
>
> —The Dunciad.

ONE HUNDRED YEARS OR SO AFTER POPE'S ONSLAUGHT DULLNESS WAS reigning more triumphant than before; secure, constipated, implacable, serene, her huge leaden feet firmly planted on the exhausted, beaten land. One or two other gallant rebels had risen since Pope to loose against that vast immovable mass of stupidity darts which fell blunted and harmless and left no mark, and Byron and Brummell had died in exile. Whistler, fifty years after them, was to attack the Dunciad's goddess with splendid savagery and Cyranoesque *panache*, and finally to get her groggy. Although mediocrity is still adored by the mass of the Islanders (as the foreigner Whistler always called us), its power is no longer absolute. Alarming fissures have been lately noted in the Public School System. The efficacy of the Team Spirit, of which the incident of the Gadarene swine is notoriously the most historic illustration, as a complete rule of life is being openly questioned. Even compulsory cricket, the most powerful method known to science of stamping out individuality in the young, next to Nazism, is losing a little of its religious terror, and its hieratic jargon of straight bats and sticky wickets is used by *The Times* today only in major national crises. If one cannot praise Whistler exclusively for all these benefits, one may award him certain honours of the pioneer. Cricket never came into his orbit, and in any case Americans do not understand its ethos, regarding cricket commonly as a form of racial catalepsy and leaving it at that. But the ritual of the Cold Tub, no less curious and sacred, aroused his interest and mirth sufficiently, as his description of the foundation of the Bath Club as "the latest incarnation of the British discovery of water" demonstrates. Had Whistler chosen to live among the Academicians in St. John's Wood those solemn tribal rites at Lord's would surely have impinged sooner or later on his consciousness, and the M.C.C. might be licking their wounds today. It is highly necessary, when contemplating this foreign iconoclast, this mocker, to realize that it was not the contemporary British attitude to art alone which drove him frantic. His high intelligence related this attitude to others of the code with which they are indissolubly linked, and he explored sources. His delight in discovering, during a voyage in a P. and O. liner, that all the British first-class passengers were sick every night in correct evening clothes ("you might as well dress to ride in an omnibus") was increased by a scientific satisfaction in finding the Samurai running impeccably true to form. The majority of these same sick but correct ones, if they ever visited one of Whistler's exhibitions, would guffaw with the Taylors, the Hamertons, the Quilters, and the other costive bonzes who lived to rue their pronouncements. The battle of the 70's and 80's was never merely Whistler *v.* British art critics, it was Whistler *v.* the Island Race.

2

The Butterly was not born with his sting, but developed and perfected it, like other *méchants*, in self-defence. This judgment runs directly contrary to the consecrated Whistler Legend, and even Max Beerbohm in his brilliant essay on "The Gentle Art of Making Enemies" seems to accept Whistler's cantankerousness and bellicosity as normal. The evidence of intimates like the Pennells, Elizabeth and Joseph, rebuts this completely. A natural charm and gaiety, that high courtesy which a certain American type shares only with the gentlemen of Spain, that distaste for crudeness, that appetite for drollery remained with him all his life, and he loved his friends. Nor was his wit, the quiddity of which may be more fully discussed in due course, dependent necessarily on the will to hurt. "What!" said one of his West Point examiners, "you don't know the date of the battle of Buena Vista? Suppose you went out to dinner and the company began to talk about the Mexican War, and you, a West Point man, were asked the date of this battle—what would you do?"

"I should refuse," answered Cadet Whistler, politely, "to associate with people who could talk of such things at dinner."

Wilde, later to be his antagonist and, it must be confessed, his master in witty slanging, might have made just that nonchalant answer. It was not for this, however, that he was sent down from the United States Military Academy, but for his airy aloofness towards chemistry. "Had silicon been a gas," mused Whistler in later life, "I should have been a Major-General." Instead of which, after a brief stay in the Coast and Geodetic Survey, where he added to an already evident sketching genius the rudiments of etching, cost the Government a great deal in ruined copper plates—his passion for hard labour was already driving him—and left behind him a joyous memory of after-hours rollicking, he went to Paris and became the complete *rapin*, the Murger Character to end all Murger characters. Anyone who has mixed with the Left Bank art colony—in Whistler's time, the late fifties, it had already established itself in Montparnasse—is aware that no Paris Bohemians have ever been more conscientiously Bohemian or Parisian than the American contingent. *Le petit Whistler* flung himself with zest into Murgerism, living in a garret up six flights, dancing at the Bullier and other students' balls with Finette and Mimi, Musette and La Tigresse, treading the Quarter in rakish sombrero and baggy corduroys, leading every studio rag, every concerted *blague*, inventing every latest *scie*, pawning his wardrobe at intervals—he who had, like so many of his compatriots, an allowance, 350 dollars a year, which was wealth in the Quarter—and working at his art like a passionate beaver the whole time, as the collection of etchings called The French Set later revealed.

These happy years gave him a reputation for idle French frivolity which was to do him no good on landing later among the serious-minded in Albion. They also developed and perfected his conversational and literary style into its final form, adding a light French grace, swing, sparkle and much *argot* to that fondness for Jacobean English which he owed to an infancy steeped in the Authorized Version.

If a similar grounding, according to Mr. Wilenski, ruined Ruskin alike in style and thought, it merely endowed Whistler, like Kipling after him, with a facility for studding his style with those Scriptural or near-Scriptural ornaments which add impressive piquancy to a phrase, and have been known to lend dignity even to a leading article in the ——.* That this literary affectation often takes little account of original meaning, and still less of context, does not deprive the page it decorates of that sonorous appeal to eye and ear for which many of the English still revere what has always been acknowledged—save by the late Professor Phillimore, a critical minority of one—the chief monument of the English tongue. Spice these solemn traditional cadences with "the finesse of the Frenchman . . . clever café cackle . . . the *chic* of great habit", and we have the main formula for that Autolycan style (Max Beerbohm) to which Whistler devoted, proportionately, as much care and craftsmanship as he devoted to an etching, or a letter to his Paris bootmaker, or the re-pasting on his walls, by a slovenly bailiff awakened for that purpose, of badly-arranged bills advertising a bankruptcy sale at the White House, Chelsea. Hence the effortless ease, the swift tempo, the sure rhythms of his writing, which might stand as one more illustration of Principle No. 1 of his Propositions, No. 2: "A picture is finished when all trace of the means used to bring about the end has disappeared."

Fools in Great Britain have never been paid a similar compliment, except by another great contemporary master of the insult.

Wilde was at the same time finding it difficult to conceal his low opinion of the pontiffs and their public as well. His exquisitely weary, cynical, olive-faced Lord Henrys and Cecil Grahams, his exquisite Ernests and Gilberts, lolling in their armchairs overlooking the Green Park, wreathed in the smoke of choice Egyptian cigarettes or toying at supper with ortolans and Chambertin, loose off innumerable darts at British stupidity and British critics ("mediocrity weighing mediocrity in the balance, and incompetence applauding its brother"); but their languid elegance is not of Whistler's world, they do not descend to the dust and heat of the arena, they sling no knobbly missiles, they lounge above the conflict like gods in a cloud, cool, superb, amused, their insults glance off the Philistine's hide and draw no blood. Moreover, Wilde rather windily held criticism itself to be a major art ("It is criticism that leads us. The Critical Spirit and the World Spirit are one"), and declared that "the really great creative artist can never judge of other people's work at all, and can hardly, in fact, judge of his own": a typically Wildean

* May be filled in by the reader, according to experience and taste.

counterblast to Whistler's key-dogma, set forth at the Ruskin trial—"I hold that none but an artist can be a competent critic"—and developed immediately afterwards in that slashing pamphlet "Art and Art-Critics". It is impossible to leave Wilde for long out of Whistler's cosmos. Infuriating as the amateur's public pronouncements on Art were to the passionate craftsman—"We are of opinion," writes Whistler to Wilde in the *World*, "that you talk like Sidney Colvin in the provinces and, with the exception of your knee-breeches, you dress like 'Arry Quilter"—Whistler recognized Wilde as an intellectual equal. So of course did the critics, to whom both were equally low comedians, eccentric and laughable to a degree. It was not long before *Punch* got them both into one joke. One must strive to get a clear picture of the background against which these two Cyranos postured and whirled their blades: the London of their day, with its dingy, insignificant main streets, rich in mud and horse-dung, its gas-lamps and hansoms, its securely fenced aristocracy which, as yet, no Assyrian or cognate tribe had subjugated in purple and gold, its leisurely traffic, its appalling underworld and dreadful charity, its few and naive amusements, its population of bipeds in top hats and trailing skirts, its gin-palaces and Kyrle Societies, its major and minor prophets, sacred, secular, and for the most part bearded, its banal Academies, the prevailing smugness of this *gens lubricata*, a kind of thick gloss covering everything, of which hypocrisy—kindly explained away by M. Georges Bernanos recently as "the effect of hereditary Anglo-Saxon shyness buttressed by education, verbal reserve, and the mute complicity of all"—was the outer layer. It is vain to sneer at the Victorians, who had so many virtues and bred such great men, but this superfatted complacency, their most obvious characteristic, was directly responsible for the ultimate revolt of Whistler. He could stand criticism from the instructed French. For some time he stood much more of it from the uninstructed English than one would think possible in a man of masterful temper fiercely and humbly devoted to his artistic faith, aware of his genius, streaked richly like most artists of stature with the temperament of the child and the *cabotin*, a painful, ruthless toiler after his ideal. Whistler had his own faults, but smugness was not one of them. His principal enemies were stiff and stinking with it, it leaps from every other page of *The Gentle Art*, it booms from Whistler's résumé of the evidence given by Tom Taylor at the Ruskin libel suit in 1878:

> "Mr. Tom Taylor—Poor Law Commissioner, Editor of *Punch*, and so forth—and so forth: 'I am an art critic of some standing. I have been engaged in this capacity by *The Times*, and other journals, for the past twenty years. I edited the "Life of Reynolds", and "Haydon". I have *always* studied art. I have seen these pictures of Mr. Whistler's when they were exhibited at the Dudley and the Grosvenor Galleries. The "Nocturne" in black and gold I do not think a serious work of art." —The witness here took from the pockets of his overcoat copies of *The Times*, and, with the permission of the Court, read again with unction his own criticism, to every word of which, he said, he still adhered. 'All Mr. Whistler's work is unfinished. It is sketchy. He no doubt possesses artistic qualities, but'," etc., etc.

Somebody with the gift of Parody should long since have described this trial in the manner of Macaulay on Warren Hastings. Well-armed as Whistler was, jaunty and quick in fence, he must have looked at regular intervals like a *maître d'armes* facing a herd of rogue elephants. The

Attorney-General, for example, rose to unprecedented heights, even for an expensive lawyer, in his address for the defence:

"Let them examine the nocturne in blue and silver, said to represent Battersea Bridge. What was that structure in the middle? Was it a telescope or a fire-escape? Was it like Battersea Bridge? What were the figures at the top of the bridge? And if they were horses and carts, how in the name of fortune were they to get off?"

Mr. Attorney-General was addressing a jury of twelve solid, reasonable, British middle-class citizens, picked at random. They awarded Whistler one farthing damages.

3

It was not until seven years after Whistler left Paris to settle in London (1860) that he opened fire on the critics. His first overtures to the Islanders had been not entirely unsuccessful. "At the Piano", rejected by the Salon, was hung in the Academy with some etchings in 1860. Within two years came the first suspicious, startled recoil of the *dilettanti*, ears laid back, whites of eyes showing. "The White Girl", rejected by the Academy and hung in the Berners Street Gallery under the title "The Woman in White", led one of the critics, bewildered, to point out in print that it seemed to have little or nothing to do ("Every Picture Tells a Story") with Wilkie Collins's novel, then popular. At this period every decent artist, and still more every Academician, was industriously digging out and pegging away at picturesque "incidents" and "bits" from Shakespeare and the world's classics, past and present, with Lemprière and the *Encyclopædia Britannica* at his elbow, and, locked jealously away in a back room lest some unscrupulous rival should divine his "subject" and sneak in first, a growing heap of period-properties, authentic and Wardour Street, tapestry, armour, costume, furniture, weapons, glass and pottery, romantic junk and tushery of every description. But the critic's natural mistake, of a kind which was later to stir Whistler to cockatoo-like screeches, moved him in 1862 merely to a polite explanation to the critic's paper. "I had no intention whatever of illustrating Mr. Wilkie Collins's novel—it so happens, indeed, that I have never read it." This mildness, almost shocking to lovers of "The Gentle Art", demonstrates that despite a few setbacks and increasing provocation—"bizarre", "smudgy", and "eccentric" were the vogue-words already applied to his work by 1862—Whistler was as yet suffering fools if not gladly, at least with masterly resignation. Even when "The White Girl" moved Mr. P. G. Hamerton to mirth he held his peace. Mr. Hamerton, art critic of the *Saturday Review* and other cultured organs, is perhaps the critic-type of the *stupide dix-neuvième*, As Léon Daudet has labelled it: a pontiff of portentous complacency, an arbiter of British taste, a dilettante of art and letters, an essayist of almost Marcaurelian nullity. Mr. Hamerton did not laugh alone. The crowd laughed as well, and the critics, perceiving they were for once (as Mr. Hamerton himself said in the *Fine Arts Quarterly* after "The White Girl" had been hissed publicly by art lovers) "quite of the popular way of thinking", began a joyous braying, soon to swell into a hallelujah chorus. And still Whistler, slaving at his art and oblivious of all else, apparently, held his peace. It was not until Mr. Hamerton gave tongue in the *Saturday* in 1867, offended beyond endurance and protesting that "Symphony in White No. 111" was not a symphony in white because there were other colours in it, that the thunder broke. In a letter to the *Saturday* which the editor was for some time afraid to print, Whistler exploded:

"*Bon Dieu!* did this wise person expect white hair and chalked faces? And does he then, in his astounding consequence, believe that a Symphony in F contains no other note, but shall be a continued repetition of F, F, F? . . . Fool!"

The war had begun. The Islanders had asked for it and they could now have it, *à outrance*.

4

The decisive engagements of the long, desultory campaign which followed (it lasted till the nineties) are recorded for all time in "The Gentle Art of Making Enemies", itself as distinctive a work of art as the Nocturnes and the Arrangements. Rolling some of its vintage insults meditatively round his tongue, the epicure of 1940 perceives that Whistler was extremely fortunate in his period. The Fleet Street of the 70's, 80's, and 90's, not yet the sedulous ape of New York tabloidery, recognized the existence of a small, cultivated, leisured evening-newspaper public and strove to meet its taste. Even at the outbreak of the Great War (1914) there were at least three evening papers, long since dead, produced exclusively by and for the educated. To appreciate the gulf between that period and now, one may recall that when the brilliant man-about-town Harry Cust, editing the *Pall Mall Gazette* in the 90's, wrote a leader on the downfall of the Casimir-Périer cabinet he gaily headlined it "Périer Joué". He also printed essays by Alice Meynell and a nightly piece of polished light verse by various hands. Moreover, the skins of the period were seemingly thicker; combatants who deemed themselves wronged in a newspaper conflict did not run instantly to their lawyers, and the hairy terror of that monstrous Chinese enigma, the British laws of libel, did not then perpetually overhang editorial desks and intimidate the stoutest. The back-files of almost any London daily or evening paper will confirm this. Living today, Whistler would not have seen five per cent of his "Gentle Art" letters appearing in the Press; whereas an editor like Edmund Yates ("Atlas") of the *World* not only printed with joy anything Whistler cared to set his pen to, mischievously egging on the merry warrior and pointing out victims he might otherwise have missed as they skulked in the undergrowth, but printed with equal relish Whistler's attacks on the *World's* own critic; a situation quite incredible to admirers, say, of some clerical star journalist of today who discharges (let us suppose) weekly missiles of the most vicious kind, to which his cautious editor would of necessity permit no reply. Whistler, then, was lucky in his Press. He was lucky also in his victims. Sir Max Beerbohm, I think, need not have tempered his just admiration of the master's sword-play in the least had he acknowledged that, barring Wilde, there was never anybody to stand up to Whistler with his own weapons. And Wilde, moreover, vanquished him with ease.

"Atlas, this is very sad! With our James vulgarity begins at home, and should be allowed to stay there."

"As for borrowing Mr. Whistler's ideas about art, the only thoroughly original ideas that I have ever heard him express have had reference to his own superiority as a painter over painters greater than himself."

To such rapier-thrusts Whistler replied with rather feeble flourishes. "The rage of the sheep is terrible!" "A poor thing, Oscar!—'but', for once, I suppose, 'your own'." Can the devoutest addict of "The Gentle Art" pretend that these were any sort of counterstrokes? The victims whom Whistler scalped with joyous ease and exultant whoops were the solemn dullards, the Tom Taylors ("tough old Tom, the busy City bus, with its heavy jolting and many halts . . ."), the ineffable " 'Arry" Quilters, the Wyke Baylisses ("champion chess-player of Surrey, member of the Diocesan Council of Rochester, Fellow of the Society of Cyclists, and Public Orator of Noviomagus"), the Seymour Hadens, and those critics, metropolitan and provincial, who were to enrich his *catalogues raisonnés* with such jewels as:

"Nobody who sets any value on the roses and lilies that adorn the cheeks of our blooming girls can accept such murky tints as these as representative of a young English lady." (*The Era.*)

"Under the same roof with Mr. Whistler's strange productions is the collection of animal paintings done . . . for the proprietors of the *Graphic,* and very refreshing it is to turn into this agreeably-lighted room and rest on comfortable settees whilst looking at 'Mother Hubbard's Dog', or the sweet little pussy-cats in 'The Happy Family'." (*Liverpool Courier.*)

"The author of several books and pamphlets on the more imaginative realm of art, he [Mr. Wyke Bayliss, Whistler's successor as President of the Royal Society of British Artists] is, one would say, as much permeated by religion as he is by art; to both of these qualities, curiously enough, his canvases, which usually deal with cathedral interiors of cheery hue, bear witness." (*Pall Mall Gazette.*)

It is hard to believe that this last extract is not a piece of grave Bellocian fantasy but a serious appreciation by a metropolitan critic, and it is mournful to think how much more Whistler might have made of Mr. Bayliss, cyclist and Diocesan Councilman, had he so chosen. The fact is, and it in no way detracts from the rare bouquet of his literary work to face it, that most of his game were "sitters".* The *World* art critic describes some etchings as "unimportant in size", and Whistler deals with him instantly:

"Seriously, then, my Atlas, an etching does not depend, for its importance, on its size. . . . Be severe with your man. Tell him his 'job' should be 'neatly done'. I could cut my own throat better; and if need be, in case of his dismissal, I offer my services. Meanwhile, yours joyously."

It is gay, it is pleasing, it is novel, it is truculent, it is pointed, it is sufficient,

---

* Two of these unexpectedly hit back and deprived the Master of breath, the one being blunt Lady Meux ("You keep a civil tongue in that head of yours, Jimmy, or I'll have in someone to *finish* those portraits of me"), and the other the excellent press-cutting firm of Romeike and Curtis, whose riposte to an airy reference to "the ridiculous Romeike" was a demand for an apology and hints of legal proceedings. But the Pennells say they never once knew him stumped.

if it is not, strictly speaking, wit. *The Times* critic, Mr. Quilter, praises highly an oil portrait of Ruskin by Herkomer. With a yell of delight, Whistler at once leaps on him in the *World*:

"'Ne pas confondre intelligence avex gendarmes'—but surely, my dear Atlas, when the art critic of *The Times*, suffering possibly from chronic catarrh, is wafted in at the Grosvenor without guide or compass, and cannot by mere sense of smell distinguish between oil and water-colour, he ought, like Mark Twain, 'to inquire'.

"Had he asked the guardian or the fireman in the Gallery," etc., etc.

Bang! Another sitter tumbles off the nest. Poor Mr. Quilter was really too easy; a heavy, humourless person, pontificating in pontificalibus, no match whatsoever for American ruthlessness plus Gallic vivacity. Nor was Mr. Attorney-General at the Ruskin trial a fencer of the calibre of a Carson crossing blades with a Wilde, and as for Ruskin himself, when the poor great man described Whistler in "Fors Clavigera" as a coxcomb flinging a pot of paint in the public's face he was under treatment for mental trouble. The ensuing action for libel gained Whistler several considerable advantages over and beyond the farthing damages awarded him by an art-loving but fair-minded jury. It enabled him to declare his gospel in public, to make a fool of a judicial system engaged solemnly in judging matters of æsthetic—the pleasing absurdity of such an idea never, oddly enough, inspired W. S. Gilbert, who preferred an easy fling at Wilde and his school—to establish himself as a public character, and to parade his *panache*. Here, perhaps, he was slightly less fortunate in his age. Today, when compulsory education, the film, the B.B.C., and other civilizing forces have practically reduced British life to a mass of even, grey uniformity, there exist few of those bright picturesque oddities, urban and rural, who flourished everywhere in the Victorian and Edwardian eras. In the London of 1940 the Whistler apparition, foppishly costumed, higher-hatted than the average, flaunting a tall cane, an eyeglass, and the famous white lock, emitting at intervals the strident, famous, and feared "Ha! Ha!", which caused poor Mr. Seymour Haden to run nervously out of a public assembly, would by reason of its rarity have been swiftly enveloped in a blinding blaze of publicity and would have become overnight the gossip-writers' idol and the constant stand-by of the illustrated Press. Even with the brisk competition of his age Whistler soon loomed nearly as large in the metropolitan eye as the Jubilee Juggins and other of his fellow-eccentrics as he strode the town, deliberately exaggerating his foreign picturesqueness and hurling his ego at the Islanders with wicked abandon; and it was the Ruskin trial which finally launched him as a public character. One may imagine the frowns and the giggles with which the sober and the light-minded respectively read that November morning of 1878 in their daily paper such passages as:

"'. . . But do you think now that you could make *me* see the beauty of that picture?'

"The witness then paused, and examining attentively the Attorney-General's face and looking at the picture alternately, said, after apparently giving the subject much thought, while the Court waited in silence for his answer:

"'No! Do you know, I fear it would be as hopeless as for the musician to pour his notes into the ear of a deaf man.'" (Laughter.)

And:

" 'Now, Mr. Whistler. Can you tell me how long it took you to knock off that nocturne?'

" 'I beg your pardon?' (Laughter.)

" 'Oh! I am afraid that I am using a term that applies rather, perhaps, to my own work. I should have said, 'How long did you take to paint that picture?'

" 'Oh, no! Permit me! I am too greatly flattered to think that you apply, to work of mine, any term that you are in the habit of using with reference to your own. Let us say then how long did I take to—"knock off", I think that is it—to knock off that nocturne; well, as I remember, about a day. . . . I had better say, then, that I was two days at work on it.' "

The fellow was obviously a clown.

" '. . . the labour of two days, then, is that for which you ask two hundred guineas?"

" 'No. I ask it for the knowledge of a lifetime.' "

Here, to the perpetual surprise of students of the Codex, follows the word "(*Applause*)". This enigma has never been satisfactorily solved. Perhaps its most feasible explanation is that it took, in the mind of the public then in court, the place of that final deafening shriek of the concert soprano which ritually evokes thunders of relieved applause from every British audience. But if the fellow was being serious for a moment, he soon resumed his form:

" 'You have been told your pictures exhibit some eccentricities?'

" 'Yes; often.' (Laughter.)

" 'You send them to the galleries to incite the admiration of the public?'

" 'That would be such vast absurdity on my part that I don't think I could.' " (Laughter.)

Rarely, one perceives, has a better "stooge" or "feed"—to use the language of the music-hall—than Sir John Holker given a performance in any Court. Undoubtedly Whistler could have easily got more laughs out of this legal beefwittedness than he did, but, unlike Wilde on a more tragic occasion, Whistler was not fencing with his adversaries partly because it was his appointed role and partly because he was driven and desperate; he was a serious artist wronged, and his smile was the smile of one of the samurai of Hokusai, whose art he so adored, in the thick of battle or in the executioner's hands; that smile which the hidalgo of Japan must never lose.

Thus Whistler thrust and parried, thus he smiled, laughed, and whooped, till, with the hanging of his mother's portrait in the Luxembourg in 1891 on its journey to the Louvre ("one of the finest paintings due to the brush of an English artist"—*Illustrated London News*), the tide finally turned. He had perceived a little before that his enemies were vanquished, when, on his being created a Chevalier of the Legion of Honour, a complimentary dinner was given him at the Criterion. The Islanders had demonstrated in their own simple traditional way, with food and drink and oratory, that the fight was over. Whistler's speech shows that he was touched.

" '. . . I may have wrapped myself, for protection, in a species of misunderstanding—as that other traveller drew closer about him the folds of his cloak the more bitterly the winds and the storm assailed him on his way. But, as with him, when the sun shone upon him in his path, his cloak fell from his shoulders, so I, in the warm glow of your friendship . . .' "

He was obviously touched. The speech is rather wordy.

5

The wit of Whistler, as may have been perceived already, is not precisely wit as the Rubrics define it, as the Olympians have used it. It is not tight-packed and diamond-hard, like the wit of La Rochefoucauld, or Beaumarchais, or Voltaire, or Congreve. It has not the neat, swift surprise-value of Sydney Smith's "I never read books I review, it's apt to prejudice me", or of Wilde's "One of those characteristic British faces which, once seen, are never remembered" (which so strongly recalls Disraeli's "features of that type which, in moments of despondency, we are apt to describe as classic"). Granted that Wilde's technique often involved mechanical verbal trickery which anybody can perform—and how many do?—there is little in Whistler's recorded conversation or letters to equal the brilliancies scattered so lavishly through the less murky pages of *Dorian Gray*, many of which jewelled darts might have been flicked at Whistler's type of enemy—for example, "one of those middle-aged mediocrities who have no enemies, but are thoroughly disliked by their friends". It would be absurd, on the other hand, not to give Whistler credit for at least one or two swift impromptus which Wilde, for all his care, could not have bettered. At a dinner-table during the Boer War somebody remarked, during a conversation which had given Whistler opportunity for more than one tricksy anti-British fling, that General Buller had retired across the Modder without losing a man, a flag, or a gun. "Or a minute," added Whistler. And there is his reply to a dissatisfied client who grumbled, "Do you call that a good piece of art?"—"Well, do you call yourself a good piece of Nature?" Nobody could much improve on that, even a professional wit, which Whistler was not. Print, moreover, robs his ripostes of a great deal. What gave his conversation its delicious sparkle and savour, Mrs. Pennell says, was his personality: the slim, beautiful, eloquent, ever-restless hands, weaving Gallic arabesques, swooping, waving and flying, giving every word significance; the deep-set, deep-blue eyes, flaming and dancing with merriment or mischief or fury; the mobile lips, the heavy, flexible eyebrows, the gaiety which even age and illness could not quench. And his writing, which so often echoes his talk, was never a planned and executed pyrotechnic display, like Wilde's. The loving care he took with it was expended on the expression of his thought in good clear native Whistlerese, not on the bedecking of his style with gauds, whether his own or—as was occasionally Wilde's habit—those of others, adapted. In his literary expression Whistler, in fact, was concerned more with making contusions than epigrams, and his taut, bright-coloured, piquant cosmopolitan style often lends an air of wit to very ordinary rudery. "The Doctor would not be so impressive," remarked one of Johnson's victims, "if it were not for his *bow-wow* way", the truth of which is patent to every Boswell student. Similarly with Whistler; and still he charms. A jovial correspondent of the *World* having caught "the sprightly and shrill McNeill" out nicely with some half-dozen mis-spellings of foreign words in an exhibition catalogue, Whistler replies in due course:

"*Touché!*—and my compliments to your 'correspondent', Atlas, *chéri*—far from me to justify spelling of my own! But who could possibly have supposed an orthographer loose! Evidently, too, 'ung vieulx qui a moult roulé en Palestine et aultres lieux.'

"What it is to be prepared, though! Atlas, *mon pauvre chéri*, you know the story of the witness . . .", etc., etc.

I have probably read this letter some 500 times and each time with equal enjoyment (which applies to the "Gentle Art" as a whole). Despite its obvious lameness as a riposte, it charms incessantly. Having just read it for the 501st time I venture to analyse its appeal as follows:

1. It opens with a gay suggestion of the *salle d'armes*, the light clash of foils, a laughing admission;
2. It evokes Paris, and particularly the affectionate mockery ("*mon pauvre chéri*") of Paris;
3. The scrap of Old French, dragged in by its heels though it may be, conveys in that one delightful world "roulé" all the rich bustling life of the highroads of the Middle Ages, Rocamadour and Compostella, Walsingham and Chartres, Bethlehem and Rome.

It is therefore the atmosphere, or atmospheres, independent of the context, evoked by this letter which lend it faint but perpetual magic, for me. For others, to whom his lavish French gestures may mean nothing more than an affectation assumed to annoy the bourgeoisie, I cannot speak; but in Whistler's most violent attacks, for example on poor stupid pompous Tom Taylor, the sudden Gallic cliché, like a half-furious, half-smiling, ironic shrug, lightens the air sufficiently, it seems to me.

"Dead for a ducat, dead! my dear Tom: and the rattle has reached me by post.

"'*Sans rancune,*' say you? Bah! You scream unkind threats and die badly.

"Why squabble over your little article? You *did* print what I quote, you know, Tom; and it is surely unimportant what more you may have written of the Master. That you should have written anything at all is your crime.

"No; shrive your naughty soul, and give up Velasquez, and pass your last days properly in the Home Office.

"Set your house in order with the Government for arrears of time and paper, and leave vengeance to the Lord, who will forgive my 'garbling' Tom Taylor's writing."

With a pathetic attempt to shrug back at this screeching Americo-Continental in his own language, poor Mr. Taylor replies heavily: "Pardon, my dear Whistler, for having taken you *au sérieux* even for a moment . . ." Thereby provoking the knockout:

"Why, my dear old Tom, I never *was* serious with you, even when you were with us. Indeed I killed you quite, as who should say, without seriousness, 'A rat! A rat!' you know, rather cursorily" (etc.).

Sir Max Beerbohm's admiration as a fellow craftsman for the technical skill of this phrasing, as the expression of a man "choking with hate", is justifiable—but "hate" is surely too strong? I find it impossible to believe that a man of Whistler's temperament hated his stockish enemies. They drove him wild with rage, he kicked them savagely in the stern, he bespattered them with abuse and ridicule, he drove them with derisive hootings back to cover, and . . . he was a great droll. The Pennells, his intimates, stand firm on this. It should be borne in mind whenever "The Gentle Art of Making Enemies" is read, and then, after the ferocity has died down, you hear the laughter; a trifle harsh, perhaps, but still genuine laughter. What child of the Muses blessed with a sense of the ridiculous, even if he belongs to the painting branch (which loves a good hairy fraternal vendetta, they say, more passionately even than the literary or musical branch), could seriously hate a professional critic? Is it possible to hate even a book-reviewer? Does a tramp hate his fleas? Did even a supersensitive introvert like Charlotte Brontë hate Mr. G. H. Lewes as she wept scalding tears over his handling of her work in *The Times*? There are two ways of dealing with a hostile critic, as Mr. Somerset Maugham has indicated; one, to fling a mental insult at the ruffian and forget him, the other—practised by those more prudent children of the Muses who study their market—to ask him to lunch and secure a more favourable notice next time. Exasperation is one thing, hatred another. Even publishers inspire only an acute dislike in those of their serfs who may hate each other with white-hot and even homicidal intensity; no publisher has ever died by an author's hand, and though Dr. Johnson certainly banged Mr. Osborne, he attached no importance to it. "Sir, he was impertinent to me, and I beat him; but it was not in his shop; it was in my own chamber." Similarly with professional critics, whose parasitic gambols may inspire a passing vexation, but cannot stir the nobler, starker emotions.

This is not the place to discuss the interesting question whether hate produces better prose than anger. The outstanding case of Pascal fails because, hating the Jesuits, he grossly misrepresented their theories, so all the rolling objurgatory music of the "Provinciales" goes for nothing. It seems clear from every page of "The Gentle Art", to one student at least, that what dictated Whistler's insults was simply anger, a virile, merry anger mixed with truculent mirth at the eternal foolishness of fools. It was anger also, the serious anger of the artist assailed by stupidity, which nerved the prose in which is expounded the Whistlerian Gospel in the pamphlet "Art and Art-Critics" and in the lecture called "Ten O'clock", which latter novelty so far stirred fashionable and artistic London with curiosity as to induce it to quit the dinner-table for St. James's Hall at the intempestive hour of half past nine; that is to say, having barely got its second wind after the sorbet or water-ice designed for that humane purpose and placed invariably midway in the repast, between the fourth and fifth courses.

These two pieces of prose express the essential Whistler. Barring an occasional addiction to alliteration for its own sake, they are entirely admirable; strong, flexible, clear, sharp-cut, masterly in choice and grouping and sound, "excellent in diction", as "Vanity Fair" confessed, rushing to succour the wounded, "broadly and boldly set down in slashing words". The "Ten O'clock", moreover, contains one justly celebrated passage of dim and delicate nocturnal beauty which no good anthology of English prose can afford to omit. By these two pieces can Whistler's prose genius be judged, and, with the letters, they supply the true word descriptive of his literary expression; which word is not "wit", in the English sense, but the subtler, untranslatable French word (which he most likely himself preferred): the word *esprit.*

SYDNEY SMITH

ERNEST NEWMAN

THE STORY OF SYDNEY SMITH'S LIFE CAN BE TOLD IN A FEW WORDS. HE was born at Woodford, Essex, on June 3, 1771. There was French blood in him on his mother's side, a fact to which he himself attributed, in part, the vivacity of his temperament. He was educated at Winchester and New College, Oxford. His own choice of a profession would have been the Bar, for which his writings prove him to have had exceptional qualifications; it was solely to comply with his father's wishes that he entered the Church. In 1794 he became curate at Netherhaven, a small village in the middle of Salisbury Plain. The squire of the place having taken a fancy to him and engaged him as tutor to his son, the pair set out in 1797 for Weimar, but somehow or other found themselves, owing to the disturbed political conditions of the time, in Edinburgh, where Smith remained some five years. In June, 1800, he married a Miss Pybus, and a couple of years later he founded, in conjunction with Jeffrey, Brougham and John Murray, the *Edinburgh Review.* Smith edited the first number, and remained a contributor to the *Review* until 1829, fighting in its columns for a number of good causes with inexhaustible ardour and unflinching courage.

In 1803 he removed to London, where he had obtained the Preachership of the Foundling Hospital, the stipend being £50 a year. Lord Holland obtained for him in 1806 the living of Foston-le-Clay, in Yorkshire, which he exchanged in 1829 for that of Combe Florey, near Taunton. (It was while he was at Foston, in 1807, that he published the famous "Letters on the Subject of the Catholics", addressed by "Peter Plymley" to "My brother Abraham, who lives in the country".) He had too much talent, or at all events the wrong kind of talent, ever to achieve a bishopric; but in 1831 he was appointed a Canon of St. Paul's, and the remainder of his days he spent alternately in London and in Combe Florey. He died on February 22, 1845. He himself reprinted in book form, in 1839, sixty-five out of the seventy-six articles he had contributed to the *Edinburgh Review*, together with the Peter Plymley Letters. The remainder of his collected "Works" consists of speeches, sermons, and public letters of various kinds.

I

None of us can define wit, though we all know wit when we see it. We can imagine definitions of it that would virtually exclude Sydney Smith. Wit of the first order is like lightning—it strikes swiftly and unexpectedly, regardless of the innocence or guilt of its victim, and it never strikes twice in the same place or in the same way. This last characteristic alone would seem, at first sight, to rule out Sydney Smith. The finest shafts of wit come inevitably, irresistibly, out of the electrical tension of a particular moment. As they are not made according to a formula, they admit of no standardization, no reduction to recipe for use on another occasion. They are first and final: they leave their victim with no chance of retort, even if the right of the matter be on his side. Judged by these exacting standards there is little in Sydney Smith that can be described as wit: as I shall try to show later, he works for the greater part of the time by formula, and his method could have been employed as easily and as effectively by others as by himself—always supposing the others had anything like his mental agility and his verbal facility. It was his good fortune never, in all his controversies, to come up against an enemy as nimble and artful as himself; had that happened, he would more than once have found himself hoist by his own petard.

A specimen or two of wit of the superlative kind I have been trying to define in the preceding paragraph will perhaps make clearer what I mean when I speak of the lightning quality of the best wit, its clinching finality, its freedom from pattern, the impossibility of reducing it to a recipe, the feeling it leaves us with that it had never happened before and will never happen again.

Meyerbeer owed a great deal of his popularity to the fact that his wealth enabled him to convince the critics of the super-excellence of his newest work even before they had heard a note of it. Heine, who had himself succumbed more than once to the logic of Meyerbeer's purse, and whose resentment was deep when the composer saw fit to suspend his persuasion in an hour when the poet's funds were particularly low, took his revenge in one marvellous quip that will survive most of what Meyerbeer wrote: "Meyerbeer," he said, "will be immortal during his lifetime, and perhaps for a little while after, for he always pays in advance."

Voltaire's wit is always swift, concise, unforeseeable, and incapable of standardization. The reader will no doubt be able to recall many examples for himself; but here is one that is perhaps not so generally known. At "Les Délices", his house near Geneva, he and his friends were running through his latest play preparatory to its production in Paris. Montesquieu, who was among those present, fell asleep during a long speech. "Wake him up!" said Voltaire: "he seems to imagine he's in the audience."

Or glance at Alexandre Dumas, senior. A play of his had just been produced in Paris, and in the foyer one night an Adolphe Dumas, who was also by way of being a dramatist, introduced himself to him. The reader probably knows that the great Corneille, Pierre, had a younger brother, Thomas, who also wrote plays but was a poor second to his senior. The other Dumas assured Alexandre of the pleasure it gave him to think that their names and fames would have the same conjoint immortality as those of the two Corneilles. Dumas bowed, but made no reply. A little while later he went up to his namesake, shook hands with him, and said gravely, "Good night, Thomas!"

Sophie Arnould, the eighteenth-century opera singer, and perhaps the wittiest Frenchwoman whose sayings have been recorded by history, achieved again and again, without effort, that swift first-and-final kind of wit that rarely came within Smith's scope. A rival actress having received from her lover a superb *rivière* of diamonds, a friend remarked what a pity it was that owing to its length it came too low on the lady's person. "*C'est qu'elle retourne vers sa source*," said Sophie. A certain Mlle Guimard, who was technically a dancer at the Paris Opéra, but whose choregraphic art consisted mostly of graceful arm movements, had an arm broken by a piece of falling scenery. "It's a pity," said Sophie, "it wasn't her leg; then it wouldn't have interfered with her dancing." Another actress was always losing both her lovers and her theatrical engagements because of the consequences to her figure of an unfortunate habit of producing a child once a year. "She reminds me," was Sophie's comment, "of those nations that are always extending their borders but cannot retain their conquests."

Coming down to our own day, there is the story of the French writer —Tristan Bernard, I think it was—who, calling on a friend who lived at the top of a block of flats, found that his progress, like that of everyone else who wanted to go up or down the stairs, was barred by a man carrying a grandfather clock which had got immovably wedged on the fourth-floor landing. Bernard watched patiently for some time the man's vain efforts to move the thing one way or the other; then he said quietly, "I say, my friend, why don't you wear a wrist-watch?"

The anthology might be extended indefinitely; but I will content myself with one more example, which shows how wit, like lightning, can illuminate while it consumes. Take the situation, not an uncommon one, of a young artist who surprises people by his precocity; and let us look at it in two vignettes. First of all there is the story of someone bringing Liszt a score by a composer whose name was unknown to him. Liszt played it through, and was astonished at the originality and audacity of the music. He asked the composer's age, and learned that he was still in his teens. Thereupon Liszt pushed the score aside. "Take it away," he said sadly; "he'll come to nothing!" He had known too many composers who were geniuses at sixteen and mediocrities at thirty-six to have any illusions as to this particular young man's future. There is not a trace of wit in Liszt's remark—only plain sense about a plain thing. But observe now how a wit like Auber dealt with a similar situation. A very young composer had produced a score full of an "originality" beyond his years. "This lad," said the cynical old Auber, "will go far when he has less experience."

2

Of the kind of wit, agile and acid, which we have so far been considering there is extremely little to be found in Sydney Smith. One suspects, indeed, that he was not particularly appreciative of it in others. He was fond of telling a story of Lord Ellenborough, in whose Court, one day, "a young lawyer, trembling with fear, rose to make his first speech, and began: 'My lord, my unfortunate client—my lord, my unfortunate client—my lord——'. 'Go on, sir, go on,' said Ellenborough; 'as far as you have proceeded hitherto the Court is entirely with you.' " "This," said Smith, "was perhaps irresistible; but yet how wicked, how cruel!—

it deserves a thousand years' punishment at least." But to take that line is to bring wit, which is purely a matter of the intellect, under the jurisdiction of a moral code that has no application to it. If the wit were to ask himself, before launching his barb, whether it is likely to give pain to the victim, the world would be poorer now by many a thousand brilliances. Nor did Smith himself ever stay his hand when he had someone whom he disliked helpless under his fire: he left the poor wretch, indeed, more full of arrows than St. Sebastian after a good day's archery practice by his persecutors. He could on occasion be not merely devastatingly critical of his adversary's principles but personally rude to him, after the robust fashion of the England of a century or so ago. One suspects that, like most artists, he had little appreciation of types of art markedly different from his own, and that his condemnation of Ellenborough's remark sprang not so much from revolt against its "cruelty" as from the consciousness that this was a brand of wit which he himself did not stock.

This conjecture is confirmed when we read his own definition of wit. The difference between wit and a bull, he said, is that while the bull is "an apparent congruity and real incongruity of ideas suddenly discovered", wit is the exact reverse of this, "for as wit discovers real relations that are not apparent, bulls admit apparent relations that are not real. The pleasure arising from wit proceeds from our surprise at suddenly discovering two things to be similar in which we suspected no similarity. The pleasure arising from bulls proceeds from our discovering two things to be dissimilar in which a resemblance might have been suspected." The limitations of this conception of wit are obvious; many of the world's finest specimens could not possibly be brought within such a definition. Smith, indeed, is once more doing what all highly individual artists are inclined to do, constructing a general theory of æsthetic out of the one practice he knows best and values most—his own. This suspicion is strengthened when we find him categorically denying the accepted view that wit is "a sort of inexplicable visitation, that it comes and goes with the rapidity of lightning, and that it is quite as unattainable as beauty or just proportion". "I am so much of a contrary way of thinking," Smith goes on to say, "that I am convinced a man might sit down as systematically, and as successfully, to the study of wit as he might to the study of mathematics: and I would answer for it that by giving up only six hours a day to being witty he should come on prodigiously by midsummer, so that his friends should hardly know him again."* There is a touch of whimsical exaggeration in this, of course; but in the main it is a frank confession and a complete exposition of his own method. For a method it certainly was, as analysis proves: the same technique of construction, the same well-tried apparatus for sparking, reappear a thousand times in his work.

Moreover, Smith's method is one which requires a certain spaciousness

* That the passages just quoted (from the article "Edgeworth on Bulls" in the *Edinburgh Review* of 1803) represents Smith's considered view of the essence of wit is shown by the recurrence of the same idea more than thirty years later in his letter to the son of Sir James Mackintosh, who had asked him to supply him with some "characteristics" of his lately deceased father. "Sir James," Smith wrote in reply, "had not only humour, but he had wit also; at least, new and sudden relations of ideas flashed across his mind in reasoning, and troduced the same effect as wit, and would have been called wit, if a sense of their utility and importance had not often overpowered the admiration of novelty, and entitled them to the higher name of wisdom."

of terrain for its full deployment, which peculiarity accounts for the fact that there are comparatively few *short* sayings of his that one can quote. Of the few that exist, two or three are first-rate—his famous parallel, for instance, between the sloth and a clergyman of the Church of England. "What is most extraordinary [about the sloth], he lives not *upon* the branches, but *under* them. He moves suspended, and passes his life in suspense—like a young clergyman distantly related to a bishop." Or his remark on that "most useless and offensive tumour in the body politic", "the titled son of a great man whose merit has placed him in the peerage. The name, face, and perhaps the pension, remain. The dæmon is gone: or there is a slight flavour from the cask, but it is empty."

"Men of very small incomes have often very acute feelings, and a curate trod on feels a pang as great as a bishop refuted" is not quite so good: we can see too plainly the machinery at work, and it creaks a little. This is better, on dull sermons: "Is sin to be taken from men, as Eve was from Adam, by casting them into a deep slumber?" And this, on his brother Robert and himself: "Bobus and I have inverted the laws of nature: he rose by gravity, I sank by my levity." Or, again, his swift scoring of a point against the talkative Macaulay: "His enemies might have said before [he went to India] . . . that he talked rather too much; but now he has occasional flashes of silence that make his conversation perfectly delightful." Neither Heine nor Voltaire could have surpassed that for lightness of touch and deadliness of effect: it deserves to be remembered, indeed, along with Voltaire's remark after an evening with the too-eloquent Diderot in which he had been unable to get a word in edgeways: asked afterwards what he thought of Diderot, he replied, "An extraordinary man! There's only one art he doesn't understand—the art of dialogue."

Conformable to Smith's definition of wit as "discovering real relations that are not apparent", and consistent with his belief that almost any man can attain it by systematic application, are a number of other good but not quite so good things, such as his remark to the child who gave as his reason for stroking a turtle that he "wanted to please the turtle". "Why, child, you might as well stroke the dome of St. Paul's to please the Dean and Chapter." And that in framing his definition he was generalizing from his own practice, elevating a personal idiosyncrasy to the dignity of a canon, is shown by the frequency with which he achieves his own brand of wit by the simple process of placing a serious and a burlesque image in unexpected apposition. As good an example as any, perhaps, occurs in his picture of the happy life of one of those transported convicts to whom Australia owes, at several removes, its present admirable population. Botany Bay was always a subject that moved Smith to riotous hilarity; and one of his best efforts in connection with it was his mock-idyllic vignette of "a London thief, clothed in kangaroo's skins, lodged under the bark of the dwarf eucalyptus, and keeping sheep, fourteen thousand miles from Piccadilly, with a crook bent into the shape of a picklock". Bishops were another source of endless amusement to him: and he scored in one hit against both the railway directors and the minor bishops when he warned his readers that nothing would be done to check the modern (1842) passion for speed in locked railway carriages until "some person of rank" happened to be cremated in an accident. "A burnt bishop" might console himself, in that event, with the reflection that "his death will produce unspeakable benefit to the public. Even Sodor and Man will be better than nothing."

One or two of his best small-scale witticisms are of the personal kind which he objected to in the instance of Lord Ellenborough; his advice to a Mr. Thomas Hope, for instance, whose novel *Anastasius* he reviewed in the *Edinburgh Review* in 1821. "Mr. Hope," he wrote, "should avoid humour, in which he certainly does not excel. His attempts of that nature are among the most serious parts of the book." And worthy of Ellenborough was the polish of the remark in which he disposed of a Frenchman, one M. Fievée, who had published a volume of *Lettres sur l'Angleterre* in 1802. "Mr. Fievée alleges against the English," says Sydney, "that they have great pleasure in contemplating the spectacle of men deprived of their reason. And indeed we must have the candour to allow that the hospitality which Mr. Fievée experienced seems to afford some pretext for this assertion."

3

In the majority of cases, however, Smith's genius does not move so lightly and swiftly as in the examples just cited. To be at his best he needs plenty of time and space in which to bring into full use the deadliest of all his controversial weapons—cumulative irony and burlesque. His total powers were never called into action except by opposition, which accounts for his so rarely achieving wit in his conversation and his letters, rich as these are in amiable pleasantry. We have to remember that when Smith took up his pen it was generally for a definite polemical purpose. There was a good deal in the England of his day which he thought could be improved upon, and to its improvement he devoted all the energies of an acutely logical intellect, a commonsense that amounted to genius, a generosity of feeling that embraced almost everybody and everything except Methodists and Freethinkers, and all the resources of his incomparable style. The astonishing thing is that although many of the matters about which he writes are of small practical interest today or no interest at all, such as Catholics and Dissenters and their legal disabilities, the stupidities and rascalities of politicians whose very names, even, are recalled with difficulty by most people now, the need for rationalizing and humanizing our criminal code, the fright the nation had during some periods of the Napoleonic wars, the pitifulness of the lot of the English curate, the comic or repellent aspects of the English bishop, novels and pamphlets and blue books buried today under a century's accumulation of dust and cobweb, and so on, his works are still readable from cover to cover—not for the sake of his subjects but in spite of them.

The majority of his writings being polemical, his wit in argument was naturally at its best when his nervous temperature rose highest. The technique of it consists largely of demonstrating, or at all events suggesting, a number of "real relations that are not apparent" between some doctrine or other that Smith has set himself to discredit and a host of imps that dance ironic attendance on it. When, for instance, a Mr.

John Bowles incautiously lays it down that the only rights of government "compatible with civil liberty" are those "recognized by the moral sense as lawful" *because they are ancient*, Smith makes him look the fool he is simply by taking him at his word and carrying his thesis to its logical but preposterous conclusion. If "every political institution," he smilingly assents, "is favourable to liberty not according to its spirit but in proportion to the antiquity of its date," then "the slaves of Great Britain are groaning under the trial by jury, while the freemen of Asia exult in the bold privilege, transmitted to them by their fathers, of being trampled to death by elephants".

Invariably he explodes a fallacy by rephrasing an abstract proposition in terms of the concrete—one of the surest ways of correcting bogus thinking. Mr. Spencer Perceval had been rash enough to assert that fidelity to the constitution and a patriotic concern for the safety of the state were dependent on every Briton being a true-blue Episcopalian. Smith turns the thesis to ridicule by arranging round it a number of distorting mirrors in which it catches its own foolish reflection whichever way it turns. He compares the ship of state to a frigate commanded by a Captain Perceval. The ship is attacked by a corsair. Instead of calling all hands on deck, inspiring them with some robust talk about old England and hearts of oak, and sending them cheering to their guns, prepared to do or die, the first thing Captain Perceval does is "to secure twenty or thirty of his prime sailors who happen to be Catholics, to clap them in irons, and set over them a guard of as many Protestants; having taken this admirable method of defending himself against his infidel opponents, he goes up on deck, reminds the sailors, in a very bitter harangue, that they are of different religions; exhorts the Episcopal gunner not to trust to the Presbyterian quartermaster; issues positive orders that the Catholics should be fired at upon the first appearance of discontent; rushes through blood and brains, examining his men in the Catechism and the Thirty-nine Articles, and positively forbids every-one to sponge or ram who has not take the sacrament according to the Church of England".

He puts his adversary to shame not by stripping off him such poor clothes as he possesses but by multiplying each wretched rag by five. One of his most brilliant achievements in this line is his sustained ridicule of the Government of the day (1807) for imagining they could beat the mighty Napoleon by a blockade that would deprive the French of certain simple medicaments. Our marvellous statesmen, it appears, "would bring the French to reason by keeping them without rhubarb, and exhibit to mankind the awful spectacle of a nation deprived of neutral salts. . . . What a sublime thought, that no purge can now be taken between the Weser and the Garonne; that the bustling pestle is still, the canorous mortar mute, and the bowels of mankind locked up for fourteen degrees of latitude! When, I should be curious to know, were all the powers of crudity and flatulence fully explained to his Majesty's ministers? At what period was this great plan of conquest and constipation fully developed? In whose mind was the idea of destroying the pride and the plasters of France first engendered? Without castor oil they might for some months, to be sure, have carried on a lingering war; but can they do without bark? Will people live under a government where antimonial powders cannot be procured? Will they bear the loss of mercury? 'There's the rub'. Depend upon it, the absence of the materia medica will soon bring them to their senses, and the cry of *Bourbon and bolus* burst forth from the Baltic to the Mediterranean."

The technique, it will be seen, resembles that of the symphony composer, with his system of endless thematic transformation. And just as even the best composer succumbs now and then to the temptation to go on varying his theme for mere variation's sake, piling modulation on modulation without achieving, past a certain point, any further real development, so Smith, as in the specimen just presented, is occasionally inclined to overwork his burlesque: the firework display, excellent as a whole, would have been even more impressive had one or two of the smaller squibs been omitted. His method has the fault of all consciously standardized methods in art: if the machine happens to be running at anything less than its full power and with anything less than ideal smoothness we become rather too conscious that it *is* a machine.

The main ingredients of the Smith technique are three in number—translation of the opponent's abstract proposition into the concrete, making the thesis in its generalized form ridiculous by breaking it up into all kinds of absurd particularities, and now and then giving extra point to the absurdity by means of alliteration. (Observe, for example, in the passage cited above, the effect of "conquest and constipation", "pride and plasters", "Bourbon and bolus".) This passage, too, is an excellent example of the Smith technique of ridicule by means of association or antithesis. The clinching effect of his use of the concrete will already be familiar to the reader, no doubt, from several examples that have become part of literary history. Could the silliness of the notion that if women were allowed to receive a proper education the very foundations of domestic life would be undermined be better exposed than in Smith's famous query—"Can anything . . . be more perfectly absurd than to suppose that the care and perpetual solicitude which a mother feels for her children depend upon her ignorance of Greek and mathematics; and that she would desert an infant for a quadratic equation?"

Yet it has to be confessed that the consummate swordsman lets us into the secrets of his gay fence a trifle too often, the master of the puppet show admits us too freely behind the scenes to examine critically at our leisure the strings by which he works his figures. Take, in proof of this, the passage in which he contrasts the freedom of the American citizen to work where he liked with the stupid laws that barred the English artisan from practising his simple trade outside his own locality. "If a citizen of the United States can make a shoe, he is at liberty to make a shoe anywhere between Lake Ontario and New Orleans—he may sole on the Mississippi—heel on the Missouri—measure Mr. Birkbeck on the little Wabash, or take . . . the length of Mr. Munro's foot on the banks of the Potomac. But woe to the cobbler who, having made Hessian boots for the aldermen of Newcastle, should venture to invest with these coriaceous integuments the leg of a liege subject of York. A yellow ant in a nest of red ants—a butcher's dog in a fox-kennel—a mouse in a beehive—all feel the effects of untimely intrusion; but far preferable their fate to that of the misguided artisan who, misled by sixpenny histories of

England, and conceiving his country to have been united at the Heptarchy, goes forth from his native town to stitch freely within the sea-girt limits of Albion"; and so on. Some of this, apart from the laboured facetiousness of "coriaceous integuments", which seems to herald the woeful verbal mechanics of W. S. Gilbert, is so good that we would be sorry to have been deprived of it; but can we persuade ourselves, for all that, that we do not see the familiar machinery at work, a trifle rustier than usual, and creaking a little now and then? And in a sentence such as this, describing the effects of the digestion on the mind—"In the same manner, old friendships are destroyed by toasted cheese, and hard salted meat has led to suicide"—we are sadly conscious that the wheels are going their customary mechanical round without a single grain of corn being ground.

4

I have already remarked that the machinery of Smith's wit always needed a certain nervous tension and temperature to make it function at its best. One reason why he is so rarely witty in his talk or his letters is that fundamentally he was a healthy, solid, easy-going, four-square man, not easily worked up even about serious things. It was comparatively seldom that he could develop enough internal combustion to summon from their lairs and marshal for assault all those separated mental images whose sudden and unexpected combination produced wit as he defined it. But certain disgraceful things in the public life of his own day always stirred him to scorn or righteous anger; and his powers both of argument and of ridicule rose with the thermometer of his mood. It is true that in proportion as his personal rather than national or broadly human interests were involved his wit tended to lose its polish and its litheness, to substitute the singlestick for the rapier; but the belabouring he gave his victims on these occasions still makes first-class reading.

He was particularly angry with the American states that had swindled him out of much of his hard-earned money by the impudent repudiation of the loans they had raised in England for the development of their trade and their amenities. He was, indeed, always refreshingly free from false sentiment where money was concerned, notwithstanding that it was his duty, as a Canon of the Church, to declare at any rate a professional belief in the blessedness of poverty and to be sceptical as to the chances of anyone who had riches entering into the kingdom of heaven. A year or two before his death his younger brother died suddenly without leaving a will, so that Sydney became entitled to one third of an estate of £100,000. "This," he wrote to John Murray, "puts me at my ease for my few remaining years. After buying into the Consols and the Reduced, I read Seneca 'On the Contempt of Wealth'. What intolerable nonsense!" And when the Pennsylvanians brazenly robbed him of his small savings in 1843 they drew on themselves a jet of caustic vituperation which, if not in his very purest vein of wit, still sticks and burns and blisters. "How a Pennsylvanian," he says, "can set himself down at an English table without feeling that he owes two or three pounds to every man in the company I am at a loss to conceive: he has no more right to eat with honest men than the leper has to eat with clean men." After which preamble the

Smith heavy tank goes into action, with all its armament of concrete illustration, antithesis and derisive alliteration. "Figure to yourself a Pennsylvanian receiving foreigners in his own country, walking over the public works with them, and showing them Larcenous Lake, Swindling Swamp, Crafty Canal, and Rogues' Railway, and other dishonest works. 'This swamp we gained' (says the patriotic borrower) 'by the repudiated loan of 1828. Our canal robbery was in 1830; we pocketed your good people's money for the railroad only last year. . . .' We all know that the Americans can fight. Nobody doubts their courage. I see now in my mind's eye a whole army on the plains of Pennsylvania in battle array, immense corps of insolvent light infantry, regiments of heavy horse debtors, battalions of repudiators, brigades of bankrupts, with *Vivre sans payer, ou mourir* on their banners, and *aero alieno* on their trumpets: all these desperate debtors would fight to the death for their country, and probably drive into the sea their invading creditors."

It is upon this technique of cumulative thematic variation, as I have called it, that Smith relies almost exclusively to batter to pieces his opponent's line of defence. It makes no difference whether he is writing merely an Album Leaf or a symphony: the procedure is always essentially the same. The Bishop of Peterborough had agitated the clerical world by propounding eighty-seven test questions for candidates for holy orders in his diocese. Smith saw at once the opportunities for fun afforded by the incongruity between the questions and the space allotted by the prelate for replying to them. "The Bishop not only puts the questions but he actually assigns the limits within which they are to be answered. Spaces are left in the paper of interrogations, to which limits the answer is to be confined—two inches to original sin; an inch and a half to justification; three quarters to predestination; and to free will only a quarter of an inch." Observe first of all the cumulative effect of the series of *reductiones ad absurdum*, then the art of the crowning touch—the reservation to the last of the most ludicrous disparity of them all between the importance of the question and the amount of space permitted for answering it.

We see the same technique in operation on a slightly larger scale in Smith's *reductio ad absurdum* of our incurable English habit of supposing that private virtue in a dull politician somehow or other makes up for his lack of political wisdom. "You spend a great deal of ink about the character of the present Prime Minister," Peter Plymley tells his brother Abraham in 1807. "Grant you all that you write—I say I fear he will ruin Ireland, and pursue a line of policy destructive to the true interest of his country : and then you tell me he is faithful to Mrs. Perceval, and kind to the Master Percevals! These are, undoubtedly, the first qualifications to be looked to in a time of the most serious public danger; but somehow or another (if public and private virtues must always be incompatible), I should prefer that he destroyed the domestic happiness of Wood or Cockell, owed for the veal of the preceding year, whipped his boys, and saved his country." Observe once more the artful crescendo of the burlesque, and the perfect timing and clinching finality of the coda of the variations.

Of the full-scale use of Smith's system of thematic variation one of the finest examples is the famous passage in which, in 1820, he warned the Americans to keep out of foreign wars, the glory of which is small compensation for the taxation they bring in their train. "We can inform Jonathan what are the inevitable consequences of being too fond of glory—TAXES upon every article which enters into the mouth, or covers the back, or is placed under the foot—taxes upon everything which it is pleasant to see, hear, feel, smell, or taste—taxes upon warmth, light, and locomotion—taxes on every thing on earth, and the waters under the earth—on every thing that comes from abroad, or is grown at home—taxes on the raw material—taxes on every fresh value that is added to it by the industry of man—taxes on the sauce which pampers man's appetite, and the drug that restores him to health—on the ermine which decorates the judge, and the rope which hangs the criminal—on the poor man's salt, and the rich man's spice—on the brass nails of the coffin, and the ribands of the bride—at bed or board, couchant or levant, we must pay. The schoolboy whips his taxed top—the beardless youth manages his taxed horse, with a taxed bridle, on a taxed road—and the dying Englishman, pouring his medicine, which has paid 7 per cent, into a spoon that has paid 15 per cent—flings himself back upon his chintz bed, which has paid 22 per cent—and expires in the arms of an apothecary who has paid a licence of a hundred pounds for the privilege of putting him to death. His whole property is then immediately taxed from 2 to 10 per cent. Besides the probate, large fees are demanded for burying him in the chancel; his virtues are handed down to posterity on taxed marble; and he is then gathered to his fathers—to be taxed no more."

Smith's definition of wit may not cover the whole ground; but in the face of a masterpiece such as this who can doubt that in the hands of an artist like himself those "new and sudden relations of ideas" of which he spoke in connection with Mackintosh can, as they "flash across the mind in reasoning", "produce the same effect as wit"? And if the resources and the technique of his wit were as limited as we have seen them to be, perhaps that was because he reasoned too well. Sophie Arnould said of Poinsinet that he had so much wit in his head that there was no room for common sense. The reverse is to some extent true of Sydney Smith.

THEODORE HOOK

A. J. A. SYMONS

"LAST NIGHT LORD HARRINGTON ENTERTAINED A SMALL COMPANY TO meet the Duke of Wellington. Those present included the Duke and Duchess of Bedford, Lord and Lady Southampton, Lord Londonderry, Lord Canterbury, Lord Lyndhurst, Lord Redesdale, Lord Charleville, Lord Strangford, Lord Chesterfield, Count d'Orsay, and Mr. Theodore Hook." A hundred years ago such notices appeared frequently in the columns of "fashionable intelligence", though not as frequently as Mr. Hook appeared at the dinner and house-parties of the great. When the long mahogany tables were set with their sparkling crested silver under the Waterford chandeliers; when the liveried servants, removing the first, placed the second service before the critical Tory grandees of the fourth

George or William, and the peeresses nodded their feathers in elegance and agreement; when the Earl of Jersey and the Marquess of Hertford "received" in their vast London houses, and the best Sillery flowed as freely as the old Lafite; at the special Sunday dinners of that Duke of Cumberland who became King of Hanover: there, prominent in gaiety, irrepressible in spirits, obese, improvident, amusing and amused, sat Mr. Theodore Hook. The Athenaeum knew him and was glad; his place by the door of the coffee-room took its name of Temperance Corner from his habit of calling, amid his jokes, rhymes and repartees, for "another glass of toast and water" or "a little more lemonade", when he desired to refresh himself with brandy or gin. His presence was a never-failing draw. If Hook was in, strangers to the wit made no bones about edging near to hear him talk, and when at last his chair fell finally vacant, the number of dinners served in the Club diminished by upwards of three hundred in a year. At the Garrick, at the Carlton—wherever his sometimes unsteady steps took him, he could always be certain of an audience eager to hear him talk; eager to hear from his own lips the story of his early hoaxes, grown almost fabulous with the years, or his fantastic musical improvisations, which strained credulity, and yet were genuine flowers of the moment, or his bewilderingly ready tongue, served by a memory which indulgence had hardly dimmed. No one who measures evidence can doubt that Hook was one of the most amusing talkers who ever lived. He charmed Greville and astounded Coleridge; Ingoldsby Barham adored him; and even conceited, upright Lockhart could not disguise his admiration. Hook wrote well enough to impress his contemporaries and to influence Dickens; he played a part in the fight for the freedom of the Press; he was that prodigy, a consistent politician; but above all he talked. He talked. He talked himself, twice, into Society; he talked himself into prison; and in the end he talked himself to death.

In his clubs, and the mansions of his frequentation, Mr. Hook appeared as an irresponsible bachelor. No wife blushed on his arm when his name was announced to his smiling host or hostess; and it was as a single man that he sparkled, bald, jocund, unrestrained, in his special masculine circles. But when hilarity ebbed and the feast was finished; when Lord Hertford's green chariot set him down in London after a roistering country session, or he returned from stage-managing private theatricals at Hatfield House, or he left Crockford's in the clear cold of dawn, then Mr. Hook returned to a binding, though legally unsanctioned, domesticity, to a wife to whom he was not married, and children lacking the authority of wedlock. Surely Hook's was the strangest of all double lives. Many men have concealed minions or misdemeanours behind a false front of respectability, but here was a friend of all the rakes of his day, the brightest spirit of the raffish overworld, who practised by stealth all the unfashionable virtues, was good to his neighbours, brimmed over with sentiment, and cherished the pleasures of heart and hearth. Extraordinary; the punning, gambling wit, the reckless jester, the madcap boon-companion, was a circumscribed and self-tormented moralist. True, he never married, though once at least he might have won beauty and companionship. But if he did not marry, neither did he desert his mistress; and his diary shows that in his merriest moments the remembrance of his undowered children sometimes struck him like a blow.

Conscience, however, though it made a victim, never made a bore of Theodore Hook, and only his closely-written private journal held the secrets of his divided mind. On parade he was the popular author, the famous diner-out, the omniscient politician acquainted with every move behind the scenes, the boisterous editor of a partisan weekly; in private he lived in semi-rural retirement in a house fronting the Thames at Fulham, unvisited by his fashionable friends, few of whom even knew the address of his retreat. Here he enjoyed the amenities of a comfortable, elegant villa; an airy, well-filled library; a walled garden with lawn sloping to the river; and the company of his family, his tame seagulls, and his dog. As a writer he was neither reluctant nor incompetent; and if he could have been contented with this ivory tower of his own building he might have been happy. He might even have been rich, for his novels were for a time second only to Scott's in the public approval, and, with his journalism, brought him in close on two thousand pounds a year. Alas for brilliant Theodore; he could not be so contented. The company of the "great" was a drug which he sometimes abhorred but never could forgo; and so, though he earned much, he spent more, for it was costly even to be a guest in that society. As he left forty behind, the range of his acquaintance with the notables of the Tory party steadily widened, and he grew more and more in demand, even with the Whigs. "Dear Theodore" was indispensable to make a party go, to persuade a duke, to be the pivot of a country stay. To sustain his double or treble role, he taxed his constitution like a wartime chancellor; his hours grew more hopelessly irregular, his work more scamped, his potations more frequent. His days and nights were crammed. After writing at speed all morning, he would drive into London to entertain an admiring circle first at one club, then another, and then another; then shine at some nobleman's feast, where for hours he would cascade impromptu merriment in talk and song; and then, when the guests departed, move on to play at dice or hazard until four or five o'clock before retreating, dispirited, home, to remember and regret his wasted hours. The remarkable thing is that, despite all this expense of spirit, he so seldom failed to dazzle. Eye-witness after eye-witness testifies to his invincible verbal dexterity, so relevant to the moment that it could not be premeditated nor recorded. Coleridge summed up these lost fireworks: "I have before in my time met with men of admirable promptitude of intellectual power and play of wit, the rays of which, as Stillingfleet says, gild whatever they strike, but I never could have conceived such readiness of mind and resources of genius to be poured out on the mere subject and impulse of the minute." Coleridge had been dazzled by Hook's ever-ready play of tongue, his ceaseless conversational high spirits, and his power of improvising elaborate metrical chants which brought in, with some apt reference or personal quip, all the persons present, however hard to manage their names might be. Once he had to cope with Rosenagen, which he introduced thus, at the end of a long string of easier patronymics:

"Yet more of my Muse is required:
Alas! I fear she is done;
But no! like a fiddler that's tired,
I'll *Rosen-agen* and go on."

Disraeli testifies in "Coningsby" to another of Hook's peculiarities: his extreme power of keeping a straight face when all his listeners were eclipsed in mirth. In the story, Theodore figures as Lucian Gay, who narrates, with implacable gravity, an elaborate fable at which it is forbidden, under penalty of forfeit, to laugh, the fable " 'of the very respectable county family which had been established in the shire for several generations, but which, it was a fact, had been ever distinguished by the strange and humiliating peculiarity of being born with sheep's tails'. The remarkable circumstances under which Lucian Gay had become acquainted with this fact; the traditionary mysteries by which the family had succeeded for generations in keeping it secret; the decided measures to which the chief of the family had recourse to stop for ever the rumour when it first became prevalent; and finally the origin and result of the legend, were details which Lucian Gay, with the most rueful countenance, loved to expend upon the attentive and expanding intelligence of a new member of the Grumpy Club. Familiar as all present were with the story, whose stimulus of agonizing risibility they had all in turn experienced, it was with extreme difficulty that any of them could resist the fatal explosion which was to be attended with the dreaded penalty".

All this, and the description of how men pinched themselves like fakirs, lit cigars at the wrong end and walked to and fro in almost frenzied efforts not to laugh at Hook, is true to fact. So also is Dizzy's sketch of yet another of Theodore's habits of entertainment: his power of producing, in parody, a complete House of Commons debate, imitating one speaker after another, not only in mannerisms but in style and subject-matter, interrupting himself, shouting himself down, taking off Peel, Palmerston or the Duke without a moment's pause. On other occasions, when a piano was available, Hook would troll out a complete comic opera, taking all the parts, and supplying recitatives and choruses with a spontaneity that had to be heard to be believed. In performances of this sort Hook has probably never been equalled; Lockhart recalls "the commentary of that bright eye—the deep gurgling glee of his voice—the electrical felicity of his pantomime—for in truth he was as great an actor as could have been produced by rolling up Liston and Terry and Mathews into one".

Apart from his histrionic talent, however, he kept all his life the habit of dramatic impudence, as when he captivated the lady of Hatfield House by his deft way of pointing out that he had been overlooked. She noticed him rocking to and fro during dinner, and asked why, to which Hook replied: "Madam, I have been accustomed all my life to those social recognitions at table which are now interdicted by fashion, and so, when no one notices me, I usually bow to the epergne, and take wine with the flowers." It was in this spirit that he interrogated an over-dressed and pompous citizen in the Strand: "Pray, sir, forgive my question: but may I ask, are you anyone in particular?" And his occasional verse epigrams were good, as on Leigh Hunt's "Rimini":

"O Crimine, Crimine,
What a nimini pimine
Story of Rimini",

or on Samuel Beazeley, "who lived hard and died easily". But it was as a ready-tongued raconteur that Theodore deserved and won his place among the wits. Like every man of his time, he was an inveterate punster; his puns, however, were almost as regular a part of his speech as his intonation, and were really a personal form of emphasis. Shrewd, eloquent, grammatical, his stories and anecdotes, witty in the manner of Defoe, not of Wilde, were the product of an extraordinary brain, as much out of the usual way as is the brain of a mathematical or scientific genius.

What a wild, vivid harlequinade jingles again in such extracts as remain from Hook's journals; what bitter self-reproaches, what a frustrated career. Why, when he earned so much, did he save so little? Incorrigibly extravagant, he lived always like an ox in summer, tormented by a crowd of midges. Creditors, bills, and notes of hand were the ground theme of this overture to greatness. Many times he was tempted to retire into pleasant, opulent privacy; but then jealousy of others to whom his place would fall, unwillingness to relinquish his unique ascendancy, enticed him again to the struggle, and, leaving his debts and duns, he would hasten to a country house party at which, the only untitled guest, he would practise again his invariable, sterile success. But even though he could evade his duns, he could not completely evade his duties. Every Thursday he must meet the printer of *John Bull*, to arrange for the week's issue. And so on Wednesday, while the company was out to hunt or shoot, he would hastily correct his proofs, scribble his editorial, wring out an article or poem, and then drive to some appointed rendezvous to meet his manager, with whom he would spend that night and the next morning in close editorial consultation. The week's work settled in this way, the portly truant would hasten back to the party, his "headache" gone, ready for frivolity, excursions, champagne by day, roman punch, gossip and gambling by night. Once more the fashionable intelligence would conclude its list of the distinguished company gathered at Coningsby Castle with the words ". . . and Mr. Theodore Hook".

2

The candle that burned so brightly in St. James's had been lit in Bloomsbury and trimmed at Mauritius. When Byron and Sir Robert Peel, who were both born in 1788, dawdled at Harrow, young Hook, of exactly equal age, dawdled also. Contemplating their careers in after life, Hook often recalled bitterly that his natural gifts were not less than theirs. They were certainly more precocious, for at fourteen handsome, curly-haired Theodore with the bright, dark eyes was a musical Crichton, or whatever more can be said of a boy with an exquisite ear for tone, a rich, controlled voice, a perfect touch at the piano, and a quick-firing ability to compose tunes and verses. A prodigy. Such prodigies nearly always draw well; and they seldom stay long at school. Hook was no exception. When his mother died suddenly, her husband, himself a composer of parts and persistence, took the boy home from Harrow, discovered his talents, and kept him for company. Precocious indeed;

at sixteen Theodore not only amused his father, but was also the author of a comic opera performed with success at Drury Lane. At seventeen he had contributed a farce applauded at the Haymarket, and more theatrical pieces, original or adapted, followed in a flood. Mathews, Liston, Bannister welcomed the bright attractive stripling with his effortless ability, and though he went up to Oxford with his serious-minded brother, after a term or two he was back in more congenial stage company.

To be a successful dramatist in his teens; to be witty, good-looking, and gifted; to possess an instantaneous charm, and the consciousness of talents beyond his own computation; it was with these advantages that Theodore Hook entered the lists of London, and what more could mortal ask? Across the interval of a hundred years still shines the light of that lucky youth, so attractive, so capable, so young. Soon he turned to a new career, and at twenty produced, under an assumed name, a three-volume novel of coincidence which, though lively, fell quite flat. Yet he did not return, directly, to farce-writing; instead, he made a boisterous farce of his own life. Here, for the first time, we glimpse some canker in the bud. What obscure form of restlessness turned this musical young dandy, with the theatre waiting for his script, towards that vexing form of illiteracy, the practical joke? Was it some insidious resentment against himself, the incipient worm of conscience reversed against his fellows? Was it a wish to out-perform his actor friends, or the knocker-stealing example of the Mohocks? Or irrepressible high spirits, the explosive force of personality, demanding some more direct expression for itself than the once-removed medium of the stage? Whatever was the cause, young Theodore flung himself into hoaxing as though it were a career; and it may safely be said, even in an age that knew Horace Cole, that no one before or since ever bent greater talents to odder ends. Many of his japes are retold in his own "Gilbert Gurney"; a few examples will give the flavour. Rowing to Richmond in company with the comedian Mathews, he was inflamed by a notice in a Barnes garden forbidding all unauthorized landings. Of course the cronies disembarked; and, converting their fishing-line into a surveyor's tape, paced the lawn solemnly, measuring and noting distances. When interrogated, Theodore proclaimed himself an agent of the Canal Company, come to determine the direction of a new cut—which, he calculated, would pass direct beneath the alderman's window, and straight through his greenhouse. The poor alderman's consternation; his attempts to placate the two unwelcome officials; his civilities, his wheedlings, and finally his pressing invitation to the dinner just about to be served were often and often retold by the ebullient Hook of later days, and even now there is something fascinating in the skill with which the queer accomplices hoaxed and yet charmed their host—till, at the end, over a last bottle, Theodore struck into extempore song which narrated the whole of the jest, winding up with the verse:

"For we greatly approve of your fare,
Your cellar's as prime as your cook;
My clerk here is Mathews the player,
And my name, sir, is—Theodore Hook!"

Some of Hook's hoaxes were more malicious. It was he who, dressed in some scarlet uniform, delivered a forged card for Carlton House to the foppish, stage-struck "Romeo" Coates, whose twin hobbies were acting Shakespeare and wearing diamonds. Convulsed in a safe corner, Theodore watched his victim enter his carriage (shaped like a cockle-shell and adorned with full-sized brass chanticleers) and, still disguised, witnessed the ignominious rejection of the poor beau. Even more mischievous was his Berners Street hoax of 1809, often imitated since. Having laid a wager that he would make a quiet little London residence famous, the jester devoted five days (or weeks: the accounts vary) to the writing of nearly a thousand letters (or nearly four thousand, according to the later version), bidding tradesmen of all kinds deliver specified wares to the address given at a particular time on a named day. Infinite trouble ensued. Dealers, merchants, and professional men of all the kinds that Hook had thought of obeyed the summons, and confounded confusion. Deep ingenuity had been used; and it is claimed that the Governor of the Bank of England was in the throng, enticed by a letter offering to reveal a complicated fraud practised by a clerk; and that the chairman of the East India Company was bagged by a similar chicanery. It is said, too, that the Duke of Gloucester started off with his equerry "to receive a secret communication from a dying woman, formerly a confidential attendant on His Royal Highness's mother". The climax of the fun, if fun it was, was the arrival of the Lord Mayor in his carriage. The Mayor's stay was short; he drove straight to the police. The hoax was a complete, far-reaching success, but if it could have been pinned on its author, Master Hook would have paid heavily for his act of humour. But he lay low, and lived to hoax another day. He made his way into a private house, which he pretended to think was an inn, and almost drove the owner into apoplexy by his curt orders and irate denunciation of the shocking service; and this was a better joke, for it depended on the impudence and personality of the joker. He won a wager that he would dine unasked in the house of a complete stranger, and actually persuaded his host that he was one of the invited guests. On another occasion, irritated before a dinner to which he *was* invited, he appeared dripping with water from head to foot, explained that he had plunged into the water-butt to cool himself, and then took his carriage unperturbed to dine elsewhere. Even his friends in the theatre were not safe from his pranks. He penetrated below the stage at Drury Lane to provide Liston, during a song, with an unexpected accompaniment from an invisible penny whistle; he confounded Dowton by appearing in a chorus coat during an act and gravely handing a meaningless note to the embarrassed principal; and at a critical moment in another play he stentoriously shouted, "Sheridan for ever!" through a prompter's trumpet which had rashly been entrusted to him. At any moment, anywhere, his freakish humour was liable to declare itself, and, like a mirthful Mr. Hyde, displace his Jekyll. Once, mounting an empty cart by a roadside, he turned down his shirt-collar and began a religious appeal in the manner of a field-preacher, until, having assembled a rustic audience, he suddenly altered the tone of his voice, thundered the most appalling curses at the congregation, and ran for his life.

These exploits set the town talking of their perpetrator; but they did less than his other gifts to make him liked. Even thus early he was a first-rate raconteur, but what charmed most was his talent for improvisation. The inspiration of the moment, as Coleridge observed, was sufficient. Greville gives an account which, though it belongs to a later date, shows clearly the impression he made: "Last night he was very brilliant. Each lady gave him a subject, such as 'The Goodwood Cup'. 'The Tithe Bill', one 'could not think of anything'; when he dashed off and sang stanzas innumerable, very droll, with ingenious rhymes and excellent hits, 'his eye begetting occasion for his excellent wit', for at every word of interruption or admiration, every look or motion, he indulged in a digression, always coming back to one of the themes imposed upon him." Such an entertainer was not likely to remain monopolized by stage circles. Sheridan took him up; he dazzled the Marchioness of Hertford; and she in turn brought him before the Prince Regent. Now he was fairly set on the tide of fashion; invitations, the sincerest form of flattery, filled his postbox, and he found himself beset by a Mayfair as eager then as ever to be amused. And, more important, the Prince himself was amused. He made enquiry concerning the situation of this favourite, and learned that he had no income and no place. "Oh," exclaimed the Regent, "something must be done for Hook." Something was. A very short time later, in 1812, Mr. Theodore Edward Hook, then twenty-four, was appointed Accountant-General and Treasurer to the Colony of the Mauritius, with a salary and allowances amounting to nearly two thousand pounds a year—that handsome income on which Hook was to remain poor nearly all his life.

This appointment was, in its way, as good a practical joke as the best of Hook's own, and lasted longer. At the end of 1813 the lucky versifier left his debts behind him, took up his magnificent post, and for five years enjoyed himself hugely in this "paradise not without angels". Life in the Colony for the lucky ones was an alternation of operas in the winter and races in the summer, with a background of balls, bathing, lounging, lovemaking, and claret at tenpence a bottle. Moreover, Hook's superior, Governor Farquhar, was distantly related to him by marriage, and therefore doubly indulgent to his idle connection, on whom the cares of office lay light as thistledown on summer air. But this long dream of tropic idleness ended the more disastrously. Farquhar fell sick, and was succeeded by General Hall. Two months later a coloured clerk in Hook's office charged him in a letter to the new Governor with extensive defalcations; and though Hook asserted (probably with truth) his complete innocence, a substantial deficit was revealed on examination, and he was hastily and ignominiously put under arrest. After the whole of his property had been seized and sold, the impeached Treasurer was delivered over to a military guard and despatched to England. On arrival at Portsmouth, however, he was released from custody, the Attorney-General finding no grounds for any criminal charge against him. His accuser, who may well have been the culprit, had meanwhile cut his throat. Nevertheless, the Board of Colonial Audit girded itself for an examination, and began a series of interrogations of Hook which lasted, off and on, for more than three years.

The penniless and disgraced wit ran to earth; and it was now, when in concealment at Somers Town, that he entered upon that attachment to which he remained so generously faithful. While sheltering from the storm, however, he soon found a profitable, if secret, purpose to which to direct his restless energy—an underground enterprise that fully satisfied the longing for personal power previously put forth in the famous hoaxes. Soon after his unwilling return from the Mauritius, Theodore took a hand in a new, short-lived periodical, *The Arcadian*; and the experience so gained was put to effective use in the weekly *John Bull*, which he helped to establish at the close of 1820. The *Bull* was an instant, an astonishing, a nation-wide success. In the contest between the Whig supporters of Queen Caroline and the private friends of George the Fourth, the former had so far by much the best of the war of wits. "The First Gentleman in Europe," with his flagrant follies, was easy prey. But now, unexpected and anonymous, came the new champion, retorting the Whig satire by an unremitting, unscrupulous investigation into the life and position of every individual who appeared in the Queen's society. Caroline, accused of adultery, was represented by her party as an injured, innocent woman; nevertheless, the great Whig ladies were loth to visit her Court, particularly when those who did so found their foibles or frailties set out in the new journal. No one knew that Hook was "Bull"; even the Government did not recognize, in the devastating *on dits*, edged personalities and reckless exposures, the hand of its ex-Mauritian Treasurer. In vain did Lady Jersey protest that no one connected with the detestable weekly should be received in her house; the next number contained a rejoinder in which the nameless editor made it clear that he was numbered among her close acquaintances. In vain did prosecution follow prosecution. The printer and publisher were loyal to their author, even in prison, and a proffered bribe of £500 failed to elicit evidence connecting Hook with the paper. The circulation soared; soon the profit of Hook's half share brought him, *sub rosa*, his lost two thousand a year; and though the Queen's death ended the original purpose of the *Bull*, its hold on the public persisted. By now, however, the secret was out, and the angry Whigs remembered Mauritius. The Audit Board suddenly concluded its inquiry into the long-debated deficit, gave judgment against careless Theodore for nearly £13,000, seized his goods and chattels (for the second time), and consigned his person, under a writ of extent, to a debtors' prison. Hook looked in vain to the King for salvation; the Tories were forced to move carefully, and in any event Queen Caroline was dead. So in prison, with varying degrees of restriction, her former enemy remained for nearly two years, when (partly through Croker's representations) he was released on parole, as it were, with the judgment against him suspended—as he hoped, for ever. Characteristically, he had charmed his gaoler, who stood his outgoing prisoner a dinner which was enlivened by a new song with the chorus:

> "Let him hang with a curse—this atrocious, pernicious
> Scoundrel who emptied the till at Mauritius."

And now, at thirty-six, this versatile adventurer in words made a new cast for fortune; he turned novelist in earnest, prompted by a friend who urged that his unceasing flow of anecdote deserved some more permanent record than a dinner-table remembrance. Was ever man more fortunate and yet more cursed than Hook? Here too he was instantly successful. "Sayings and Doings" appeared in 1824, with no author's name, offered as "A series of sketches from Life". In reading these stories today, it is not at first easy to understand the enthusiasm with which they were received. The clock must be put back; it must be realized that, in their day, they were something new in fiction; almost as new as the Sherlock Holmes stories were in the 'nineties. In political conviction Hook was the bluest, Blimplike Tory; his moral philosophy was flatly, school-girlishly conventional; as a story-teller he had no true power of invention. But he was a very shrewd observer, and a very good raconteur; he had come to know more sides of the world than most men; he had been a research worker in scandal for five years. From these advantages he produced a new literary *genre*; the unromanticized close-up of the shabby side of social life. The middle-class met its betters on equal terms in his pages, and was delighted by the privilege. Hook is less a pointer to Bulwer and Disraeli than to Dickens; and though his work has not lasted well, no close student of the novel ought to ignore it. Indeed, despite a morality so insistent as sometimes to seem canting, there is enjoyment to be savoured still from Hook's animated portrait galleries, from his queer inventions, farcical contrivances, and detailed descriptions of dinners. The strange thing is that his novels are so much more full of purpose than of wit. Their humour is the humour of character and situation rather than of phrase.

Freed from prison, and once more in funds (for if *John Bull's* earnings had fallen off, the novels made up the difference, and the magical two thousand a year was once more his), Theodore took a pleasant house at Putney, and began to re-enter Society, which he had shunned since his Mauritius débâcle. As one of the best-selling authors of the day, he was again a person of consideration; his consistent Toryism brought him new friends in high places; and his talent of entertainment was undimmed. After a year or so he flew his kite higher, and became tenant of a fine, fashionable house in Cleveland Row. Here he was extravagantly hospitable, elaborately the bachelor (but with his family of four girls and a son tucked away in the wings), with all the fitments, from a neat carriage downwards, of the man of fashion. Who could have supposed that the Fleet prisoner of three years before, with that vast load of debt to the Crown hanging over his head, could have given so recklessly little thought for the morrow? Soon, as we all do, he had succeeded in repeating his own history. The names in his visitors' book grew so numerous and so eminent that Lockhart was astonished when he came to go through it, but the new debts kept correspondence with the noble names, and after four years Hook was forced to retire from St. James's to that Fulham retreat which has already been described, and "to wonder", in his diary, "when I look back, that I should have been so foolish as to waste the prime of life in foolish idleness". In that wondering consciousness of waste he remained to the end; that useless wonder of men who are their own enemies, whose industry turns bankrupt in their hands. He hoped, too, to the end; hoped that the King or his counsellors would once more feel that "something must be done for Hook". And once something nearly was. In 1834, when his schoolfellow Peel formed his first government, the post of Inspector of Plays was offered to the faithful flame-thrower, if George Colman could be persuaded to relinquish it. But Colman was an old friend, and Hook, who had come to dislike the theatre, did not even try.

3

In his youth gay Theodore, happy, handsome Theodore, had needed no stimulants beyond the high spirits and intelligence with which he was gifted by nature; but when his hair fell the bald, bluff wit drank, as he talked, incessantly. On one occasion he questioned a bill for ten brandies preferred by the club waiter, claiming that he had taken only nine, and was forthwith reminded of the one that he had enjoyed before he sat down. On another, he spent the whole afternoon with an American *bon vivant*, drinking experimental gin and maraschino cocktails by the *pint*—and then dined, calm and sober, at Lord Canterbury's, where he ascribed his poor appetite to "a biscuit and glass of sherry rashly taken at luncheon". Yet these excesses seemed only to stimulate his indefatigable brain; and he would call over the names of all the shops in Oxford Street in their order, recount the advertisements in *The Times* after a single reading, or submit to some more difficult test to prove it. Now and again, however, it could be seen that the gold was wearing thin. At one literary dinner (times change, but not dinners), after his health had been toasted enthusiastically, Theodore rose with an air of heavy sternness, and began irascibly what was taken as a spoof speech protesting against the liberty taken with his name. The laughter grew louder and louder as Hook's phrases increased in what seemed their tempo of mock-temper; but those near him were soon uncomfortably aware that the rage was real, if a reflection of the bottle; the realization spread, and he had to apologize in the morning.

No constitution could endure this pace for long; and that Hook should have maintained it for ten years was not the least of his feats. But when pain added itself to remorse and the consciousness of wasted gifts, it became plain, even to himself, that he was mortal. The liver, that bastard enemy of good living, betrayed him in the end. He dined out almost to the last, but with doom written on his face. When a friend, admitted by error, caught the fading wit in *déshabillé*, Hook, who looked horrible, observed sombrely: "Well, you see me as I am at last—all the bucklings and paddings and washings and brushings dropped for ever—a poor old grey-haired man, with my belly about my knees." To another friend, in whose mirror he had caught sight of himself, he remarked, "Ay, I see I look as I am; done up in purse, in mind, and in body too at last." He was indeed; within a week he was dead. He died on August 24, 1841, not quite fifty-three. In a last spasm of spite, the Lords of the Treasury revived their claim against his estate, sold off for the third time all that he possessed—all the books, bijouterie and furnishings of the Fulham villa—and seized the resultant money in reduction of the long-forgotten Mauritius debt. As he had always feared, his children were left completely unprovided for: or would have been, had not old friends raised a subscription for their benefit. Nearly three thousand pounds were gathered, though apart from the King of Hanover few of Hook's grand acquaintances contributed to it, and none of them followed his corpse to its place of burial.

Who shall pronounce the epitaph of Theodore Hook? Not Thackeray, certainly. Thackeray, who transposed his now faded Yellowplush from Hook's Mrs. Ramsbottom, who became the minor despot of the Garrick Club when Hook had been silenced by death, has left in Wagg of "Pendennis" and "Vanity Fair" a caricature in libel-colour of the wit whose ascendancy he would have copied if he could. Following him, it became the fashion to call Hook a snob. The charge is harsh. Poor men as well as rich may like fine porticoes, grand façades, and all the panoply of magnificence, and Hook was such a man. He liked high company; but he also liked low, and he can be tested by his friends. To the end of his life he retained and cherished intimacies with the struggling as well as with the successful and the great. He was open to anyone who laughed or listened, and was happier with Broderip, Hill, Jerdan, Barham or Maginn than with any of the social eminences whose patronage of him surprised Lockhart and annoyed Thackeray.

Such a career as Hook's shows how little, even now, and despite the psychiatrists, we comprehend the mechanism of the unusual mind. Perhaps he should be called witty, rather than a wit, for the essence of his jests, of his puns and improvisations, was a rapidity of thought and expression which gave his words the force, but not the didactic weight, of epigram. Some passage in the brain, usually or partly impeded in most of us, was clear in him; and so, like Macaulay's, his memory seemed limitless; so, like Fox, his flow of speech seemed never to halt. This facility must have been inherited; his father, who wrote thousands of songs (including the familiar "Lass of Richmond Hill"), evidently shared it. His mother, too, was talented and articulate, and the family ability shone in the respectable and fortunate elder brother, who early quenched his flame in holy water, and died at fifty-five Dean of Worcester. Theodore talked like a book; like the best part of his own books, shrewd, apposite, with a garnishing of mimicry and a prolonged, impressive relevance. Lacking any depth of thought, his wit was restricted to personal themes. It flowered and faded in the heated moments that called it forth; and now little beyond the recorded wonder of his contemporaries, his youthful farces and his silver-fork novels, remains to remind the world of Theodore Hook. But if the bloom was short-lived, it was none the less real; and the legend will long remain of the queer fish who all his life swam so desperately in the shallow waters of his own laughter.

CHARLES LAMB

ROBERT LYND

THERE IS ONLY ONE STORY TOLD OF LAMB'S CHILDHOOD THAT GIVES ANY foretaste of the wit and humorist he was to become. As little more than an infant, he was walking through a graveyard with his sister Mary, ten years his senior, and reading the epitaphs on the universally belauded dead—for he was a precocious reader, who, it is said, "knew his letters before he could talk". As he came away, he turned to his sister and asked: "Mary, where are the naughty people buried?" This, we may be sure, though a joke to the reader, was not uttered as a joke by the small child. At the same time, it is evidence that even then he possessed that balancing and corrective kind of observation out of which humour grows.

It was, perhaps, significant that his first witticism came to birth in such melancholy surroundings. For Lamb's humour is that of a man whose nature was enriched by suffering—who confronted tragedy at the outset of his manhood and who lived under the perpetual shadow of disaster.

He was born in 1775, a Cockney, the son of a scrivener who had become servant and assistant to a lawyer in the Temple. His father, he declared, "had the merriest quips and conceits", and he had enough literary ambition to publish a book of verse. At the age of eight Charles entered Christ's Hospital, where Coleridge, aged nine, was a promising scholar, and where his friendship with Valentine Le Grice infected him with a love of punning. He left school when he was only fourteen years old, was given a job in a counting-house, became a clerk in the South Sea House at the age of sixteen, and about a year later entered the service of the East India House, which was to provide him with a livelihood for the rest of his existence. Shadows worse than that of servitude began to fall early. We find him at the age of twenty-one writing characteristically to Coleridge: "The 6 weeks that finished last year and began this your very humble servant spent very agreeably in a mad house at Hoxton—I am got somewhat rational now, and don't bite any one." In September of the same year his sister Mary in a fit of madness stabbed her mother to the heart. "My poor dear dearest sister," he wrote to Coleridge, "in a fit of insanity has been the death of her own mother. I was at hand only enough to snatch the knife out of her grasp." This was the testing time of Lamb's life and he rose to it. He could not endure the prospect of his sister's being confined permanently in an asylum, though his elder brother was in favour of this, and, giving "his solemn agreement that he would take her under his care for life", he set up house with her at the age of twenty-four, and remained her devoted guardian till his death thirty-seven years later. Mary had many relapses, and Barry Cornwall has told how, at the approach of one of her fits, "Lamb would take her under his arm to Hoxton Asylum. It was," he goes on, "very affecting to encounter the young brother and his sister walking together (weeping together) on this painful errand. . . . They used to carry a straitjacket with them."

That is the biographical background which enables us to appreciate the truth of Valentine Le Grice's description of Lamb's wit. "His wit," says Le Grice, "flashing out of his melancholy, was as the summer lightning, playing innocuously round the very cloud that gave it birth. And thus it is the overburdened spirit relieves itself: a pun may discharge a whole load of sorrow: the sharp point of a quibble or a joke may let out the long-gathered waters of bitterness."

2

There are critics who dismiss Lamb as a maudlin sentimentalist with a vein of tipsy jocularity, implying that he was a man of shallow nature and of equally shallow mind. If he had been so, it is unlikely that Coleridge and Wordsworth would have loved him, that Shelley would have longed for his society, or that Landor would have adored him at first sight. Among the great men of his time, Lamb was an equal among equals. He did not live under patronage and was resentful when he felt that Coleridge was not only patronizing but libelling him for addressing him as "my gentle-hearted Charles" three times in one poem. "For God's sake (I never was more serious)", he wrote to the well-meaning Coleridge, "don't make me ridiculous any more by terming me gentle-hearted in print, or do it in better verses. . . . In the next edition of the 'Anthology' . . . please to blot out *gentle-hearted* and substitute drunken dog, ragged-head, seld-shaven, odd-eyed, stuttering, or any other epithet which truly and properly belongs to the gentleman in question." Much though Coleridge meant to him, Lamb constantly allowed his comic spirit to play on that fragmentary man of genius. His description of Coleridge as "an archangel a little damaged" is a perfect example of witty portraiture. We find an example of the same spirit of irreverence in the story Leigh Hunt tells of a meeting at Highgate at which Coleridge pontificated at length on the eternal verities. When he had gone, Hunt asked Lamb irritably, "What makes Coleridge talk in that way about heavenly grace, and the holy church, and that sort of thing?" "Ah," replied Lamb, with a stammer, "there is a g-good deal of fun in Coleridge!"

Lamb's playful attitude to Coleridge is, perhaps, best exemplified in a story he once related to an American visitor. He told him how one day on his way to the City he met Coleridge "brimful of some new idea, and in spite of my assuring him that time was precious, he drew me within the door of an unoccupied garden by the roadside, and there, sheltered from observation by a hedge of evergreens, he took me by the button of my coat, and closing his eyes commenced an eloquent discourse, waving his right hand gently, as the musical words flowed in an unbroken stream from his lips. I listened entranced; but the striking of a church clock recalled me to a sense of duty. I saw it was of no use to attempt to break away, so taking advantage of his absorption in his subject, I, with my penknife, quietly severed the button from my coat, and decamped. Five hours afterwards, in passing the same garden, on my way home, I heard Coleridge's voice, and on looking in, there he was, with closed eyes —the button in his fingers—and his right hand gracefully waving, just as when I left him. He had never missed me!" The story may not have the truth of history, but it has certainly the truth of caricature.

As for Wordsworth, he must have been exceptionally fond of Lamb, if the story is true that Lamb once pulled his nose with impunity. Haydon also tells us of a party at which Lamb, a little tipsy, challenged Wordsworth: "Now, you old lake poet, you rascally poet, why do you call Voltaire dull?" and of the good humour with which Wordsworth entered into the spirit of the occasion. Probably he knew that Lamb disliked Voltaire and spoke only from a spirit of contradiction. Lamb's attitude to Voltaire was perfectly expressed in his remark to a man who was attacking Voltaire and comparing him unfavourably with Jesus Christ, that "Voltaire was a very good Jesus Christ—*for the French*".

Lamb's light conversation—many of his friends liked his serious conversation better—ranged from sheer nonsense and puns to wit and humour such as we find in his letters and essays. His puns were not particularly good, and few of them would have been recorded if they had not been uttered by Charles Lamb. Still, he showed ready wit when, having fallen downstairs after a convivial evening at a friend's house, and hearing his friend calling from above to ask him what he was doing, he called back: "Yser rolling rapidly." Some of his contemporaries groaned over his puns. Thomas Moore, while praising him, described him as "full of villainous and abortive puns, which he miscarries of every minute". Hazlitt imputed his love of puns to humility. Lamb himself in his thumbnail autobiography suggests that his conversational extravagance was the result of his stammer. "Stammers abominably," he wrote of himself, "and is therefore more apt to discharge his occasional conversation in a quaint aphorism, or a poor quibble, than in set and edifying speeches; has consequently been libelled as a person always aiming at wit, which, as he told a dull fellow that charged him with it, is at least as good as aiming at dullness." Of all the hostile accounts of Lamb as a wit Carlyle's is at once the most condemnatory and the most brilliant. Carlyle was thirty-five years old and Lamb fifty-six at the time of their meeting at Enfield, and it may be doubted whether Carlyle's features relaxed even once into a smile in the course of the visit. "Charles Lamb I sincerely believe to be in some considerable degree insane," he wrote. "A more pitiful, ricketty, gasping, staggering, stammering Tomfool I do not know. He is witty by denying truisms and abjuring good manners. His speech wriggles hither and thither with an incessant painful fluctuation, not an opinion in it, or a fact, or a phrase that you can thank him for—more like a convulsion fit than a natural systole and diastole. Besides, he is now a confirmed, shameless, drunkard; *asks* vehemently for gin and water in strangers' houses, tipples till he is utterly mad, and is only not thrown out of doors because he is too much despised for taking such trouble with him. Poor Lamb! Poor England, when such a despicable abortion is named genius! He said 'There are just two things I regret in England's history: first, that Guy Fawkes' plot did not take effect (there would have been so glorious an *explosion*); second, that the Royalists did not hang Milton (then we might have laughed at them) &c. &c.' *Armer Teufel!*" Carlyle, worshipper of heroes, clearly found it difficult to recognize a hero except among the dead. It is pleasant to think of Carlyle sitting with his expression growing more and more scowling as Lamb tried to make him see the fun of that hypothetical explosion.

Hazlitt, who could scowl as fiercely as Carlyle, knew Lamb better—knew him well enough, indeed, to appreciate him as "the most delightful, the most provoking, the most witty and sensible of men". "He always," said Hazlitt, "made the best pun, and the best remark in the course of the evening. No one ever stammered out such fine, piquant, deep, eloquent things in half a dozen half-sentences as he does. His jests scald like tears, and he probes a question with a play upon words. What a keen, laughing, harebrained vein of home-felt truth! What choice venom!"

Few people associate Lamb's humour with venom; and certainly his jests rarely left a wound. At the same time, he had what people call a rough edge to his tongue, as appears in his remark to a friend with whom he was playing cards: "M——, if dirt were trumps, what hands you would hold!" His nonsense must sometimes have appeared rude to his listeners, as when a lady asked him. "Mr. Lamb, how do you like babies?" and he replied: "B-b-boiled, ma'am." Grave conversationalists must often have been disconcerted by his nonsensical interruptions of the debate. One evening Coleridge and Holcroft were discussing "man as he is and man as he ought to be." "Give me", said Lamb, breaking in on them, "man as he ought not to be." There was a lively vein of mischief in his nature. He used to like to force his way into the Misses Norris's school at Goddard House, and make discipline impossible, teaching the girls a new version of the Church Catechism. He also took great pleasure in teaching a small girl to say the Lord's Prayer backwards. Devoted though he was to children, he did not hesitate to propose the toast of the "m-m-much ca-calumniated good King Herod" on one occasion, and in the same mood he wrote approvingly of the Massacre of the Innocents.

The word "whimsical" has become such a term of reproach in modern times—and, indeed, there is nothing more nauseating than pseudo-whimsicality—that one feels reluctant to speak of Lamb's "whimsicality". Yet whimsicality was of the essence both of his style and of his character. It was the half-deliberate play of an intensely serious nature—a nature that had gone through the fires of suffering, but had no mind to inflict his sufferings on the world at large. He found relief from his troubles in eccentricity and could turn even a painful experience into a joke. Consider his behaviour after the failure of his play "Mr. H." which was hissed into ruin by the first night audience. Lamb, we are told, joined in the hissing from his seat in the Drury Lane pit, explaining afterwards that he did so because he was so damnably afraid of being taken for the author. In a letter written to Thomas Manning at the time, Lamb let himself go about the audience in a fine outburst of grotesque vituperation. "Damn 'em, how they hissed! It was not a hiss neither, but a sort of frantic yell, like a congregation of mad geese, with roaring something like bears, mows and mops like apes, sometimes snakes, that hiss'd me into madness. 'Twas like St. Anthony's temptations. Mercy on us, that God should give his favourite children, men, mouths to speak with, to discourse rationally, to promise smoothly, to flatter agreeably, to encourage warmly, to counsel wisely; to sing with, to drink with, and to

you like it, you will love him. If you can see nothing in it, you had better turn to another author. "I like," he wrote, "to meet a sweep—understand me—not a grown sweeper—old chimney-sweepers are by no means attractive—but one of those tender novices, blooming through their first nigritude, the maternal washings not quite effaced from the cheek—such as come forth with the dawn, or somewhat earlier, with their little professional notes sounding like the *peep peep* of a young sparrow; or liker to the martin lark should I pronounce them, in their aerial ascents not seldom anticipating the sunrise? I have a kindly yearning towards these dim specks—poor blots—innocent blacknesses—I reverence these young Africans of our own growth—these almost clergy imps, who sport their cloth without assumption; and from their little pulpits (the tops of chimneys), in the nipping air of a December morning, preach a lesson of patience to mankind."

It is interesting to notice how Lamb, who as a talker was a stammerer of detached sentences, loved to prolong the flow of his fancies and images when he took a pen in his hand. He had an artist's pleasure in the flavour of words, and lingered over them affectionately like a wise child sucking a sweet. He loved to elaborate. Most of his written humour is a matter of fantastic elaboration, as when, having put his dog Dash in the care of Patmore, he wrote to ask whether the dog was safe from the then prevalent hydrophobia. "Goes he muzzled, or *aperto ore*?" he asked. "Are his intellects sound, or does he wander a little in his conversation? You cannot be too careful to watch the first symptoms of incoherence. The first illogical snarl he makes, to St. Luke's with him! All the dogs here are going mad, if you believe the overseers; but I protest they seem to me very rational and collected. But nothing is so deceitful as mad people to those who are not used to them. Try him with hot water. If he won't lick it up, it is a sign he does not like it. Does his tail wag horizontally or perpendicularly? That has decided the fate of many dogs in Enfield. Is his general deportment cheerful? I mean when he is pleased—for otherwise there is no judging. You can't be too careful. Has he bit any of the children yet? If he has, have them shot, and keep *him* for curiosity, to see if it was the hydrophobia."

4

Lamb's life was as fantastic as his writing. He looked fantastic with his beautiful head, his eyes of different colours, his spindle shanks, and his dress like a Methodist minister's. He could not even smoke except fantastically. Talfourd tells us that when Dr. Parr "saw Lamb smoking the strongest preparation of the weed, puffing out smoke like some furious Enchanter, he gently laid down his pipe, and asked him how he had acquired his power of smoking at such a rate? Lamb replied, 'I toiled after it, sir, as some men toil after virtue.'" A story of his snuff-taking—Mary also "took snuff liberally"—shows equally how Lamb's naturally comic behaviour struck humour out of those who knew him. Hone of the "Every-Day Book" tells it. "One summer's evening", he says, "I was walking on Hampstead Heath with Charles Lamb, and we had talked ourselves into a philosophic contempt of our slavery to the habit of snuff-taking, and, with the firm resolution of never again taking a single pinch, we threw our snuff boxes away from the hill on which we stood, far among the furze and brambles below, and went home in triumph; I began to be very miserable, was wretched all night; in the morning I was walking on the same hill, I saw Charles Lamb below, searching among the bushes; he looked up laughing, and saying, 'What, you are come to look for your snuff box too!' 'O no,' said I, taking pinch out of a paper in my waistcoat pocket, 'I went for a halfpenny worth to the first shop that was open.' "

His freakishness in company must often have been a cause of embarrassment. As one of his contemporaries wrote, "there was a whimsical recklessness which would occasionally beset him". To give an example, the writer continued: "He dined one day at the house of a friend of ours, and on entering the drawing-room after dinner, saw a gentleman standing in the middle of the room whose bent shoulders, in schoolboy leapfrog phrase, 'made a back'; the temptation was too great for Lamb, he placed his hands on the unconscious victim and flew over his head, to the astonished indignation of many and amusement of the few. This perhaps may be called a mere disregard to the proprieties of time and peace; but Lamb was at times less excusably aggressive." This story is evidence of Lamb's physical vigour. He was proud of his feats as a pedestrian, measuring, it is said, the distance he walked by ale-houses. "I have walked a pint," he would say.

Some critics have called Lamb affected as a writer, but we have only to read his life to see that his freakish humour was no superficial acquirement, but was as much a part of his nature as his breath and blood. His essays, the golden harvest of three years, are merely the perfect self-expression of the Lamb we find in the life and letters. You will find him in the letters, for example, discoursing humorously on eating. In the essay "Grace Before Meat", you will find him doing the same thing better. "I am no Quaker at my food," he writes. "I confess I am not indifferent to the kinds of it. Those unctuous morsels of deer's flesh were not made to be received with dispassionate services. I hate a man who swallows it, affecting not to know what he is eating. I suspect his taste in higher matters. I shrink instinctively from one who professes to like minced veal. There is a physiognomical character in the tastes for food. C—— holds that a man cannot have a pure mind who refuses apple-dumplings. I am not certain but he is right. With the decay of my first innocence, I confess a less and less relish daily for those innocuous cates. The whole vegetable tribe have lost their gust with me. Only I stick to asparagus, which still seems to inspire gentle thoughts."

One of Lamb's essays, "Distant Correspondents", is merely an elaboration of a letter he had written five years earlier to Barron Field, who had gone to Australia, then associated with convicts. In the letter he wrote: "Well, and how does the land of thieves use you? and how do you pass your time in your extra-judicial intervals? Going about the streets with a lantern, like Diogenes, looking for an honest man? You may look long enough, I fancy. Do give me some notion of the manners of the inhabitants where you are. They don't thieve all day long, do they? No human property could stand such continuous battery. And what do they do when they an't stealing?" In the essay the same fancy becomes: "I see Diogenes prying among you with his perpetual fruitless lantern. What must you be willing by this time to give for the sight of an honest man! You must almost have forgotten how we look. And tell me, what your Sydneyites do? Are they thxxvxng all day long?'

There is always this close correspondence between Lamb the writer for the public and Lamb in private life, both in his serious and in his jocular character, Lamb, the tenderly devoted brother, we find equally in "Old China" and in Cowden Clarke's earwitness story of how Lamb once said to his sister, "with his peculiar mode of tenderness, beneath blunt, abrupt speech: 'You must die first, Mary.' She nodded, with her little quiet nod and sweet smile: 'Yes, I must die first, Charles.' " That story gives us a glimpse of the harrowed soil from which Lamb's wit and humour were harvested, and which, as a result of the deepening of his sympathies, enabled him to bring London and its queer people more vividly before us and more ingratiatingly into our hearts than any other writer but Dickens.

SHERIDAN

CAMPBELL DIXON

A WIT, OF ALL PEOPLE, SHOULD NOT BE A SNOB; BUT SHERIDAN, LIKE CHESTERfield and Wilde and Congreve (and Squire Shakespeare living down his shady Bohemian past?), was determined to be a gentleman. We know what Voltaire thought of Congreve's snobbishness, and of Shakespeare's taste. It would be amusing to have his opinion of a code that approved of a gentleman's saving an innocent young girl from a seducer by running off with her himself, and victimizing tradesmen to pay card debts to wealthy rakes.

Amusing; but not, of course, conclusive. By the standards of his time, Sheridan was a man of honour. He was also, though Harrovians sneered at him for having an actor-father, of gentle birth, if of no great family. The castle owned by the family at some period unspecified, the "large estates assigned to them by ancient geographers", the descent from royal and hypothetical O'Sheridans—these we needn't take too seriously; but we do know that for at least two generations the Sheridans had been men of culture and even scholarship. Richard Brinsley's grandfather, Dr. Thomas Sheridan, was a friend of Swift's; at the doctor's little farm, Quilca—later to loom in the family legends as Quilcagh House, a sort of boggy Trianon—Swift wrote "Gulliver's Travels". None of the Sheridans was fortunate in his friendships. Dr. Sheridan was begged by Swift to watch for signs of his meanness becoming a positive vice, and was simple enough to warn him. "Did you never read 'Gil Blas'?" sneered the Dean, and promptly dropped the "vaporing scab". Dr. Sheridan's son, Thomas, might act and even recite for a living, and still be a friend of Dr. Johnson's; but then he had the impudence to bring out a dictionary, and accept a pension from Bute; and that was too much. Mendelians can make what they like of Johnson's verdict that the son of one wit who had few equals, and the father of another who had none, was of a dullness beyond the reach of nature unassisted by art and patient effort.

Sheridan's parents seem to have intended christening him Richard Brinsley Butler. Possibly the actor fluffed his lines at the font. The infant emerged with the names Thomas Brinsley; the Richard came later, and the Butler was never used in signatures at all. He was sent to Harrow, and seems to have had a thin time there. Fifty years later a master, Dr. Parr, recalled with satisfaction that behind laziness and ignorance he had discerned "vestiges of a superior intellect", and wrote archly of raids on neighbouring orchards, and of how he had threatened, "but without asperity, to trace the depredations through his associates up to their leader". Alicia Lefanu, Sheridan's niece, paints rosy pictures of the young hero, admired and beloved by masters and boys at school, and in the holidays entertained at Richmond by his father's friend, Aikenhead, "a splendid West Indian, an amateur of fashion in the literary and theatrical history of the day"; whatever that might be. Poor Richard, if he may be allowed to speak, strikes a jarring note. He said he formed no friendships, was low-spirited and "much given to crying when alone", and was so "slighted by masters and tormented by the boys as a poor player's son" that he came to loathe the stage. The hurt to his pride went deep, and never fully healed. Nothing but necessity could have driven him to the theatre, and not till he rehearsed "The Duenna", or so he declared long afterwards, did he ever see a play right through. Lord Holland found this incredible. So may we; but the fact that he said it at all is deeply significant. As for hospitality, we have a letter dated March 2, 1765, in which the lonely boy asks for "cloaths" he can wear without shame, and fancies he will "spend his holydays again at Harrow", for he has not heard from Mr. A. since August—"though," he adds, "I had rather stay at Harrow than go to Richmond". So much for the splendid West Indian and the value of sentimental memories of the great.

It was at Harrow that Sheridan heard the "mellancholly knews" of his mother's death. Poor Sherry spelt badly at fourteen. At forty he did not spell much better. That he had a more exact scholarship in the dead languages is unlikely, but this did not prevent his airing the classics in after life and collaborating with Halhed, at Harrow and just afterwards, in a translation of the trivial "Love Epistles of Aristoenetus". Halhed supplied the scholarship and Sherry a Greek grammar. Between them they Englished such pretty conceits as "a whimsical account of a lover and his mistress, who admitted him to every favour but the last", with a Snark-like lament, in the penultimate verse, for lovers who "seek it with labour and pain", where they might have tried forks and hope.

Nothing, in his whole career, is more characteristic of dashing, brave, theatrical Sherry than his first marriage. In 1770 Thomas Sheridan opened an Acadamy of Oratory in Bath. ("Sir, it is burning a candle at Dover to show light at Calais", mocked Dr. Johnson, more witty then wise.) The one bright feature of his Attic Nights was the singing of Elizabeth Linley, a sixteen-year-old girl with a lovely face and figure, and a voice described as angelic. Face to face with "St. Cecilia's" battery of charms and virtues, the gallants of Bath were mown down. Her purity did not prevent her consenting to marry a wealthy squire of sixty, Walter Long; but when she refused a pre-matrimonial experiment

—at his lodgings, the thrifty old dog!—he seems to have broken the engagement. Talk of a lawsuit was dropped when he paid £3000 to her father, and £1000 worth of jewels, besides collateral, to the girl. On these terms outraged virtue agreed to say no more about it; but the affair was naturally the talk of Bath, and through Foote's comedy, "The Maid of Bath", enough to set all London laughing.

One seducer removed, another sprang up in his place. Lord Grosvenor, who had just prosecuted the King's brother for obtaining from his wife favours valued by the best judges at £10,000, suggested a settlement on the Maid, in writing. And no sooner was he repulsed at this moral Thermopylae than Captain Mathews, who so nearly killed Sheridan in a duel, made a pass at her. The *London Magazine*, reporting the struggle as the Press now would a Test match, says that "the censorious, as usual, took the alarm, and became very anxious for her virtue, without knowing whether it was in danger".

The curtain is up, the heroine discovered with villain. Enter the hero, twenty-year-old Dick Sheridan. As a friend, and a disinterested man of the world, he persuaded the Maid to fly to a convent at St. Quentin, hired a woman companion (of whom we hear no more, if she ever existed), and set out for London. There, probably to better his chances of a loan, he introduced the girl to a relative as an heiress who had consented to marry him in France. After a stormy passage that offered the runaways no temptations—the Maid was as sick as a dog the whole way across the Channel, and indeed looked like dying—they reached France. What happened on that corrupting soil is not certain. Moore's comment that "the chivalrous and disinterested protector degenerated into a mere selfish lover" is justly regarded as ungenerous; but it has a grain of truth. Mrs. Lefanu says Sheridan told the girl she couldn't possibly return to London except as his wife, and refers to a marriage by a priest, at or near Calais, who seems to have specialized in the carriage trade.

The ceremony over, one might have expected nature to take its course. Not so. The *General Evening Post*, which presumably had its own sources of information, informed an anxious public on July 4, 1772, that "nothing criminal passed between Mr. S. and the Maid of Bath during their late tour of France. At every place they put up at, he requested the landlady's company, and took care to have Miss Linley constantly provided with a bedfellow". Such thoughtfulness is surprising in a husband of whom the bride was to lament later that he was constantly providing bedfellows for himself, and sometimes, as in the case of the governess, being clumsy enough to get himself caught by the guests. Or it would be surprising, if the French marriage ever took place. Sherry's anxiety when there was talk of Elizabeth's marrying Sir Thomas Clarges, the couple's long separation, and then their marriage, all suggest that it did not, though the opposition of the Sheridan and Linley familiy to what both considered a *mésalliance* may be a sufficient explanation. The *Morning Chronicle*, with the thoroughness of the time, records that they were married at Marylebone, dined at the Star and Garter on Richmond Hill, and had a ball, "after which the family and friends returned to town and left the young couple at a gentleman's house at Mitcham to consummate their nuptials".

Sheridan's duels with Mathews, marked equally by posturing and reckless courage—in the second the older man got Sherry down and, when he would not beg for his life, hacked at him ferociously with a broken sword—are not without significance. They are part of the pattern of his early life, of his design, planned as a whole if the incidents often sprang from impulse, to dissociate himself from the player class and establish himself as a man of honour and of fashion. His wife was the most famous singer of her day; she could have earned a fortune. He forbade her to sing in public, even for a fee of £3000 for twenty concerts. For this he was warmly commended by Dr. Johnson. "I know not", said the doctor, giving rein to a pleasing fancy, "I know not if I should not prepare myself for a public singer as readily as let my wife be one." Sherry refused even to let his wife sing at private parties. "What reason," grumbled Sir Joshua, "could they think I had in inviting them to dinner, unless it was to hear her sing?—for she cannot talk." Very astutely, the Sheridans waited until they had a house in Orchard Street and could give parties of their own. Their "concerts given twice a week to the nobility", on top of the bride's beauty and the bridegroom's wit, were all that was needed to establish the attractive young couple in Society. By 1775 they were the talk of the Town.

2

Only one thing was wanting. All his life, from his light-hearted, impudent descent on London to the last miseries in Savile Row, Sheridan needed money. The bride's father furnished the house in Orchard Street, perhaps out of the £3000 earned so curiously by his daughter. How was a penniless young man of 23 to find the thousands a year required for a life of fashion? To Sherry it seemed simple. He wrote a book, which he hoped would bring him credit, and a comedy, from which he expected only cash. "Harris [of Covent Garden] tells me," he wrote, "that the least shilling I shall get (if it succeeds) will be £600."

"If it succeeds"—but it didn't. "The Rivals" was a flop. Luckily the manager still believed in it, and with some scenes rewritten, others tightened up, and Clinch in place of Lee, who had somehow contrived to be dull as Sir Lucius O'Trigger, the play was presented a second time. For once the public reversed its verdict. Later in the same year came "The Duenna", with music composed, or arranged, by his father-in-law. Linley seems to have had no faith in the production: he asked that his name should not appear. "The Duenna" had a record run of 75 nights—twelve more than "The Beggar's Opera"—and Sheridan, probably the least surprised man in London, found himself the rage.

So now-a-days, As 'twas in Gay's,
The world's run mad agen-a;
From morn to night, Its whole delight
To cry up "The Duenna".

To crown it all, Garrick retired, and Sheridan, at 25, had the audacity to take over Drury Lane. How did he find the money? People have been wondering ever since. More than thirty years later Lord

Glenbervie recalled that he had been told by the Princess of Wales, whose informant was Miss Hayman, her maid of honour, who had it straight from the victim's mouth, that Sheridan had forced his wife to "grant the last favour" to the Prince of Wales in return for £20,000. Here, it was suggested, was the answer to the question how Sheridan managed to buy out Garrick and entertain what Fanny Burney charmingly calls "leaders of the *ton* and their followers and slaves".

This invention was perhaps inspired, as Mr. R. Crompton Rhodes suggests in his authoritative biography, by half-remembered gossip of the Prince's little transaction with "Perdita" Robinson, in which Sheridan may have been one of the go-betweens. In any case it may be dismissed as perhaps the most unpleasant invention of an age rich in libels. There was no mystery, really. Sheridan established his home on credit; he lived on credit to the end. ("I've just bought a new house," he told Lord Guildford. "Now everything will go like clockwork." "Ay," said his witty lordship. "Tick-tick.") For his half share in Drury Lane Garrick was paid £35,000. Dr. Ford, the Court *accoucheur*—brought in, suggested Kitty Clive, in a letter to Garrick, "to prevent miscarriages"—found £15,000, and Mrs. Sheridan's father £10,000. The remaining £10,000 was raised by Sheridan himself: £1,300 in cash, possibly his own savings from royalties and his wife's £1,000 from Mr. Long, and the rest borrowed with the theatre's earnings as security. As patentee of one of the two Theatres Royal, the only theatres open all the year round, he enjoyed a semi-monopoly; and the investment normally brought in 10 per cent. Salaries and ground rents were low, and the takings surprisingly high—from £225 to £292 a night in the case of "The School for Scandal" during intermittent runs spread over three or four years. Add the book and song rights to the regular receipts from his own and other people's plays, mostly non-copyright, and there is no more mystery about Sheridan's income than about Mr. Coward's. The fact that he lived like a prince, had his theatre twice destroyed, gambled rashly, and yet was only £3,000 in debt at the end, speaks for itself.

Wits, like lyric poets, tend to flower early and wither young. Wycherley, Vanbrugh, Farquhar, superior Congreve and waspish Pope—none of these reached the heights as young as Sheridan. At 17, in a farce begun at school, he had given hints of his flair for dialogue; at 23, with "The Rivals" he stormed London; at 26, with that superb satire on contemporary journalism, "The School for Scandal", he reached his zenith. Two years later came "The Critic" and his career as a playwright was practically over.

It would be tempting to examine the plays, to trace their origin, watch their shaping and analyse their wit. I have not the space, but I must say a word about the odd notion that Sherry was an inspired buffoon, tossing off masterpieces between four bottles and a hangover, or (as some said) stealing them piecemeal from Molière, Congreve and Vanbrugh, and wholesale from women who entrusted their plays to him. It is true he learned his trade with marvellous quickness; but learn it he did. "The Rivals" taught him to take pains. Mr. Cochran planning a revue could not be more precise or practical than Sherry's instructions to Linley for "The Duenna", explaining (no doubt with his wife's expert help) how to get the right variety of mood and tempo, and the best out of popular but limited singers like Leoni. "The School for Scandal", too, was tailor-made to fit the King's Company at Drury Lane—Mrs. Abington (Lady Teazle) with her "brilliant loquacity", Smith (Charles Surface), the genteel, the airy and the smart", Dodd (Sir Benjamin Backbite), "unrivalled in genteel fops", and so on. Discouraged playwrights may be comforted if they compare this masterpiece with early drafts, disfigured by faulty construction and clumsy devices. He kept changing even the names, Charles Surface is successively Clerimont, Florival, Captain Harry Plausible, Harry Pliant or Pliable, Young Harrier, and Frank.

The one thing he never was stumped for was wit. The wit of Pope, Byron and Swift was literary, smelling of the lamp; Johnson's was philosophic and didactic, expressing itself more often in pregnant apophthegms than in lightning repartee. From Sheridan it gushed like an Oklahoma well, and burned as brilliantly; he let it flow, as he did wine and money, like the prodigal he was. Johnson, even though he didn't appreciate the service and once irritably ordered Boswell back to his chair, had always a reporter at his elbow, pencil eagerly poised. What treasures of wit and fun (a quality given to few great wits) Sherry must have lavished on friends who laughed at his *mots* and forgot them, or repeated them as their own. Like himself, his wit was essentially social, and generally goodnatured, even when he was rebuking insolence. ("I say, Sherry", said one of two Royal dukes meeting him in Piccadilly. "We're just discussing whether you are more rogue or fool." "Why, faith", said Sherry, taking each by the arm, "I believe I am between both.") It was also remarkably clean. Only a critic who has never tried to compose a drawing-room limerick as funny as the smoking-room sort could ever rank Sheridan below Wycherley and Congreve. His comedies, unaided by obscenity, are the funniest in the language as certainly as Sherry was, by the evidence of judges like Byron, the most entertaining talker of his age. He was even witty drunk, when most men only think they are. Picked up by the watch in the street and asked his name, he hiccupped and solemnly said, "Wilberforce."

Though "Pizarro" was a box-office success for half a century, "The Critic" was Sheridan's last important contribution to the drama. The rest is politics and oratory, the exacting routine of a theatre manager, and the more-than-exacting, the ruinous, life of a man about town. We may think it a melancholy thing that a first-rate genius should have been at such pains to become a frustrated politician; still, his motives were honourable enough. The "player's boy" was conscious of great powers. What more natural than that he should wish to make his mark in the world of affairs, and in so doing serve his country?

3

In 1780 Parliament was dissolved. Sheridan thought he saw his chance. Touring the West Country in search of a "free and independent borough", he picked on Honiton, and was supported by the Linleys' old friend Ozias Humphrey, the miniature painter, as a man "beloved and almost adored by all parties". At the polls the "damned fellows of

Honiton chose a Scotsman—and a Mac, too"; but the day that brought the bad news brought also the offer of another seat. Through Fox and the Duchess of Devonshire he was invited to stand for Stafford. Twenty-five years later, when his romantic marriage had been wrecked by tomfoolery, and his adored Elizabeth was dead of consumption at thirty-eight, and he had long since written himself out, and hope of high office had grown dim, Sheridan told Creevey that the day he stole off alone to rejoice at the news of his election and dream about the future was the happiest of his life. A statement of his annual expenditure on his borough casts a bright light on politics before the Reform Bill:

"Expenses at the Borough of Stafford for election, anno 1784. 248 burgesses paid £5/5 each. . . .

£1302. 0. 0."

In 1780, when he was unknown to them and had only £1000 to spend, burgesses came cheaper or needed less convincing of his worth.

Still conscious, perhaps, of being the player's son, Mr. Sheridan, M.P., at first took himself very seriously indeed. He rebuked Courtenay, which was never a safe thing to do, for mocking a bill of Burke's; adding, more characteristically, that the most serious part of Courtenay's argument seemed to him the most ludicrous. (Cf. his devastating "The hon. member is indebted to his memory for his jests, and for his facts to his imagination.") Courtenay retorted that "the honourable member seemed inimical to mirth and wit in any house but his own". But Sheridan soon found the confidence to be himself. We find him crossing swords with Pitt, whose shield of scornful hauteur was no defence against his rapier. Sheridan, sneered the 24-year-old Prime Minister, should keep his jests and dramatic turns for his theatre. Sheridan, always oddly self-controlled in debate, genially replied:

"Flattered and encouraged by the right hon. gentleman's panegyric on my talents, if ever I again engage in the compositions he alludes to, I may be tempted to an act of presumption, to attempt an improvement on one of Ben Jonson's best characters, the character of the Angry Boy in *The Alchemist*."

Wordy and florid, of course; but even genius uses the idiom of its time. Shakespeare would have had fewer lines in need of blotting if he had not lived in an age of detestable Euphuism. Sheridan's jests are mostly neatness itself—e.g. (on Lauderdale's threatening to repeat one of his best things) "Pray don't: a joke in your mouth is no laughing matter"; to the servant who rushed into the dining-room at Somerset House crying, "Sir, the house is on fire": "Bring another bottle of claret: it's not my house"; and his attempt to escape the old maid who said it had cleared up enough for a walk: "It has cleared up enough for one, but not enough for two." His speeches are not to be judged by modern standards, still less by the standards of the library. Burke bored the House with philosophic essays that might have been sent straight to the publisher, and probably were. Sheridan realized that speeches, like plays, were meant to be heard. He had a fine voice, a most engaging manner, and the art of the actor: he knew how to put a line across. So we read that his thrust at that "dog" and "scoundrel" Pitt delighted a

House which admired the insolent prodigy, but never learned to love him; and to the end of his life Sheridan recalled it with boyish pleasure.

Sheridan did not make his mark in Parliament all at once. His first speech, a defence (a little difficult, one might have thought) against a charge of corruption in the Stafford election, was heard with "particular attention, the House being uncommonly still while he was talking". Yet Woodfall, the veteran gallery reporter, was not impressed, and long afterwards he had the honesty to admit it. "I am sorry to say I do not think this is your line," he told the young M.P. bluntly. "You had much better stick to your former pursuits." Sherry accepted the verdict as he had the public's on "The Rivals"; his head sank upon his hands. Then he looked up and cried: "It is in me, however, and, by God, it shall come out!"

It did. Burke's impeachment of Warren Hastings provided the opportunity. His mind, generous and chivalrous if inconstant, was powerfully stirred by the wrongs of the Begums of Oude, imprisoned and forced to pay their English oppressor £1,200,000; and on February 7, 1787, he delivered the speech that became a legend. He spoke rapidly for five hours and forty minutes, freely departing, as he always did, from his notes; and the effect was indescribable. Cicero's indictment of Verres, St. Just's of Danton, were no more terrible. It was the sort of speech that sends men to the scaffold.

His triumph was complete. Within twenty-four hours he had been offered £1,000 for the copyright. (Alas, owing to the poor reporting of the time, there was no text to sell.) Fox told Holland twenty years later that it was the finest speech he had ever heard. Windham thought it the finest in the memory of man. Logan, who had been one of Hasting's defenders, is said to have heard the first hour with the comment, "All this is declamatory assertion without proof"; the second hour with "This is a most wonderful oration"; the third with "Mr. Hastings has acted very unjustifiably"; the fourth with "Mr. Hastings is a most atrocious criminal"; and the end with a cry of, "Of all monsters of iniquity the most enormous is Warren Hastings." When Sheridan sat down, we are told, the whole House, with peers and strangers, "involuntarily joined in a tumult of applause, and adopted a mode of expressing their approbation, new and irregular in that house, by loudly and repeatedly clapping with their hands". But perhaps the greatest tribute of all, so far as I know unique, is that its hearers were so profoundly moved and excited by what Byron (putting it a little high, perhaps) called "the delegated voice of God", that they felt incapable of reaching a fair decision. The House adjourned.

The trial in Westminster Hall, of which Sheridan was one of the managers, might easily have been an anti-climax. Actually he achieved another *tour de force*. What a glittering and dramatic show it must have been—Warren Hastings, icily composed as the cold-blooded, immensely able tyrant always was, facing the greatest array of orators ever assembled for a prosecution, with the Queen, royal dukes, 170 peers, M.P.s, and the rank and fashion of England packing the galleries and hanging on every word. Burke, after treating them to a dissertation on India, geographical, historical, philosophical and political, which may have been something less than electrifying, was lifted by indignation to the top of his form, and his peroration was superb. It so affected ladies "perhaps not unwilling to display their taste and sensibility", says Macaulay, that smelling-bottles were pulled out, hysterical sobs and screams were heard, and Mrs. Sheridan was carried out in a fit. She had plenty of time to recover. Fox followed Burke; then Sheridan launched the case for the Princesses of Oude, and it was Mrs. Siddons's turn to be carried out in a swoon. I don't suppose she ever gave a better performance. Sheridan spoke for four days, the Hall was crowded the whole time, and fifty guineas were offered for a seat. Macaulay comments that at the end Sheridan "contrived with a knowledge of stage effect which his father might have envied, to sink back, as if exhausted, in the arms of Burke, who hugged him with the energy of generous admiration". A nice touch; but the prolonged nervous and physical strain may well have left Sheridan in collapse. Burke called this speech "the most astonishing effort of eloquence, argument and wit united, of which there is any record or tradition". Pitt was generous enough to declare that it surpassed "all the eloquence of ancient and modern times", and had "everything that genius or art could furnish to agitate and control the human mind". Well might Betsy Sheridan write to her sister-in-law in an intoxication of pride and happiness: "It is impossible, my dear woman, to convey to you the delight, the astonishment, the adoration, he has excited in the breasts of every class of people. Every party prejudice has been overcome by a display of genius, eloquence, and goodness, which no one, with anything like a heart about them, could have listened to without being the wiser and the better for the rest of their lives." Mrs. Oliphant, who disliked Sheridan's character from the depths of her prim Victorian soul and seems to have thought Mrs. Sheridan a ninny for speaking of his "goodness", wonders whether the enthusiasm in the speech was not as much for Brinsley Sheridan as for the Begums of Oude. The taunt is ungenerous, but may be supported by Creevey's anecdote of Hastings' visiting the Prince of Wales at Brighton seventeen years later and being introduced to Sheridan. Creevey, probably missing Sherry's point that he had no personal dislike for a man he had never met, says he "lost no time in attempting to cajole old Hastings, begging him to believe that any part he had ever taken against him was purely political, and that no one had a greater respect for him than himself, etc." Hastings gravely replied that "it would be a great consolation to him in his declining days if Mr. Sheridan would make that sentiment more publick". Not even the author of "The Rivals" could find a retort to that.

Victorians, whose influence still lingers, had no great opinion of Sherry. What could they think of a man who was unfaithful to his wife, diddled his creditors, and kept letters, when he could afford to pay the postman, unopened in a box? Had he been farther off, like Charles II or Cœur de Lion, they might have romaniticised him, or at least seen faults and virtues in proportion; they might have realized that even in his vices Sherry, far more than Disraeli's dukes and Ouida's guardsmen, was the very embodiment of the Romantic tradition. He had carried off a beauty and fought duels over her, he was the wittiest man of his time and the most loved, he had written three plays each the best of its kind in the language, and in the public's eyes his Begum speeches made him, as a servant told old Tom Sheridan, the first man in England. Practitioners in the Gothick like Walpole and Beckford never dared to create a hero so extravagantly endowed. Why, then, did his oratorical triumphs bring no reward but fame? The English notoriously distrust brilliance, which makes Disraeli's career all the more astonishing; yet it is probable that in almost any other age, and I think certain that today, Sheridan would have gained high office. It is said that his judgment was sometimes faulty. Of how many politicians can one say they were always right? The Tories detested Sheridan as a climber and a radical; the Whig bourgeoisie distrusted him; Burke, when he heard him speak on the French Revolution, jumped up and announced that their friendship was dead. Yet Sheridan's, not Burke's, is the verdict of posterity. Making all allowances for his very real defects of intellect and character, he was one of the unluckiest statesmen in our history. He had, in two senses, the misfortune to back the wrong horse, and the principle to stick to it. In the first place he attached himself to the Whigs just when the Tories were beginning a domination that was to last a quarter of a century. Twice, before the Angry Boy was in the saddle, he was given junior office, the first time under Rockingham, the second in the Coalition. But in four months Rockingham was dead, and when Fox's East India Bill was thrown out by the Lords, and its author dismissed by the King, Sheridan loyally followed his friend and leader into the wilderness. Sheridan's second tactical blunder—and it was this that finally spoiled what chance he ever had—was in attaching himself to the Prince of Wales. George, in those days, distantly resembled the Florizel his toadies painted when he was fat and fifty; he could be very charming when he chose, and, lacking talent himself, he had taste enough to relish it in others. The player's son would have been more or less than human if he had not felt flattered by his future king's friendship—never, as Creevey admits, presumed upon. Besides, as an incurable romantic, he thought he perceived in the Prince the character and ability needed to restore the glory of England, in need of a bit of furbishing after the American War, and usher in a new, more liberal age.

There were two periods when it looked as if his loyalty would be rewarded. The first was in 1788, when the King began raving at the dinner-table and shaking hands with oaks, and Parliament its passionate debates on the Regency. Pitt and Lord Chancellor Thurlow ("a great rogue", thought Sherry, who was rash enough to hint at Tower Hill if the old man opposed the future king) asserted Parliament's authority; Burke, Fox, and Sheridan demanded the fullest powers for the Prince of Wales. It was taken for granted that the Regent would send for the Whigs, and the delightful game of cabinet-making was in full swing, with Sheridan, as the Prince's favourite, destined to the Exchequer if he wanted it, when the worst happened. By the grace of God the King was restored to his normal stupidity, and the Whigs were back where they started.

Under the stress of disappointment, the Whigs began to break up. Fox still befriended Sheridan; the rank and file followed Burke. In 1792 Betsy Sheridan died, after a long illness that reduced her erring husband to the depths of despair and remorse; and he drank harder than ever to forget, lost ruinous sums at cards and neglected Drury Lane and Parliament. His grief was real but his temperament was mercurial.

Two months later, at 41, we find him madly in love with Pamela, believed to have been Mme de Genlis's daughter (by Philippe Egalité?), a tearing beauty of eighteen. He captivated the girl, as he captivated everybody, by his wit and charm; she returned to France and they were to have been married a fortnight later. Then fate played Sheridan a trick so strangely melodramatic that a dramatist would hesitate to use it. When his wife was most hurt and hopeless over his infidelities she apparently consoled herself briefly with Lord Edward Fitzgerald. Whom should Pamela meet in Paris but the same gay, romantic adventurer, and one can imagine Sherry's feelings when he heard that they were married.

Still, as we have seen, his was not a heart to break. In 1795 the dissipated roué, as Mrs. Oliphant saw him, acquired a second infatuated wife, and made some speeches with his old fire. He took a statesmanlike view of the country's relations with France, pleading for peace, but at the same time warning Chauvelin that it would be madness to hope for any English aid for an invasion.

Yet slowly his fame grew tarnished, his motives more suspect. Men said he was insincere. (How could he be so charming if he weren't?) They said he was a drunkard and a rake. (What was Walpole? What was Fox?) They said he was an intriguer. (How many statesmen, from Burghley to Pitt, were not?) They said, making a virtue of their own dullness, as politicians and publicists always do, that he was an irresponsible buffoon. (Yet his administration seems to have been as efficient as his colleagues'; his share in the indictment of Warren Hastings was by far the most efficient; and he had the judgment to support Wellington when other politicians wanted to recall him.)

Cant, all cant, perhaps unconscious. Sheridan had a head for affairs all right, when he chose to think about them; and few men of his age had as strict a sense of humour. His failure to gain the highest rewards was not due to lack of principle, or his vanity and indiscretions, or even his proud and obstinate adherence to his Prince, damaging though this was. How easily all these would have been forgiven if he had been a Cavendish or a Pelham. Sheridan's real crime, as Creevey says, was the same as Burke's; it was presumptuous in men without family to aspire to offices desired by noblemen and great landowners with gold for the party funds and boroughs in their pockets. Lady Holland puts it beautifully: "His defenders (and their number is but slender) say that all his bad conduct has proceeded from his struggling against the meanness of his origin and the littleness of his means." The Hollands are full of complaints about his faithlessness to Fox; but when the test came the betrayer was not Sheridan. Pitt, so long, so heartbreakingly long, the lion in the Whig's path, died in 1806. Fox, leading the Ministry of All the Talents with that cold mediocrity, Grenville, at last had the power to give his old colleague the Cabinet rank he had always promised. Instead he offered a sinecure carrying £2,000 a year for life. Sheridan refused. He accepted the Treasuryship of the Navy instead—an appointment that moved even the directors of the Bank of England, not as a rule merry men, to the pleasantry of running out of the room with their books and papers when Sheridan appeared to open the Navy account; and he outdid all his colleagues with his magnificent banquets at Somerset House.

4

But the sands were running out. With Fox's death the Prince of Wales ceased to support the Whig party: a heavy blow. Then one night in 1809, while Sheridan was attending a debate on the Peninsular War, a red glare told that Drury Lane was on fire. M.P.s, sympathetic, and perhaps unwilling to see the spectacle, wanted to adjourn. Sheridan would not hear of it. Watching his hopes go up in flames, through a window in Covent Garden, he was rebuked by some solemn owl for calmly drinking. "Surely," he protested, "a man may be allowed to drink a glass of wine by his own fireside." For brilliance and bravery where is there a saying to beat it?

One more betrayal was to come, and politically it was a death sentence. All his life Sheridan had been the Prince's close friend and most loyal supporter. He put George's case in Parliament even when, as in the row over Mrs. Fitzherbert, he had no case to put. The Prince, threatened with the penalties of marriage to a Catholic, including the loss of the Crown, had denied the marriage to Fox, and Fox denied it in the House. The affronted lady raised hell, and George hysterically demanded that Sheridan should save her face. Sheridan must have been only too conscious of the ridiculous figure he cut, denying a marriage in one breath and in the next asserting that Mrs. Fitzherbert's position was "truly respectable". The situation recalls that in "The Critic" where "the two Nieces draw their daggers to strike Whiskerandos, the two Uncles at the instant with their two swords drawn catch their two Nieces' arms, and turn the points towards Whiskerandos, who immediately draws two daggers, and holds them to the two Nieces' bosoms"—except that to solve that deadlock Puff had "a very fine contrivance", and the deadlock of the marriage was beyond contriving.

Again in 1810, when the King went mad for good, it was Sheridan who advised the Prince and drafted his letters to the Cabinet. What more natural than that the old and trusted servant should expect reward? The sequel was heart-breaking. Falling out with Grenville, and seeing both Grenville and Gray jealous of Sheridan's influence, the Regent decided to dish the Whigs impartially and keep Perceval in office. It was the beginning of the end. The directors of the new Drury Lane, led by Caroline's friend Whitbread, refused Sherry any say in the management; through Whitbread again, he was for some time denied £12,000 owing to him, lost his seat in Parliament, and, being no longer immune, was arrested for debt. The claim proved fraudulent, and he was freed. He still cherished hopes of a seat (the Prince seems to have given him £3,000 to buy one at a cut rate from his old friend Norfolk, but the money was taken for debts); and he saw a successful revival of "The Rivals". There is a touching story that he disappeared during the performance and was found in the green room, happy in the homage of actors and writers, including the generous, affectionate Byron.

The rest is horror. Sherry should have died, as he lived, carelessly, in the limelight, sinking into a colleague's arms at the end of an oration with cheers growing dimmer in his ears. What happened was pure Hogarth—obscurity, pain, humiliation, the neglect of friends, a visit from a lawyer wearing his best "will-drawing face", and ghoulish dunning by creditors trying to beat the grave. As a final touch of ignominy, the bailiffs were about to carry the dying man to prison in his blanket when a doctor came to the rescue with threats of a murder charge. It was a relief to everyone when, on July 7, 1816, he died, and his corpse was smuggled away in the darkness out of reach of body-snatching bailiffs.

Five peers and a bishop were his pall-bearers; two royal dukes and half the peerage followed him to the Abbey. Many of his old friends had the grace to be ashamed, but the general opinion of contemporaries, and of Victorians, was that Dissipation Never Pays, and he was probably overrated anyway. Mrs. Oliphant, by no means the most critical of his biographers, sums it up, after a kindly account of his sufferings: "He had a fit of writing," she says, "a fit of oratory, but no impulse to keep him in either path long enough to make anything more than the dazzling but evanescent triumph of a day."

"Of a day"! What other writer, before or since, has achieved the very highest rank as a dramatist, a wit and an orator, and at the same time played so conspicuous a part in public life? None; but that is not enough. He must go on churning out plays like Dion Boucicault, orations like Mr. Gladstone, jokes (louder and funnier) like Joe Miller. His critics hadn't the wit to see that though the mediocrity may be a machine the genius is always a man. And Byron's "poor dear Sherry", in particular, was very, very human.

JOHN WILKES

OLGA VENN

IN LUDGATE CIRCUS THERE STANDS A SMALL AND DINGY OBELISK, DEDICATED to the Right Honourable John Wilkes, Esq., Lord Mayor. An appropriate enough symbol in its way, its chief use today is to indicate that comfort for gentlemen may be found beneath it. Though they may pass it a dozen times in the week, few of the City whose independence he glorified or of the Street whose liberty he established give a thought to the man it commemorates, a figure who bulked as large in his time as half a dozen statesmen now flawlessly embalmed for posterity. History has conspired to bury that lively corpse as contemporaries conspired to damn the man. Occasional exhumations there have been, attended by the oddly blended odours of sanctity and corruption. Unlike more decent remains, this cadaver retains disconcertingly galvanic properties. One set of morticians compose it lovingly into a sanctimonious attitude, only to find one of those squinting eyes opening upon them in a conspiratorial leer; a rival set, holding their nostrils and flinging the bones summarily back into the felon's pit, are horridly fixed by the other eye, this time an orb glowing with the most honest reproach.

What are the school textbooks to make of a people's representative who, rising in the House to tell the Speaker: "Sir, I hold in my hand a petition from a most intelligent, independent and enlightened body of men," had just informed him privily that he had a petition to present from the greatest set of scoundrels on earth: who sincerely declared: "It will ever be my ambition to transmit my name to posterity as that of a man sincere and honest in the public cause, and inflexible in the defence of our laws and liberties, over which we cannot keep too watchful an eye, when we observe all the neighbouring nations sunk in abject despotism," and yet assured gullible Gibbon, who called for his tablets and goggling set it down, that he was in the political game to make his fortune?

The truth is that Wilkes is the original 'Orrid Example held up to all of us in our youth, of the awful consequences of being Too Clever, *anglice*, too witty; of the shocking dangers of Trying To Be Funny and of Going Too Far; and of the ultimate horror of Joking About Serious Things. Wilkes invariably Went Too Far, heedless of the enemies he was making, and Joked About Serious Things, unconscious that his casual ironies would be taken down and grimly used *in perpetuo* as evidence against him; for he was quite without the saving grace of hypocrisy. "He had such a flow of spirits," records Charles Johnston, "that it was impossible ever to be a moment dull in his company. His wit gave charms to every subject he spoke upon; and his humour displayed the foibles of mankind in such colours as to put folly even out of countenance. But . . . his spirits were often stretched to extravagance to overpower competition. His humour was debased into buffoonery, and his wit was so prostituted to the lust of applause that he would sacrifice his best friend for a scurvy jest." Today Wilkes would be classed as an exhibitionist. His tongue was unbridled by discretion, and for this reason he is not an anthology subject. His wit survives in comparatively few self-contained epigrams; it must be looked for in his reputation, in his conduct, and in his role, to extend the content of a phrase that fits him aptly enough, as the life and soul of the Party.

By all accounts he was cursed from birth by a most unnatural ugliness. Reynolds describes "his forehead low and short, his nose shorter and lower, his upper lip long and projecting, his eyes sunken and horribly squinting". So posterity, remembering Hogarth's virulent cartoon, will always visualize him. That cartoon, of course, was a calculated and revengeful slander, and unless all other contemporary portraitists stooped to the most servile flattery his was not such a bad face, with its compound of grit, sardonic humour and even a certain kindliness. However, we will accept the ugliness as Wilkes himself accepted it, bearing in mind his claim that it took him only half an hour to talk away his face, given which start he would back himself for a lady's favours against the handsomest man in England.

2

Born in 1727, Wilkes came of the authentic bourgeoisie and was a compound of its contradictory elements. His father, a wealthy distiller, provided him with strong Whig views and considerable social pushfulness; his mother, a strict Calvinist and a woman of flinty character, with a stern upbringing that was later to have its reaction. Both agreed that he was to be the gentleman of the family, and at the age of twenty, after a year or two at Leyden University, he was manœuvred into a marriage of suitability with Mary Mead, daughter of one of his mother's Dissenter friends, a costive creature ten years his senior who accepted him with unconcern, achieved an apathetic parturition, and relapsed into that monumental lethargy from which none of life's major experiences ever succeeded in budging her. The young man endured a few years of this existence, spending half the year at the Prebendal House at Aylesbury, living the life of a typical country squire, improving his estate, administering local charities, a well-liked member of county society; the other half at his mother-in-law's home in Red Lion Square, whose intimidating atmosphere quickly froze out the raffish collection of friends he introduced there, so that he escaped as often as possible to the club, the coffee house and the bagnio. Eventually the pair separated. These years left him three legacies: a daughter, Polly, his lifelong devotion to whom even his bitterest enemies acknowledged; an established position as Squire of Aylesbury; and the acquaintance of Thomas Potter, scapegrace son of the Archbishop of Canterbury, who, for all he maintained that Wilkes had "done everything in his power to destroy his health by strong soups, filthy claret, rakish hours and bad example", was, in fact, proudly instrumental in introducing the young wit not only to the most dissolute company of London, Bath and Tunbridge Wells but to the notice of his Buckinghamshire neighbour, Lord Temple of Stowe, and to Temple's brother Grenville and brother-in-law Pitt, and thus launching him upon a political career.

To this powerful triumvirate the young man recommended himself as a useful recruit, and in 1754, to oblige them, he went north to contest the rotten borough of Berwick. In a famous address he told the electors: "Gentlemen, I come here *uncorrupting* and I promise you I shall ever be *uncorrupted*. As I will never take a bribe so I will never offer one." Meanwhile, for a consideration, the captain of a ship bound from London with a load of his opponent's voters was dumping his puzzled cargo on the coast of Norway. Losing the election nevertheless, Wilkes did not scruple to petition against the more successful bribery of his rival.

Three years later, however, a reshuffle left the Aylesbury seat vacant. Wilkes weighed in "with the utmost spirit, particularly the true Aylesbury way of *palmistry*", and carried it "by sheer weight of metal"; and, for an expenditure of £7,000, to find which Potter obligingly introduced him to the lifelong acquaintance of the moneylenders, took his place in Parliament under the Pitt-Newcastle Ministry.

For several years his parliamentary activities were confined to recording a dutiful vote and fulfilling the ruinous claims of hospitality which led him to protest that no Member concerned for his purse or his cellar should represent the borough in which he resided. He had no personal ambitions, and he made himself useful by taking a commission in the Buckinghamshire Militia, a home defence scheme of Pitt's. As usual in administrative work, he distinguished himself by courage, conscientiousness and a humane regard for his men. As usual, he led a double life. His Colonel, Sir Francis Dashwood, a professional rake with a reputation on both sides of the Channel, took a fancy to the young man and introduced him to the most esoteric of the circles he had founded: the notorious Company of the Monks of St. Francis, which simple souls referred to as the Hellfire Club. The dozen hardened profligates composing this order, among them Potter, the half-witted Lord Orford, the brutal Sandwich and that Lord March who was to ogle his senile way to perdition as the infamous "Old Q", used to meet at Medmenham Abbey, near Marlow, for what were popularly assumed to be diabolical orgies. In other words, they tippled, tumbled their mistresses and possibly dabbled in the few remaining conceivable vices, though Wilkes observed that "they seem to have sinned *naturally*". The inscription "Fay ce que voudras", borrowed from Rabelais' Abbey of Thelema, gave a clue to the atmosphere, and an elaborate mock-ceremonial was practised, dedicated to the Goddess of Love and parodying the ritual of the Roman Catholic Church. Wilkes seems to have thrown himself into the proceedings with gusto, born in part of pure delight in the social eminence of his companions. Many of the ingeniously indecent inscriptions which adorned the place are assumed to be his work, not forgetting his extension of the classic exceptions to *omne animal triste* . . . to include . . . *et sacerdotem gratis fornicantem.* It was under the stimulus of this company that he produced those improper parodies which amused his patrons at the time but were later to come home to roost; and he possibly devised a pastime which enjoyed an ephemeral popularity, that of reading newspapers across the columns instead of down, which sometimes produced such fruitful results as:

> "This morning the Right Honourable the Speaker
> was convicted of keeping a disorderly house."
>
> "This day His Majesty will go in state
> to fifteen notorious common prostitutes."
>
> "A certain commoner will be created a peer.
> *** No greater reward will be offered."

Wilkes never ceased to appreciate the amenities of this high-class brothel: "that amusement," he once wrote to a friend, "I must have, and it is almost the only one I take"; but its pretentious diabolism soon ceased to impress one whose tastes in debauchery, if inexhaustible, were simple, and who, retaining a primal innocence of outlook on such matters, needed no adventitious trappings of sin and shame to spur his unjaded appetites. He began to amuse himself at the expense of these laborious panters after unrighteousness and finally called their bluff by a pleasantry which had the result of breaking up the order. For it was Wilkes who smuggled into the Abbey a large black baboon, which he dressed as the devil and hid in a chest, releasing it at the moment when the company were offering a mock invocation to Beelzebub; a concrete response to their devotions which had a permanently chastening effect. This story died hard, and was still going the rounds not many years ago, its hero being Edward VII when Prince of Wales.

At Medmenham Wilkes contracted a friendship with the poet Churchill, popularly known as the Bruiser. Like so many of his friends, he was an unfrocked clergyman, coarse-mouthed, dissolute and diseased, but with a gift of savage satire which, had it been expended on less ephemeral subjects, might have perserved his name to this day. He sprang into fame in 1761 with the publication of the "Rosciad", the first of a spate of satires which precipitated with the *Critical Review* (a journal which observed of his "Night": "This Night, like many others at this time of the year, is very long, cold, dark and dirty") that Grub Street combat known as the Battle of the Wits, his chief adversary in which, Arthur Murphy, was to figure in later journalistic scuffles.

Meanwhile the public stage was being set for Wilkes's entrance. The curtain rose in 1760 on the death of George II and the accession of his grandson.

3

In his mother, "*cette diablesse, Madame la Princesse,*" as her father-in-law used to call her, "that grave, lean, demure elderly woman," as Thackeray characterized her, the 22-year-old King had a determined mentor who filled his uneducated mind with ideas of absolute monarchy by divine right, and, to guide his stumbling and obstinate feet, set his ex-tutor, the vain and narrow Scot Lord Bute, to watch over him. Bute's job was to recapture for the King the power now held by the Whig oligarchs; his first step to undermine Pitt's popularity, bound up with the triumphs of the Seven Years' War, by working for a premature peace. Within a few months the Great Commoner had been jockeyed into resigning on the issue of relations with Spain. He was justified within another few months, when England was forced to declare war on France's new ally.

Wilkes, so long content to fritter away his time in ignoble diversions, suddenly leapt into the arena in defence of his patron. He descended upon the House and harangued it. Finding that he commanded little attention there, for his oratorical gifts were not great, he turned to his more effective weapon, the pen. A Government White Paper had been issued on the Spanish situation, a glib production which sought smoothly to justify the Administration. Wilkes tore it to shreds in an anonymous pamphlet. "Observations on the Papers Relative to the Rupture with Spain". The repercussions were immediate. A new power was alive in political journalism.

The riddle of its authorship set the town debating. Wilkes enjoyed the situation and could not resist improving upon it. Discussing the question with the lickspittle parson James Douglas during a casual encounter in the Park, he hinted darkly of reports that Douglas himself was the culprit. The wretched man, in trying frantically to combat a rumour so damning to his hopes of advancement, obligingly spread it abroad, finally appealing to Wilkes. "I am entirely satisfied with your authentic assurances on this subject," was Wilkes's comforting reply, "and on every occasion will contradict so groundless a report . . . for, undoubtedly, the author of the 'Observations' has no chance of favour from any of the present powers."

Wilkes had found his medium. He knew what to do when, a month or two later, Bute openly took over the power he had so far been content to wield from behind the scenes. Bute's first act was to back the issue of a ministerial weekly, *The Briton*, whose editor was Tobias Smollett and whose purpose the vilification of Pitt. Wilkes and Churchill got together, and the following Saturday there appeared the first number of the *North Briton*, a sheet that was to galvanize many a Saturday morning to come and to set in motion results beyond its authors' wildest dreams. The title of *North Briton* was, of course, a mocking choice. Bute was a Scot, and, what was more, a Stuart, and to understand what a godsend that fact was to his detractors it is necessary to remember the violence of the contemporary feeling against the Scots. The union of the two kingdoms was not so very remote, and the two Jacobite rebellions, only a few years behind, together with Scotland's traditional friendship with France, England's enemy in the current war, favoured the general impression that every Scotsman was a potential fifth columnist. Furthermore, personal economic jealousies were becoming acute, and in London then, as in Fleet Street now, there were murmurings that all the best jobs were being snapped up by the Scots, driven from their own country, it was savagely maintained, by that devastating barrenness which was the favourite butt of eighteenth-century jokes.

It was with malicious irony, therefore, that Wilkes produced the first few numbers of the *North Briton* in the fictitious character of a Scot, "with this most singular circumstance belonging to me, that I am *unplaced and unpensioned*: but I hope that this reproach will soon be wiped away, and that I will no longer be pointed at by my sneering countrymen". The irony was gross, but telling. Succeeding "letters" from this elated but somewhat dull-witted Caledonian summoned his fellow-countrymen to share the pickings now that a Stuart was in charge of the public treasury. The rallying-cry was Virgil's *Nos patriam fugimus*, translated, "We all get out of our country as fast as we can." All this, of course, was only the sugaring. The pill was bitter and salutary. At a time when the reporting of parliamentary debates was forbidden, official news reserved for the *Gazette*, and pamphleteering at once personal and pusillanimous, the *North Briton* gave the public news, culled by Wilkes himself, and comments marshalled with courage and force. Its sales multiplied, and the coffee-houses went into a huddle over every new issue.

The real fun began with the publication of the twelfth number, by which time the pseudo-Scot had been dropped as a device that had served its turn. Part of the number was devoted to baiting Dr. Johnson, that inveterate loather of "patriotism" in the contemporary sense. Wilkes had already thrown one small squib under Johnson's feet in connection with the unfortunate observation in his Dictionary that "H seldom, perhaps never, begins any but the first syllable," commenting in the *Publick Advertiser*: "The author of this remark must be a man of quick apprehension and compre-hensive genius, but I can never forgive his un-handsome be-haviour to the poor knight-hood, priest-hood, and widow-hood, nor his in-humanity to all man-hood." This time the occasion was the pension which Johnson had just accepted from Bute. The *North Briton's* comment was to quote the lexicographer's own definitions; as: "PENSION: an allowance made to any one without an equivalent. In England it is generally understood to mean pay given to a state hireling for treason to his country. PENSIONER: 1. One who is supported by an allowance paid at the will of another: a dependant. 2. A slave of state, hired by a stipend to obey his master."

The rest of the paper dealt with an incident which had delighted the London crowds at the recent coronation. The Lord Steward of the

Household, the exquisite and arrogant Lord Talbot, had, with a nice sense of punctilio, taken some pains to train his horse always to back respectfully from the royal presence. The poor creature, however, had lost its head and reversed the procedure, backing *into* the presence and throughout all subsequent manœuvres presenting an uncompromising rump to the royal personage, amid hilarious Cockney cheers. "A politeness equal to that of lord TALBOT's—*horse*," commented the *North Briton*, "ought not to pass unnoticed. At the coronation he paid a new, and, for a *horse*, singular respect to his sovereign. I appeal to the applauding multitudes, who were so charmed, as to forget every rule of decency, and to *clap* even in the *Royal presence*, whether *his* or his *lord's* dexterity on that day did not surpass any courtier's. Caligula's *horse* had not half the merit. We remember how nobly *he* was provided for. What the exact proportion of merit was between his lordship and his *horse*, and how far *the pension* should be divided between them, I will not take upon me to determine . . . In my private opinion, however, the merit of *both* was very great, and neither ought to pass unnoticed. The impartial and inimitable pen of *Cervantes* has made *Rozinante* immortal as well as Don Quixote. Lord TALBOT's *horse*, like the great planet in Milton, *danc'd about in various rounds his wand'ring course*. At different times he was *progressive*, *retrograde*, or *standing still*. The *progressive* motion I should rather incline to think the merit of the *horse*, the *retrograde* motion, the merit of the *Lord*."

From this passage arose a farcical duel with the outraged peer, a duel which began with two months of preliminary skirmishes and ended with Talbot's declaring Wilkes the noblest fellow God ever made.

4

As the summer of 1762 wore on Bute's manœuvres for peace became more and more open. The Opposition, divided and uncertain, looked in vain to their leaders. Pitt had retired into an enigmatic aloofness, Newcastle as usual maintained a masterly indecision. Only Wilkes, Wilkes and that unprivileged ninety per cent of the populace splendidly dismissed as The Mob, proclaimed the personal ambitions behind the mask of the peace-giver and the iniquity of England's bartering away her conquests to a beaten enemy for the ignoble furtherance of a party intrigue. Bute called in Fox to save the situation, placing unlimited funds at his disposal, and "in a single fortnight", Walpole records, "a vast majority was purchased to approve the peace." To such a House, met to condone a felony already compounded, Pitt made his dramatic appeal, carried in from his sick-bed, livid-faced, dressed in black from head to foot. But Bute had done his work, and the Peace was approved by 319 votes to 65. "It is certainly the peace of God," was Wilkes's comment, "for it passeth all understanding."

The Opposition's retreat became a rout. Newcastle, Rockingham, Grafton, Devonshire and a host of others, with their friends and dependants down to the lowest menial, were stripped of their offices. "Every person brought in by the Duke of Newcastle," wrote Wilkes, "is to be turned out—except the King." Almost alone, he refused to acknowledge defeat, and even in the first dark days rallied the spirits of his friends and discomfited his enemies by a characteristic piece of foolery. Arthur Murphy's *Auditor*, a ministerial sheet which Bute had long since called into being as a reinforcement to the battered *Briton*, received a letter from a gentleman signing himself Viator who professed great indignation at the efforts of the Opposition to depreciate the value of the territories Britain had gained by the Peace. For instance, Florida (at that time almost uninhabited) would prove a valuable acquisition by reason of its peat bogs, which could be made to furnish badly-needed fuel for the poor and shivering planters of the West Indies. Murphy published the letter in good faith with some supererogatory comments of his own. It received from the Press the attention it deserved. "Did any Man, before this egregious Wight," asked the *St. James's Chronicle*, "ever think of kindling Fires, or as he calls them, *comfortable* Fires, in a Country, where every Art is tried to moderate the perpetual, unremitted, and almost intolerable Heat of the Climate?" It only remained for Wilkes to add a postscript to the next *North Briton* thanking Murphy for inserting his letter "and for the *full credit* he has given to the several *facts* it contains".

The *Briton* and the *Auditor* ceased publication in February 1763, with the signing of the Peace Treaty. Wilkes was given some credit for their demise.

But Wilkes was after bluer blood, and before long he drew it. On March 15 the *North Briton* published an introduction to Ben Jonson's tragedy, "The Fall of Mortimer", dedicated to Lord Bute, whose weakness for amateur theatricals was a standing joke. It drew an audacious, albeit unavowed, parallel between Bute, whose ascendancy over the King's mother had long invited the popular interpretation expressed in the "Boot and Petticoat" slogan, and the murderer of Edward II, who, as the lover of his widow, had ruled England for three years, while Edward III "was held in the most absolute slavery by his mother and his minister, the first nobles of England were excluded from the king's councils, and the minion disposed of all places of profit and trust". "I absolutely disclaim the most distant allusion," Wilkes shamelessly declared, "and I purposely dedicate this play to your lordship because history does not furnish a more striking contrast than there is between the two ministers in the reigns of Edward the Third and George the Third. . . . Let me entreat your lordship to assist your Friend [Murphy] in perfecting the weak scenes in this tragedy. . . . It is the warmest wish of my heart that the Earl of Bute may speedily complete the story of Roger Mortimer, . . . Such a work will immortalize your name in the literary as the peace of Versailles will in the political world; and wherever the name of Roger Mortimer shall be mentioned, that of Bute will follow to the latest times."

"It is wormwood," commented Walpole, and the town with him. Bute was crimson, the King livid. But Wilkes casually mentioned to a government hack that "it is usual to give dedicators something; I wish you would put his lordship in mind of it". A little later he was asked by a Frenchman how far the liberty of the Press extended in England. "I do not know," he answered. "I am trying to find out."

It was not long before he did. In April Bute resigned, perhaps because his task was done, perhaps, as many claimed, because Wilkes had written him out of office. But the speech from the throne at the close of the parliamentary session was an echo and justification of his policy. With the authority of Temple, and possibly also of Pitt, Wilkes produced the last and most famous issue of the *North Briton*, Number 45.

It was an issue far less tendentious than many of its predecessors. Its first words, "The *King's Speech* has always been considered by the legislature, and by the public at large, as the *Speech of the Minister*", not only fixed a constitutional point but appeared to safeguard the author from any charge of *lèse-majesté*. Another passage which was found actionable made the distinction with equal clarity: "A despotic minister will always endeavour to dazzle his prince with high-flown ideas of the *prerogative* and *honour* of the *crown*, which the minister will make a parade of *firmly maintaining*. I wish as much as any man in England to see *the honour of the crown* maintained in a manner truly becoming *Royalty*. I lament to see it sunk even to prostitution." But Wilkes had at last gone too far. Perhaps stung to fury by the affront to his personal vanity, perhaps exasperated that not even the resignation of Bute could buy a surcease from the gadfly's attacks, the King gave orders that Wilkes was to be prosecuted. A general warrant was drawn up in the name of Lord Halifax, Principal Secretary of State, for the arrest of the "Authors, Printers & Publishers of a Seditious, & Treasonable Paper, intitled, *The North Briton*, Number 45".

The proceedings were farcical from the first. Forty-eight persons were arrested before an attempt was risked on Wilkes himself. The chief government runner became conveniently ill. The messengers could not bring themselves to arrest him, their explanation being that he was "in liquor". They were equally obliging next morning when he passed them with the casual remark that he would be back to breakfast, so that he was able to go down to the printing shop, borrow a ladder to enter an upper room "pie" the type for the next issue of the *North Briton*, destroy any compromising papers and return home as casually as he had come. There the messengers were waiting for him. He demanded to see their warrant, and, in view of its general terms, asked why they chose to serve it on him rather than on the Secretaries of State, Lord Bute or his next-door neighbour. Finally he inveigled them into his house to discuss the matter, and there held the pass verbally against an assault of messengers, sub-messengers and assistants. Friends who dropped in were embroiled or sent off to secure a writ of habeas corpus. At one point Churchill looked in. "Good morrow, *Mr. Thomson*", Wilkes greeted him. "How does Mrs. Thomson do today? Does she dine in the *country*?" The Bruiser took the hint and left the house and London precipitately.

The messengers were becoming frantic, and still Wilkes would not be arrested. To a personal invitation from Halifax, who lived a few doors away, to step in and see him, he replied that he had not been introduced. Finally, on the arrival of a force of police, and the threat that a platoon of guards would be called out if necessary, he yielded. Even so he insisted on a sedan chair to carry him the few yards to Halifax's house. Here there awaited him Halifax and his fellow-Secretary, Egremont, backed by an imposing array of Under-Secretaries, law clerks and solicitors to the Treasury. Wilkes was unimpressed. To a battery of questions he replied that at the end of the interview "all the quires of paper on their lordships' table should be as milk-white as at the beginning". To Halifax's conciliatory offer of a choice of prisons he replied that he never accepted obligations except from a friend; but he did ask to be placed in a room where no Scot had ever been a prisoner, "if it is possible to find one".

So on Saturday night Wilkes was packed off to the Tower. His house was ransacked in his absence, and all his papers taken. Temple was ordered to cashier him from the Militia, and, when he did so only under protest, was himself deprived of his Lord-Lieutenancy. On the following Tuesday Wilkes made a formal appearance in court; and on the Friday presented his appeal against unlawful arrest. "The liberty of all peers and gentlemen," he told the court, "and, what touches me more sensibly, that of all the middling and inferior set of people, who stand most in need of protection, is in my case this day to be finally decided upon: a question of such importance as to determine at once whether English liberty shall be a reality or a shadow." Lord Chief Justice Pratt summed up with caution and at first discouragingly. But he could not accept the libel complained of as treason, felony or a breach of the peace; therefore, in view of his parliamentary privilege, Wilkes must be released. A roar of triumph arose from the "middling and inferior set of people", and the great cry of "Wilkes and Liberty!" was raised. And Hogarth slipped away from behind a pillar with the sketches for his famous cartoon.

Wilkes's first act on his release was to write to the Secretaries of State demanding the return of his "stolen property". He also applied for a search warrant against them, but this was refused. Forthwith he sued Halifax and his Under-Secretary for unlawful arrest, and most of the other forty-eight sufferers followed suit against an army of government officials. Some of these cases miscarried, but others, thanks to the enthusiasm of London juries, reaped a handsome harvest of damages. The general warrant, to the relief of Englishmen to this day, was dead.

The next attack upon Wilkes was prepared with more care. He had recklessly laid himself open to it by setting up a private printing-press in his house, where he had reprinted Number 45, and also, for distribution among his old friends the Medmenham Monks, a few copies of his "Essay on Woman", and some shorter poems. By a systematic campaign of bribery the authorities managed to possess themselves of these, and planned a double attack, with one assault on Wilkes's public actions and another on his private morality.

The "Essay", generally considered unprintable, was a close parody of Pope's "Essay on Man", dedicated to Fanny Murray, a famous courtesan of a past generation. The notes were wantonly ascribed to Bishop Warburton, annotator of Pope. Whatever the poem's indecencies, they were not of a nature to shock that least queasy of ages and the public horror expressed at them was a piece of politic hypocrisy that deceived no one. A comparable situation might arise if a certain contemporary member of Parliament, who has more than once shown a Wilkesian wit and ingenuity in the defence of minor but still cherished English liberties, were for his nuisance-value to be publicly branded and expelled from the House on the strength of an amusing and undoubtedly improper little poem, the authorship of which he has not hesitated to admit.

On the opening of the parliamentary session a motion was carried condemning Number 45 as a "false, scandalous and seditious libel" and ordering it to be publicly burnt; an order whose execution was thwarted by The Mob, who burned instead Bute's symbol, a large jackboot. At the same time the unspeakable Sandwich, with many lip-smackings and gross affectations of horror, was reading the "Essay" to the Lords, to audible comments from Dashwood (now Lord Despencer) as to Satan's rebuking sin. Why Sandwich should have led the attack against his old friend is not clear, though a reason has been found for it in a fragmentary "instruction" which had been discovered among Wilkes's papers, addressed to Sandwich on the occasion of his appointment as ambassador to Spain: "It is beneath your lordships to measure swords with the men, and we do most expressly restrain you to make all your thrusts at the women. . . . I hope . . . you will first carry the breastwork, then take the demilune, and at last plant your victorious standard in the citadel of every fair Donna." In any case Wilkes's was the ultimate revenge, for he damned Sandwich for ever in one of the most stinging repartees in the English language. "I am convinced, Mr. Wilkes," Sandwich told him languidly, "that you will die either of a pox or on the gallows." "That depends, my Lord," was Wilkes's instant reply, "whether I embrace your mistress or your principles."

Wilkes did not hear the contemptuous and contemptible speech in which Pitt, while ostensibly defending him, cast his loyal supporter to the wolves: he had been seriously wounded in another duel, and proved the fact to a doubting House by calling in two doctors who, "since they were both Scotsmen and attached to the Royal Household, must surely be acceptable as suitable spies". Shortly afterwards he left for France to find a chaperone for his daughter and stayed there to seduce her when found. Whether or not the illness that kept him from returning was genuine, he was still in Paris when, in January 1764, the House of Commons expelled him and when, a month later, Lord Mansfield in the Court of King's Bench issued a writ for his arrest. He had still not made up his mind what to do by the end of the summer, and in October sentence of outlawry was passed upon him.

5

He was an exile. His friend Churchill had just died. His financial situation was ruinous. Wilkes went to Italy, "to economise". He went, though, in the uneconomic company of Gertrude Corradini, a stormy creature who "had the divine gift of lewdness", allied to the kind of piety that held out against all assaults until Wilkes carried the fortress by the well-timed gift of a crucifix: and which impelled her, in a boudoir whose uncurtained windows invited shameless publicity, to veil the plaster eyes of a madonna statuette. The piety was probably part of the stock-in-trade, however, for she left him when she had run through his money. The news that the government had fallen and that the Whig leader, Lord Rockingham, had been asked to form a ministry appeared to offer consolatory prospects of a recall. But in point of fact four years were to pass in half-promises and repudiations, and Wilkes was to make several flying visits to London to be cold-shouldered by his former friends, before, in 1768, he damned them all, returned to England and announced himself as parliamentary candidate for the City of London. Mixed as were the feelings of his official friends, the people welcomed their returned hero with delirious enthusiasm, and the Joiners made him an honorary member of their company to qualify him for election. But his supporters were poor—when told that they were turncoats Wilkes pointed out, "Impossible. None of them has a coat to turn"—and vested interests were powerful. Wilkes's name came last on the poll. He set his famous jaw, begged a qualifying strip of land from Temple and addressed himself to the electors of Middlesex. With his lieutenants, Glynn and Horne, he campaigned tirelessly. Hecklers were handled with mastery. "I would rather vote for the devil than for John Wilkes," one fellow told him. "And if your friend is not standing?" asked Wilkes. His supporters went wild. Thousands of tavern signs sported his picture; "Aye, there he swings, everywhere but where he should," grumbled one old woman he was fond of quoting. The number 45 acquired a cabbalistic significance. Handel's " 'Tis Liberty alone that gives fresh beauty to the Sun" was found to contain just forty-five bars; Magna Carta's "No Freeman shall be taken or imprisoned . . . unless by the legal Judgment of his Peers, or by the Law of the Land" was the forty-fifth article; clergymen preached on the text, "And he said, if I find there the forty and five, I will not destroy it", or offered prayers for "the restoration of liberty, depending upon the election of Mr. John Wilkes"; the mystic number, if we are to believe the evidence of contemporary songs, even set a new standard in the bedchamber.

When Wilkes's victory was announced there was delirium. Coaches were mobbed, and "45" or "Wilkes and Liberty!" scrawled upon them. The Austrian ambassador was dragged from his coach and "45" chalked on the soles of his shoes. If the King had had a bad character and Wilkes a good one, suggested Benjamin Franklin, George III would have been turned off his throne.

On the first day of the Easter Term Wilkes went to the Court of King's Bench and surrendered himself. Lord Mansfield, in acute embarrassment, dismissed him on the count that, as an outlaw, the court could not technically take cognisance of his presence. Wilkes therefore arranged for a writ and an arrest in due form. This time the court, refusing bail, committed him to prison pending its decision. The Mob drove off the police and took the horses from the shafts of the prison coach. It was Wilkes who had to placate them, and Wilkes who, slipping away at night in diguise and in a private carriage, knocked up the prison and let himself in.

Mansfield's decision was given a few days later. A packed court held its breath while a preamble of masterly legality delayed the ultimate explosion: the outlawry was voided by a technical error in the writ. Ten days later Wilkes came again into court to receive his sentence for the proved charge of libel. He was fined a sum which his supporters found, bound over on recognisances which his friends paid, and sentenced to twenty-two months' imprisonment.

It is said that Wilkes and a friend once issued a manifesto from a tavern room beginning, "We the People of England, . . ." If the story is true he had some justification, for from his room in the King's Bench Prison, where he received his friends and mistresses at ease and feasted off the innumerable gifts that poured in from every part of the country and even from America, he controlled the popular sentiment of the country. Manifestoes, petitions, appeals, accusations, streamed out of the room, and gifts, money and resolutions of solidarity streamed in. A week after his arrest Wilkes appeared in person to make his petition to the House. They rejected it and expelled him. He offered himself to Middlesex for re-election and was returned. Again the House expelled him. He was returned for the fourth time, with a majority of 1143 to the 296 of Luttrell, his officially-backed opponent. Parliament declared him permanently disqualified and carried a motion that Luttrell should sit in his place. The issue had ceased to be personal and had become constitutional. Protests and petitions poured in. Wilkes's long-deferred case against Lord Halifax came to a decision and Wilkes was awarded £4000 damages. The whip of Junius cracked in his defence. Burke cited his case as one of the "causes of the present discontents". The great Chatham emerged from his silence, and he, who six years previously had repudiated his champion, now repudiated that repudiation. The ministry toppled and fell.

The City of London, whose merchant-class had long found in Wilkes the champion of their liberal principles, and whose privileged independence was always jealously watchful of royal encroachment, made a gesture. Wilkes was elected Alderman of Farringdon Without, and the society known as the Supporters of the Bill of Rights was formed to pay his debts and support his cause. When he left prison in 1770 he was able to renew a guerilla warfare against his old enemy, George III, from a new vantage ground. But the enemy, meanwhile, was strongly entrenched; the King had found in North a docile Prime Minister, and had at last achieved his ambition of unchallenged power: unchallenged until "that devil Wilkes" once more entered the arena; that devil Wilkes, who made no bones of his opinions and when asked to take a hand at whist had replied, "Pray, madam, do not ask me, for I am so ignorant I cannot distinguish between a king and a knave."

Having set rolling the avalanches of the illegality of general warrants and the urgency of electoral reform, Wilkes kicked off a new one: the liberty of the Press. The reporting of parliamentary proceedings, technically illegal, had for some time enjoyed unofficial toleration. Now the House of Commons saw fit to denounce for this offence Thompson and Wheble, printers of the *Gazeteer* and the *Middlesex Journal*, and to issue a proclamation for their arrest. Wilkes immediately ordered the pair into hiding and a week later Wheble was "arrested" by one of his employees and brought to the Guildhall, where the officiating justice, by a curious coincidence Mr. Alderman Wilkes, dismissed the case, the arrest on the strength of an illegal proclamation being, as he explained in a letter to the wretched Halifax, again Secretary of State, "in direct violation of the rights of an Englishman and of the chartered privileges of a citizen of this metropolis". Thompson was brought before Oliver at the Mansion House, and the procedure gravely repeated. The arrest of a third printer, Miller, of the *London Evening Post*, was ordered and a messenger dispatched to apprehend him. Miller, finding the officer had no warrant from a City magistrate, refused to accompany him and instead gave him in charge for assault; and the Lord Mayor, Brass Crosby, supported by Wilkes and Oliver, committed the man to jail. In the end the Serjeant-at-Arms had to come posting down to the City to bail his messenger out. The elated trio of cits were peremptorily summoned to the House. Crosby and Oliver attended, stood their ground and were committed to the Tower, where they were sustained and fêted at the City's expense until the end of the session. Wilkes ignored three summonses, refusing to attend except in his capacity as Member for Middlesex. In the end the House extricated itself by summoning him for a certain date and then hastily adjourning.

A few months later Wilkes captured the next stronghold by getting himself elected Sheriff. There was a Court Party in the City, however, as well as at Westminster; a reactionary Court of Aldermen as well as a democratic Livery. The old processes of betrayal and sharp practice began to be repeated. His bid for Lord Mayoralty, which inevitably followed, therefore followed as inevitably the all-too-familiar pattern. According to the practice, the new Lord Mayor was chosen by the Court of Aldermen from the two men who headed the poll, and each party normally put up two candidates in the hope of securing representation by one or the other. Wilkes secured a majority, followed by Townshend, the other party candidate. To the astonishment and fury of his supporters, a Court of anti-Wilkes Aldermen nominated Townshend. The next year Wilkes stood again, naming Bull as his fellow-candidate. Again he headed the poll, and yet Bull was chosen over his head. It was another Middlesex election. When he stood a third time, as of course he did, he again chose Bull to stand with him. The reason was not clear until the Court of Aldermen were once more preparing to return the second candidate; but at that juncture an Act of Common Council of the reign of Henry VIII was produced for their disconcerted inspection. It enacted that the same Lord Mayor could not be elected for two consecutive terms. Bull was therefore disqualified, and amidst rejoicing that put even the Middlesex celebrations in the shade Wilkes was elected Lord Mayor on October 1774.

The Lord Mayor's show was a Roman triumph; the banquet which followed, although "their Royal Highnesses the Dukes of Gloucester and Cumberland, the Lord Chancellor, Chief Justices of the King's Bench and the Common Pleas, Secretaries of State, and most of the nobility were suddenly *taken ill*, which prevented them accepting the Lord Mayor's invitation to dine at Guildhall", a feast of victory.

It is time to mention here that Wilkes's progress through the City offices was not that of a careerist. As Alderman he had successfully checked profiteering in corn prices and had challenged the press-gang abuse. As Sheriff he had instituted notable reforms in prison conditions. As Lord Mayor he drastically reduced the price of bread, democratized the electoral system, did much to shore up the crumbling power of the workers' guilds, and above all rallied the City to a point where it took the initiative over political issues. There was solid achievement, therefore, behind the social brilliance which marked his term of office; behind those Guildhall banquets, with Polly as hostess, which became a by-word for City hospitality (and for subsequent hangovers, since Wilkes, in reply to Walpole's accusation that he was a French agent, banned all French wines from the mayoral table and replaced them with the traditional heavily-fortified sherry and port); behind those shows and processions and state visits to Bartholomew Fair; behind the swagger with which the Lord Mayor sported his latest mistress, Marianne Geneviève de Charpillon, a woman who had not only resisted Casanova but reported him to the police for molestation, and with whom Wilkes took over her mother and grandmother too, three generations of solid professional talent which had blazed a triumphant trail among the crowned heads, diplomatic corps and nobility and gentry of Europe, from Berne to Paris and from Paris to London; and behind that "belly truly aldermanic" now sported by one who before his term of office had been "thin as a shotten herring".

6

Two weeks after his election as Lord Mayor Wilkes was once more returned to Westminster as Member for Middlesex. This time he came, not as a camp follower, but as the leader of a party; for about a dozen Wilkites, the Twelve Apostles, as they came to be called, were elected to support a programme in which electoral reform and the American question took precedence. This time he took his seat without opposition. His first act was to spread a rumour that he intended to propose as Speaker an ex-waiter who had somehow been returned for a rotten borough. His first speech proposed that the anniversary of Charles I's execution should be kept not as a fast but as a day of rejoicing. He lost little time in introducing the first of his famous annual motions for the expunging of the House's ruling on the Middlesex election. But it was soon obvious that he had more serious business in hand, and here the charge of demagogue, if not already demolished, must fall to the ground. Mutual encouragement and support had long pledged him to the cause of the American colonists, and to that cause, at the sacrifice of personal triumphs and even of the cherished programme of electoral reform, he devoted almost all his parliamentary energies. His speeches in the Commons, like Chatham's in the Lords, fell like Cassandra's prophecies on the deaf ears of the "set of idle, listless, loitering, lounging, ill-informed gentlemen at Westminster". History upholds him but contemporaries got tired of him. It is true that at first popular opinion ran with him; vested interests were opposed to the war and the City was an American stronghold. But as jingoism grew, and contractors battened on the usual artificial boom, feeling ran the other way. Before long the "demagogue" found himself on the unpopular side.

The first indication was his defeat for the office of City Chamberlain, a sinecure which his pressing financial needs made doubly desirable. It was a bitter blow, and perhaps it was to regain popular favour that shortly afterwards he did introduce a Bill for electoral reform, and in a speech that returned to character. "No less than twenty-two towns," he declared, "sent members to Parliament in the twenty-third, twenty-fifth and twenty-sixth of Edward I which have long since ceased to be represented. The names of some of them are scarcely known to us, such as those of Canebrig and Bamburg in Northumberland, Pershore and

Brem in Worcestershire, Jarvall and Tykhull in Yorkshire. What a happy fate, sir, has attended the boroughs of Gatton and Old Sarum, of which, though *ipsae periere ruinae*, the names are familiar to us, the clerk regularly calls them over, and four respectable gentlemen represent their departed greatness as the knights at the coronation represent Aquitaine and Normandy! The little town of Banbury, *petite ville grand renom*, as Rabelais says of Chinon, has I believe only seventeen electors, yet it gives us in its representative [North] what is of the utmost importance to the majority here, a First Lord of the Treasury and a Chancellor of the Exchequer." The Bill proposed that rotten boroughs should be abolished, unrepresented towns enfranchised and the vote given to "the meanest mechanic, the poorest peasant and day labourer", since "some share in the power of making laws . . . should be reserved even to this inferior but most useful set of men in the community". It received "very jocular treatment" and was rejected without a division.

There were certain subjects upon which Wilkes's intervention was dreaded. One was the Civil List. When Parliament was asked to pay the King's debts Wilkes cast an expert eye over the accounts and pronounced them "loose, unsatisfactory, perplexed, and unintelligible"; "the nation, sir, suspects that regular Ministerial majorities in Parliament are bought by these very grants." There was no answer to his public congratulations on the royal fecundity, which had produced twelve children in sixteen years: "The gratitude of this House to heaven increases every year with the fortunately prolific annual increase of the royal offspring. We triumph in those endearing pledges of our monarch's love, and the public felicity which an all-bounteous Providence continues to bestow on this peculiarly favoured nation. The kingdom at large contemplates with rapture His Majesty's numerous, and still, I hope, increasing progeny, as insuring even beyond our children's children, to the *nati natorum et qui nascentur ab illis*, the blessings and glories of his reign." This was the Wilkes who "so loved his King that he hoped never to see another"; who toasted George III ostentatiously in front of his rival, the Prince of Wales, and, when asked whence dated this anxiety for the King's longevity, replied, "Since I had the honour of Your Royal Highness's acquaintance."

Wilkes's reputation as a "blasphemer of his God" rests on Chatham's phrase and was one that he bitterly resented. He made, Heaven knows, no pretensions to piety—"The word *Liberty* is as ridiculous in his mouth," he said of Johnson, "as *religion* in mine"—but he was not fundamentally an irreligious man. He may have been unorthodox: witness his observation to Boswell that "I should no more value being raised in the same body than being raised in the same coat, waistcoat, and breeches." "But upon my word, Sir, the doctrine of some, who call themselves orthodox, and deal out damnation so liberally, makes a humane man tremble." He had been known to speak out, even, in defence of his creed. "Where was your religion before the Reformation?" a Catholic once asked him. "Where was your face before you washed it this morning?" was his reply. Nevertheless, the reputation stuck, and by a crowning irony it was his intervention on behalf of religious toleration that put an end to the "Atheist's" career.

This happened at a moment when, after years of disaster abroad and discouragement at home, when his personal plans had come to naught, his prestige was low and his finances lower, when the prudent Mrs. Stafford, the first woman who might have been a friend as well as a mistress, had been alienated by the intervention of a virtuous friend, the tide had begun to turn. In 1778 he had once more rallied a somewhat disillusioned City on the question of the war. His power there was on the increase again, and in the autumn of 1779 he was at last elected Chamberlain. The urgent need for economy had revived the question of ministerial expenditure, and that same winter no fewer than three reform bills were introduced and Wilkes's friend Dunning carried his famous motion that "the influence of the Crown has increased, is increasing and ought to be diminished". At such a moment the Gordon rioters marched on London with their cry of "No Popery!" For a week the city was at their mercy. It was Wilkes, the idol of the people, the demagogue, the opportunist and the atheist, who saved it; Wilkes and George III. While all other authority was paralysed the King turned out troops, and Wilkes collected a militia, patrolled the city and saved the Bank from an infuriated mob. He had pledged himself to religious toleration, and he swore that he would not leave a rioter alive. One of the men he sent to prison for destroying a house was a former printer of the *North Briton*; the house was Lord Mansfield's. His old enemies, and the apostles of moderation, had reason to be grateful to him, but The Mob had finished with him.

7

One thing remained to be done. In 1782 the news of the defeat at Yorktown drove North from office, and Rockingham, Shelburne, Fox and other Whigs returned to power. For the last time, Wilkes produced his now-hoary motion on the Middlesex election; and this time it was carried, and the record expunged. After this, although his familiar figure, with the scarlet coat and cocked hat of the militia colonel, a little gouty now and "growing more like Hogarth's portrait every day", as he ruefully admitted, was still seen in the House, it caused little stir there, and in 1790 Wilkes retired from Parliament; in his own words, "a spent volcano". Once an old market woman raised the cry of "Wilkes and Liberty!" at the sight of him. "Be quiet, you old fool," he muttered. "That's all over now." His wit, however, had not deserted him. In the City, where he continued unflagging in his duties as Chamberlain, his quips were still a by-word. Bets were made that from leaving his house to reaching the Guildhall he could not meet a person but he would leave that person chuckling. At City dinners he laid about him with gusto: comparing them unfavourably, when one guzzler disgusted him by roaring for his meat, with a bear garden, where the bear was brought to the stake, not the steak to the bear; concurring, when one dignitary protested he would be his butt no longer, with, "With all my heart. I never liked an empty one"; answering some young toady's, "I was born between twelve and one on the first of January, isn't it strange?" with, "Not at all. You could only have been conceived on the first of April." The apprentices over whose court he presided adored him, and fifty years later Charles Mathews could convulse a room with an imitation of the old man solemnly admonishing an unruly youngster, while one squinting eye conveyed sly encouragement to the sinner and the other the admonishment to the master.

Wilkes had mellowed with years. Old enemies who now met him for the first time were astonished at his breeding and charm. Lord Mansfield declared him "the pleasantest companion, the politest gentleman, and the best scholar I ever knew. Even George III was forced to admit he had never seen so well-bred a Lord Mayor. And no one will ever forget the famous meeting with Johnson: Boswell's tortuous contrivance of it; the agonized suspense when the irresistible force met the immovable post; then Wilkes's assiduous, "Pray give me leave, Sir:—it is better here—A little of the brown—Some fat, Sir—A little of the stuffing—Some gravy—Let me have the pleasure of giving you some butter—Allow me to recommend a squeeze of this orange;—or the lemon, perhaps, may have more zest." Johnson's "surly virtue" giving way to complacency, until the two of them were laughing their heads off at the expense of the Scots. And Johnson's verdict: "Jack has great variety of talk, Jack is a scholar, and Jack has the manners of a gentleman . . . I would do Jack a kindness, rather than not."

So Jack came to terms with respectability, though he often sneaked off for carousals with boon companions, Miles Peter Andrews, Captain Ayscough, Edward Topham, the amorous Chase Prince, Lord Irnham, that amusing old scoundrel who had once challenged his beastly son Luttrell to a duel and had had his challenge refused on the grounds that he was not a gentleman. Some evenings he would dine quietly at home with Polly, others as quietly at Kensington Gore with his homely mistress, Amelia Arnold, consoling her for a malicious paragraphist's taunts on her plainness with, "You see, my dear, there has never been any *difference* between us." Part of the time he retired to his "villakin" at Sandown, where the younger Reynolds found him concerned over his pigeons and "the difficulty he had experienced to make them stay with him. Every bird that he had procured from England, Ireland and France having flown back to its native land the moment the latch was raised, he was about to abandon his scheme as impracticable, 'when,' he continued, 'I bethought myself to procure a cock and hen pouter from Scotland; I need not add that *they never returned*.' "

Wilkes was once asked if he would go through the storms of his political life over agian. "Not at all," he replied. "Adversity may be a good thing to breakfast on; nay, a man may dine upon it; but believe me, my good friend, it makes a confoundedly bad supper."

In 1797, at the age of seventy, he caught a chill and died a few days later. There are many epitaphs to choose from: his own "a patriot by accident"; Boswell's "good without principles"; or that he himself left, "A Friend of Liberty".

HENRY LABOUCHERE

W. W. HADLEY

NEARLY THIRTY YEARS AFTER HIS DEATH, FEW WILL CHALLENGE THE TITLE of Henry Labouchere to a place in this collection of English Wits. Yet it may be that after thirty years more the title will have lapsed. His wit was natural and unforced, flowering from childhood to age, in writings and speeches, and most abundantly, in the ease and freedom of social intercourse. His speeches were almost exclusively political and, admirable as they often were, are already forgotten. His writings are mostly to be found over a quarter of a century in his own paper *Truth*. He wrote as easily as he spoke and, even when most diffuse, was never dull. He had an uncommon gift for narrative; he was a *raconteur* of the fi- order; and when he wrote of his own variegated adventures it was with an engaging air of taking the reader into his special confidence.

He wrote for pleasure and found more satisfaction in the act of writing than in the use that was made of the resultant script. In early years he acquired a simple, colloquial style that was always lucid and vivacious and derived a special attractiveness from his unconventional frankness. Collection of his best *Truth* articles in two or three volumes might have given him lasting fame, but he would never take the trouble to do it and the process of revisio- would have bored him. Why in the leisure of his years of retirement at Florence he did not write his memoirs is an interesting problem. Few men of the time equalled his variety of experience, and those who knew how rarely the urge to write had left him up to then expected a book that would live. He didn't write it, and the explanation is, I think, that when he ceased to be an actor the need for self-expression ceased; and he was unlikely to feel any call to amuse a posterity that would not amuse him. But posterity loses much. Labouchere had been a cool, sharp-eyed observer of life, his range of interests was wide, and in whatever role he appeared his personality compelled attention. "Labby" stories in the newspapers were innumerable. They began with his preparatory school, thickened about him as his career opened out, and had become legendary before he reached middle age.

It is nearly sixty years since, a boy in Northampton, I first set eyes on Labouchere. He had been returned to the House of Commons by that borough a year or two before, with Charles Bradlaugh as his colleague. Bradlaugh was an atheist and, because of that, was prevented from taking his seat throughout the Parliament of 1880-85. This kept Northampton politics in a continual ferment; there were occasional by-elections in which the town was frenzied with excitement. In my recollection of the period, Labouchere appears as the only person whose equanimity was always undisturbed. He lounged through the most exciting scenes, his manner bland, his voice unraised. Off the platform he was continually smoking cigarettes, a new-fangled habit which, in the eyes of his Nonconformist supporters, was unquestionably naughty. There were shocking stories, too, of his gambling habits, but these, it was said, he had abandoned—and much could be excused in one who had lived so long abroad. Moreover, it was counted to him for righteousness that in a hard-drinking generation he had little use for alcohol. And how well he quoted the Scriptures! The most austere of the Puritans who then ruled the political roost in Northampton persuaded themselves that he really was a brand plucked from the burning.

There must be some explanation of Labouchere's unlikeness to all the other politicians I knew in the '80's, and I found it, of course, in his French origin. In the seventeenth century the Laboucheres were Huguenot cloth merchants at Orthoz in Bearn. One of them, Matthieu, was educated in England and settled in Holland about the middle of the eighteenth century. It was his second son, Pierre-César Labouchere, who by marrying a daughter of Sir Francis Baring founded the English branch of the family. He was a bold adventurer in international finance during the Napoleonic wars and after, amassed a large fortune and ended his days in England. This Pierre-César had two sons, Henry and John. Henry won distinction in society and politics, had the honour of defeating Disraeli in a by-election at Taunton, sat in Whig Cabinets and went to the House of Lords as Baron Taunton. John combined philanthropy and religion with banking; his house in Portland Place was filled with the odour of sanctity. There his eldest son, Henry, was born in 1831. Mr. Algar Thorold's excellent biography (which I have used as *aide mémoire*, and more) tells us nothing of the child's home life, which is a pity, for one would like to trace the beginnings of the alienation from his father and his father's faith. John Labouchere must have been shocked by his boy's precocious pranks at Eton and horrified by his doings at Cambridge, where his gambling debts amounted to about £6000. One morning, when Henry was on an illicit visit to Town, they met in the Strand. Henry (I quote from Mr. Thorold) returned his father's cold greeting with a surprised stare. "I beg your pardon, sir," he said, "I think you have made a mistake. I have not the honour of your acquaintance"; then he left him and, running to the station, caught a train for Cambridge. His father followed in the next train, found his son in his rooms absorbed in study, and convinced himself that in the Strand he had been the victim of hallucination.

A spirited combat with Authority caused Henry's departure from the University early in his third year. He then led what he described as a life of profligacy in London until his father sent him abroad in the care of a Mentor from whom he soon parted. Writing to *Truth* from Wiesbaden long after he said: "I remember being here nearly forty years ago. I was then a lad travelling on the Continent with a bear-leader to enlarge my experience. The bear-leader and I never could quite agree what spot would prove the most improving. He wished to study still nature, I wished to study human nature. So, like Abram and Lot, we generally separated. He betook himself to the Carpathian Mountains, I sojourned here."

A Mentor with him again, he next went to South America, where his family had large commercial interests and he would meet the right people. They did not keep him out of mischief; nor was the bear-leader more successful than in Germany. For a year or two Labouchere wandered about Central America, keeping strange company. Some of the stories told of his doings during this period are probably imaginary, but there appears to be evidence for the one that he had an affair with a lady of the circus and for a time travelled about with the troupe. He himself used to tell how he joined the circus without pay and figured on the playbill as "The Bouncing Buck of Modern Babylon". Then, seeking a quieter life, he spent several months with a party of Chippeway Indians. Meantime, his friends in London were trying to find him befitting employment, and while he was still in America—in July 1854—he learned that he was in the Diplomatic Service and had been most considerately appointed an *attaché* at Washington.

Though his duty at Washington lasted less than eighteen months it made liberal contribution to the record of his exploits. Naturally courteous, he was politely uncommunicative to the inconsiderate or rude. This was noted when he was a very small boy at preparatory school. Asked in the morning if he had cleaned his teeth he admitted he had not. There followed a sharp admonition during which Henry kept silence till he was asked plainly *why* he had so neglected the teeth; and then he gave the startling reply, "Because I haven't got any!" The first set had gone and the second had not come. The same disconcerting technique was applied to an assertive American who called at the Legation at Washington and asked to see the Boss. Labouchere explained that the Minister was not in—could he himself oblige the gentleman? The suggestion was ill received and the visitor said he would wait. Two hours later he lost patience and asked when the Boss would be back. Labouchere thereupon informed him that the Minister was on vacation and was expected to return in about six weeks.

Another story of this period he used to tell himself. Sent to Boston to look after some Irish patriots, he gambled his money away, was turned out of his hotel and, at the end of a foodless day, went into a restaurant and ordered dinner. The waiters were Irish and he observed that they were continually staring at him. "At last one of them approached me and said, 'I beg your pardon, sir; are you the patriot Meagher?" Now this patriot was a gentleman who had aided Smith O'Brien in his Irish rising, had been sent to Australia and had escaped thence to the United States. It was my business to look after patriots, so I put my finger before my lips and said 'Hush!' while I cast up my eyes to the ceiling as though I saw a vision of Erin beckoning to me. It was felt at once that I was Meagher. The choicest viands were placed before me and most excellent wine. When I had done justice to all the good things I approached the bar and asked boldly for my bill. The proprietor, also an Irishman, said 'From a man like you, who has suffered in the good cause, I can take no money; allow a brother patriot to shake you by the hand.' I allowed him. I further allowed all the waiters to shake hands with me and stalked forth with the stern, resolved, but somewhat condescendingly dismal air which I have seen assumed by patriots in exile."

He left Washington at the end of 1854 and during the ten years following served in Munich, Stockholm, Frankfort, St. Petersburg, Dresden and Constantinople. There is evidence that his official duties were done with competence, though his own reminiscences of the period suggest that social diversions were his main concern. His knowledge of the casinos of Europe was said to be unsurpassed. Two of his stories are concerned with his relations with the Foreign Office. After leaving Frankfort and while he was on holiday at Florence, he was notified of his appointment as Secretary of Legation to the Republic of Parana. "After diligent inquiry I learnt that Parana was a sort of Federal town on the River Plate, but that a few months previously the republic of that name had shared the fate of the Kilkenny cats. So I remained in Italy, and comfortably drew my salary like a bishop of a see *in partibus infidelium.* A year later came a despatch couched in language more remarkable for its strength than its civility, asking me what I meant by not proceeding to my post. I replied that I had passed the twelve months in making diligent inquiries respecting the whereabouts of the Republic of Parana, hitherto without success, but if his lordship would kindly inform me where it was I need hardly say that I would hasten there."

Lord John Russell, then Foreign Minister, swallowed that affront, but not the one that followed. In 1864 at Baden-Baden, Labouchere was officially informed that he had been appointed as Second Secretary to the Legation at Buenos Aires. He was enjoying Baden-Baden and was determined not to go to Argentina. But refusal outright was not his way. He begged to inform the Secretary of State that if he could fulfil the duties of the Buenos Aires appointment at Baden-Baden he would be pleased to accept it. The Foreign Office had no further use for his services.

2

Labouchere was then thirty-three. His father had died a year before. He was sufficiently well off to have free choice of a career, and when he inherited the bulk of the fortune of his uncle, Lord Taunton, he was a rich man. Eton and Cambridge had done little for him, but, in his unconventional fashion, he had educated himself well. In the finishing school of the Diplomatic Service he had become an accomplished man of the world with an established reputation as a wit.

He still wanted to be amused; he still wanted to extend into new fields his studies of human nature; but these were no longer enough: his wild oats sown, he must do things that others, at any rate, thought worth doing. He turned first to politics. Uncle Taunton was overjoyed to find that his heir was giving his mind to serious things and asked if he could do anything to help him in his candidature for Windsor. "Really, I think not," the nephew replied, "but I don't know. If you would put on your peer's robes and walk arm-in-arm with me down the High Street it might have a good effect." He and Sir Henry Hoare, both Liberals (though Labouchere already thought of himself as Radical), were nominated against two Conservatives at the general election of 1865. Personation and "bottling" were then regular electioneering devices. Labouchere used to tell how one man, beginning early in the morning, voted for him several times, always as a clergyman. "I remonstrated with him, but uselessly," he said. Some Tory electors had to be kept from the polling booth by hook or by crook. One of them was taken out in a punt and kept in the middle of the river till the poll was closed. "Another aged and decrepit Tory was kept in the house by having cabs run at him whenever he tried to issue from his door." By these and other means the two Liberals got in, but only for a short time. There was a petition, and they were both unseated for illegal acts committed by their agents on the instructions of a candidate-elect who did not go to the poll. Attempts to bring a particular act of bribery home to Labouchere failed; he told counsel that the alleged bribery—the gift of a silk dress to the wife of an elector—was an affair of gallantry which had no relevance to the election inquiry. "The lady in question," he explained, "was extremely good-looking, and I have frequently noticed that a present of finery is a simple way to win the female heart. I regret that, in the particular case, I was unsuccessful, but, good God, you do not insinuate for a moment, do you, that I intended her husband to know anything about the affair?"

He was returned for Middlesex without a contest in 1867 but lost the seat in the following year, and a dozen years passed before Northampton gave him a long-term career in politics. For a time he was proprietor and manager of the Queen's Theatre. It was a costly enterprise. In one trying week actors complained that they could not play to empty houses. "Why don't you draw?" Labouchere replied. "Draw! Confound it, why don't you draw?" His own journalistic enterprises did draw. In 1868 he became part proprietor of the *Daily News*, received his share of substantial profits for nearly thirty years and then sold his interest in the paper for many times what he paid for it.

It was his association with the *Daily News* that provided the occasion for his first notable achievement in journalism. Being in Paris in the autumn of 1870 when the Germans were closing in on the city, he persuaded the resident correspondent of the paper, G. M. Crawford, to follow the French Government to Tours and to leave the representation of the paper to himself. The arrangement was a fortunate one for the *Daily News*. By balloon post Labouchere supplied it with reports which set a new standard in war correspondence. He was still studying human nature, and his letters not only described events but revealed a people. Humour relieved the gloom of the darkest days. His money was running short and "unless rats are reasonable I shall not be able to afford myself the luxury of one oftener than once a week". Donkey meat was a delicacy: "at Voisin's there was always every day a joint of cold donkey for breakfast, and it was greatly to be preferred to anything else." A few days after Christmas he had a slice of Pollux for dinner. Pollux and his brother Castor were two elephants which had been killed; the meat was tough, coarse and oily, and he did not recommend it for English families so long as they could get beef or mutton. And the monsters taxed severely the resources of the Paris cooks. Fuel was scarce and they were recommended to use lamps; "but although French cooks can do wonders with very poor material, when they are called upon to cook an elephant with a spirit lamp the thing is almost beyond their ingenuity". In another despatch he described his feelings when under fire. "The first time, I felt that every shell whizzing through the air would infallibly blow me up"; and, remembering that he was a non-combatant, he retired, "in an unconcerned sort of way as if I had business to attend to elsewhere. . . . But as no shell had blown me up I came to the conclusion that no shell would blow me up and accepted afterwards as a natural state of things which did not concern me the fact that these missiles occasionally blew up other people."

A few years later, in July 1874, Labouchere introduced himself to the readers of Edmund Yates's *World* as an authority on finance. "In casting about for the City editor of our journal," he wrote, "we have fallen upon a gentleman who, by promoting rotten companies, puffing worthless stock and other disreputable but strictly legal devices, has earned a modest competence. He resides in a villa at Clapham, he attends church every Sunday with exemplary regularity and is the centre of a most respectable circle of friends; many of his old associates still keep up their acquaintance with him and therefore he is in a position to know all that passes in the City. This reformed speculator we have engaged to write our City article." Lively, provocative articles they were; and Labouchere found the work so entertaining that at the beginning of 1877 he established his own paper. He wished to give it the title of *The Lyre* but was persuaded to call it *Truth*, which meant, he explained, a new and better *World*. It was a success from the start and was soon making large profits. Labouchere wrote the City article, was the paper's dramatic critic and contributed amusing paragraphs about all manner of subjects and people. No one could do such things better. He was the complete cynic, disliking and distrusting enthusiasm and delighting in the deflation of pomposity and the exposure of pretentious humbugs. It is in *Truth*, too, that one finds most about himself. His reminiscences appear in unexpected places. Writing as dramatic critic on the début of Kyrle Bellew at the theatre, he filled several columns with a droll account of a visit to Palestine with the actor's father, the Rev. J. M. Bellew. One day in a Venice restaurant, Labouchere saw a stranger pay his bill and heard him say that he was going to the Holy Land. "Wait five minutes," Labouchere said to him, "and I will come with you"; and here in the middle of a theatre notice is the account of their strange companionship. It was Bellew's habit occasionally to preen himself before a looking-glass. Labouchere came to hate this mirror, and one day he "sent it to join Sodom and Gomorrah" beneath the waters of the Dead Sea. "Some day," he moralized, "an explorer will fish it up and we shall have archæologists divided in opinion, one half proving that it belonged to a lady of Sodom and the other half that it was the property of a gentleman of Gomorrah."

Labouchere's editorship of *Truth* was nominal. He worked only at what interested him, as writing always did, and the routine of editorial duties would have bored him stiff. The acting-editor on holiday once received a letter from him saying that things were dull and he didn't think he would bring out the paper next week. The unfortunate man rushed back to the office, and for years after spent every vacation within easy distance of London.

3

When he returned to the House of Commons in 1880 Labouchere ceased to contribute regular articles to *Truth* on finance and the theatre and, instead, wrote on politics and Parliament. The Lobby side of Parliamentary journalism had not then been developed and his candid and spicy commentary was eagerly welcomed. But the readers of *Truth* were never given his frank account of how he became "the religious member for Northampton", as Lord Randolph Churchill called him.

The Northampton Liberals knew that if they were united they could return both its members. But they were very much disunited. Charles Bradlaugh, whose candidature put two Conservatives in at the previous general election, was determined to stand again. Because of his atheism, a considerable section of Nonconformist Liberals had been bitterly opposed to him. They were still unwilling to go on his platform, but Gladstone's trumpet was sounding to his last battle with Disraeli, and they must not fail their leader now. If two official Liberals were nominated, with Bradlaugh also in the field, the two Conservatives would again be elected. So there was a sort of understanding that only one candidate should receive the party certificate, leaving Bradlaugh to do his best or worst as a free lance. A deputation from the Liberal Association explained the position to Labouchere in London. He knew they were seeking a candidate worthy to represent the Christian electors of Northampton: and Barkis was willin'. There is no reason to believe that he told the deputation—he certainly did not tell the electors—that in religion he was as much an unbeliever as Bradlaugh himself. Anyhow, he accepted the call, went down to Northampton to survey the field and at once decided to make common cause with Bradlaugh. They were both elected with Labouchere at the head of the poll, as he always was, for the devout Christians who could not conscientiously support the atheist never failed to vote for the agnostic.

Having chosen the role of independent Radical, Labouchere was extremely fortunate in finding a constituency which was itself Radical and independent. Though the Caucus had spread from Birmingham, the party in Northampton was free both from central control and from the influence of local territorial magnates. Nobody and nothing came between member and constituents, and they quickly established relations of mutual admiration and trust. In a letter to *The Times*, Labouchere said he told them that his voice would be raised "against any Government that lags on the path of progress or falls into error. My constituents have been good enough to leave it to me to decide what is lagging and what error."

The contrast between the two members was so complete that there could be no question of jealousy between them. Each was the complement of the other; each brought new strength to the other. Physically and intellectually, Bradlaugh was a giant: the greatest mob orator since O'Connell, but he was more than that, and could state a case in highly concentrated form with tremendous force. Those who had relations with him found that though he rejected all the creeds there was in him a strong core of Puritan morals. Labouchere had no faintest trace of Puritanism. Enthusiasm was distasteful to him, the display of emotion embarrassing. Nor was he capable of veneration for a cause or a person: when he saw it in others he itched to disillusion them. At the funeral of Mr. Gladstone in Westminster Abbey there were two veteran Liberals from his own constituency; and after the service he gave them luncheon at the Reform Club. His guests were sorrowful and sad and still under the spell of the scene in the Abbey, and they never quite forgave Labouchere for torturing them in that hour by belittling gossip about the great leader just laid in the grave.

But though Labouchere lacked much that the English value, his own positive qualities were impressive. He had a personality of much charm, fine manners and the desire to be agreeable to all. His mind was powerful and quick in action, he possessed wide general knowledge and was precisely informed about many things. His speeches had the qualities of his writing: unfailing lucidity, disregard of some common conventions and a confiding manner which persuaded his audience that he had special knowledge and that they would make a sad mistake if they failed to trust him. And they trusted him none the less because he joked and jested and mercilessly mocked at people they disliked—keeping up always, when in this vein, the quiet, bland, rather superior manner that he made so effective. I remember one meeting when there was a violent attack on the editor of the local Conservative paper. Labouchere pretended sympathy with him. "The poor man is doing his best," he said. "I am really sorry for him; indeed I am willing, as it is rather in my line, to give him some help and to show him how this sort of thing should be done." He addressed an open-air meeting from a wagonette in which he had a bodyguard of deacons, society stewards and Sunday-school superintendents. A Conservative complained that Liberals were enemies of sport, particularly racing. "You are mistaken, my friend," replied Labouchere, and he went on to speak of a recent visit to Epsom. "It's not you I'm complaining about: it's your friends—*look at them!*" Labouchere surveyed their austere visages and again told the heckler he was mistaken. "You may take it from me that there isn't a man among them who doesn't have a bit on his fancy."

Had he still been in public life when the suffragettes began their campaign of violence they would have made a dead set against him; for he was one of the stiffest opponents of votes for women. In Northampton he kept them at a distance as long as he could, but at last a deputation of two ladies found him in at his hotel and were shown to his sitting-room. Labouchere received them with grave courtesy. Each in turn stated the reason why in their view they should have the vote. Silence followed for a minute or so. Labouchere, who had listened with the closest attention, and appeared to be carefully considering their appeal, then leaned forward and murmured: "Pretty dears!"

At one election he was told that the cabdrivers would vote solidly for him. "Yes," he replied, "they do seem to like me—I don't know why. It isn't that I use cabs a great deal. In the morning at ten o'clock I ring the bell, and when the waiter comes I say, 'George, will you please call a cab?' A few minutes later I find it waiting outside the hotel. I say to the driver, 'Will you please take me to my committee room?' I get into the cab and a few seconds later get out, for the committee room, as you know, is only a few yards along the same street; and then I always give the driver half-a-sovereign. The poor man must live. It is interesting to know that they like me."

For five-and-twenty years he played a conspicuous part in the House of Commons: distinctly a "character", one of the few private members that strangers asked to have pointed out to them. He was the last of the independent Radicals, for the party machine is a leveller, and even while he was in the House it was only one or two resolute and adroit veterans in the Liberal party who went their own way with or without the blessing of the Whips.

He had at last found a career which fully engaged his interests, and being one of the cleverest men at Westminster, he could reasonably expect the seat on the Treasury Bench which is the reward of well-doing in the House of Commons. It was Queen Victoria who kept the prize from him. He had been a persistent opponent of Parliamentary grants to members of the Royal Family and he thought this was the reason of her hostility. It was not; at any rate, the Queen did not say it was. Her objection to him was that he was editor and "chief writer" of *Truth*. The only political reward that came to him was the Privy Councillorship after he had retired from Parliament.

The great disappointment of Labouchere's political career was the 1886 crises on Irish Home Rule which drove Joseph Chamberlain out of the Liberal Party. He had pinned his faith to Chamberlain as the Radical leader and strove his utmost to keep him in the Liberal fold. From the hour trouble began till the schism was complete, he plied Chamberlain with argument, cajolery, blandishments, promises and, towards the end, with veiled threats. It was in vain. Chamberlain broke away, pursued by the bitter reproaches which for years Labouchere incessantly cast at him. The long correspondence with Chamberlain in 1885-6 which is given in Mr. Algar Thorold's biography of Labouchere reveals astuteness and skill in the arts of intrigue. Chamberlain was told that if he remained faithful he was the inevitable successor of Gladstone; meantime let him be patient and take the long view. In public no one insisted more than Labouchere on the necessity of Home Rule—in these letters it was "but a pawn in the game". In public no one more regularly sounded the praises of Gladstone—here he was an old man afflicted with the "almost insane desire" for office. A few months later: "If the G.O.M. loses his Bill it will be from not having been able to be clear for five minutes in his seventy-five years." In the counties Jesse Collings's "three acres and a cow" had worked wonders. On urban cows, wrote Labouchere, "Mr. Gladstone would be very much in your hands, for to get into power I really believe that he would not only give up Ireland but Mrs. Gladstone and Herbert."

Labouchere found no other leader who filled Chamberlain's place, and there were long years during which he and his party were ploughing the sands. But he had his moments, and enjoyed the reputation he had acquired in the country and the genuine regard in which he was held at Westminster. The House always filled to hear his speeches; the Smoking Room was never livelier than when he was pouring out gossip and anecdote and reminiscence. From this vivid life he retired without warning at the end of 1905 and left the country. The rest of his days—he died in 1912—were spent quietly at Florence, where, nearly half-a-century before, he had leisurely pursued his inquiries as to the whereabouts of Parana. On the day before his death Mr. Thorold (nephew as well as biographer) was sitting by his bedside. A spirit lamp which was burning was accidentally overturned. Labouchere opened his eyes, murmured, "Flames?—not yet I think," laughed and went to sleep.

MAX BEERBOHM

GERARD HOPKINS

"I WAS A MODEST, GOOD-HUMOURED BOY", WROTE SIR MAX BEERBOHM IN one of his rare passages of autobiography: "it is Oxford that has made me insufferable." This attitude to his University of regretful suspicion is expressed more than once in the body of his writing. As far back as 1895, in the essay on "Dandies and Dandies", we find the following premonitory whisper: "Any parent intending his son to be a dandy will do well to send him first into the Army, there to learn humility as did his Archtype Apollo in the House of Admetus. A sojourn at one of the Public Schools is also to be commended. The University it were well to avoid." Twenty years did nothing, it seems, to soften the felt need for stricture, nor is the reason difficult to understand. Those early portraits of himself which Sir Max loved to scatter through the first collections of caricatures show him ever as the unspoiled boy. The gaze of the large, round, long-lashed eyes is innocent; the mischief in the face is young. He presents himself as the precocious member of the Sixth, never as the jaded undergraduate. At the worst he could be taken for the freshest of freshmen, his disenchantment all before him. At school a man finds his feet. At Oxford or at Cambridge he too often loses his balance, and balance is, of all things, what Sir Max through his literary life has most consistently valued. It is no accident that his appreciation of dandies should have appeared prominently in his first published volume. The dandy is an artist working in a limited field. In Max (no lover, however grateful to Majesty for a deserved honour, can long use, unselfconsciously, the title) love of artistry has always been dominant, and if his field has never ceased to be limited, that is because he has been ever scrupulous to remain within the bounds of what he knew, of what he could control. At first it was worse. In the first phase, as so often with young men of brilliance, the mere fun of their use and marshalling was apt to kick up its heels in exuberant fantasy. He could play, in that dawn of his career, with such phrases as "the inilluminate parchment",—"the scud-a-run of quivering homuncules over the vert on horses"—with words like "comprimend" and "couth", nor has he ever lost wholly the taste for placing, with meticulous delight, the unexpected vocable. "The Works" were mannered: they have been outgrown, but they have never been repudiated. The old Max—if such an adjective be tolerable—has in no instance (unlike those "doubles" of his well-known series of cartoons) snubbed or rejected the young. Looking back now at that first volume we can see that the preciosity was no mere ornament of its period, that Max's earliest book was never wholly Yellow. Something of the times he had caught (as what beginner of genius will not?), but the articulated skeleton of the wit is his own. In later years the tightness has grown less or, perhaps, the ease of achievement greater. The constriction has vanished, but not the trimness. The clothes on the mature writer sit with a looser elegance, but the cut is the same, the choice of cloth and colour. And Max has always chosen, picking daintily what he could use, refusing contact with what would use him. No greater lover of the proportioned style is to be found in the centuries of our literature—not even in the eighteenth. Something in his work, as in his distant heredity, is faintly un-English. His least line is balanced and deliberate. He long ago realized that the too constant glare betrays the artificer. Like his own Brummell he has "turned full and square towards his art, and looked life straight in the face out of the corners of his eyes". Not that the oblique glance is ever blunderingly paraded. Part of his endless power to charm comes from the strict claim which he makes on his readers' attention. We need to keep wide awake as we follow him. The killing phrase, the clinching word, lies often coyly hidden, as when he says, of 1880—"to give an accurate and exhaustive account of that period would need a far less brillant pen than mine", or, when commenting on Madame Bernhardt's playing of Shakespeare, he remarked—"the only compliment one can conscientiously pay her is that her Hamlet was, from first to last, *très grande dame*". It is never safe to read Max lazily.

2

But there have been other careful users of language. One of the remarkable things about Max has been the way in which he has carried over his sense of form into his life. There have been no unsightly passages in his career, as in that of most working artists, of intrigue, bitterness and savage competition. Happy is the writer without a history. Many great authors have died leaving instructions that no biography was to be attempted, but one cannot help feeling that, for all the gesture, the knowledge of two stout volumes of "Life and Letters" would do much to lay their uneasy ghosts. Max, honest in this as in all else, has solved the problem by leaving his prospective executors nothing to record. Essayist, story-teller, draughtsman, dramatic critic and parodist—all of him that need be known is ranged for posterity between covers. All else is for himself alone. As long ago as 1895 he saw clearly what should be his chosen path. At the end of that first volume he wrote: "Already I feel myself to be a trifle outmoded. I belong to the Beardsley period. Younger men with months of activity before them, with fresher schemes and notions, with newer enthusiasms, have pressed forward since then. *Cedo junioribus*. Indeed, I stand aside with no regret. For to be outmoded is to be a classic if one has written well. I have acceded to the hierarchy of good scribes and rather like my niche." But how many men like at forty what they thought they would like at twenty? Admirably consistent in all but the actual date of retirement, Max has been as good as his juvenile word. He has never fought to keep his head above the contemporary waves—and, consequently, he has never been in danger of sinking. Somewhere about 1912 he retreated to Italy. Tidings, an occasional volume, a collection of caricatures, came now and again to gladden us. But the boat had slipped into the backwater. Rightly its pilot felt himself to be of the "Beerbohm period", and, because of his steadfast refusal to join the ever-quickening race of reputations, the Beerbohm period has remained for us a glory and a delight. In thinking of Max, returned, even now, when politics have closed the Riviera to him and forced him into the refinements of the Home Counties, we can understand with rather more sympathy Congreve's intention when he shocked Voltaire by asking to be regarded not as an author but as an "English gentleman".

And so, to return to the earlier argument, Oxford delayed if it did not destroy that fine sense of limitation which is so essential to the artist. The joy of Oxford for the emancipated schoolboy comes from the consciousness it breeds in him of a glorious and new indiscipline. As an adolescent the young Max doubtless rejoiced in the freedom: as an artist he probably deplored it. It was to John Lane and Vigo Street rather than to Pater (whose moustache was one of the first severe shocks of his life) and the High, that he owed the development of his gifts. It was London that made him, as he might, in his first manner, most carefully have written, so much more than sufferable. Yet Oxford had bred in him a love which could not but be a torment, because, until 1911, it remained indigested and unadjusted. For an artist of Max's sensitiveness a great passion must be an agony as well as a danger. Oxford clearly must be dealt with, but how? Clearly no undergraduatish novel, all bump-suppers and epigrams, tobacconists' daughters and college portraiture, could do the trick. Max's muse, even in rompers, was mature, and Oxford as a subject for art presents to the adult mind insuperable difficulties. It is the measure of Max's real importance that he solved them, and made from the unsuitable material of adolescent freedom a work of art that stands alone in its field. "Zuleika Dobson" is a perfect work. To add that it is the best book ever written about Oxford is pathetic. The magic of the place is caught in it and preserved, but it is also, as is but just in art, faintly distorted. The streets, the quadrangles, the colleges frequented by Zuleika and her Duke are moulded into a pattern of artifice which wholly satisfies. We can never be sufficiently grateful that Max waited until he was in his thirties before tackling the Oxford problem. Rightly he has sacrificed realism to reality. Here is no "reportage", here no easy satire, but considered art. Who but Max would have thought to mock at Ouida in his hero, and yet, while keeping the mockery, have succeeded in making him profoundly moving in a way that Ouida must have envied as something entirely beyond her compass? Her aristocrat might have died for love full panoplied in all his Garter robes, but he would have been ridiculous. Dorset, striding to the river beneath the ominous thundercloud, in all his bravery of velvet, tasselled mantle, osprey plume and silk, may be a figure of fantasy but he is never a figure of fun, though fun, watchful lest a threat of emotion break the mould of the tale, is allowed to frolic round his advancing pomp.

". . . It was with a measured tread, as yesterday with Zuleika, that he entered the avenue of Elms. The throng streamed past from behind him, parting wide, and marvelling as it streamed. Under the pall of this evil evening his splendour was the more inspiring. . . . And, just as yesterday no man had questioned his right to be with Zuleika, so today there was none to deem him caparisoned too much. All the men felt at a glance that he, coming to meet his death thus, did no more than the right homage to Zuleika—aye, and that he made them all partakers in his own glory, casting his great mantle over all commorients. Reverence forbade them to do more than glance. But the women with them were impelled by wonder to stare hard, uttering sharp little cries that mingled with the cawing of the rooks overhead. . .

". . . To-day by scores of women it was calculated not only that the velvet of the Duke's mantle could not have cost less than four guineas a yard, but also that there must have been quite twenty-five yards of it . . ."

There is more in that than mere bravura with a flick of humour in the tail. And who but Max would have enlisted for chorus to his action those stone Emperors who preside over the dignities of the Sheldonian? That single touch of genius makes Zuleika the one true Oxford novel, not merely the best novel about Oxford.

". . . A moment later a certain old don emerged from Blackwell's where he had been buying books. Looking across the road, he saw, to his amazement, great beads of perspiration glistening on the brows of those Emperors. . . .

". . . Yes, as the landau rolled by, sweat started from the brows of the Emperors. They, at least, foresaw the peril that was overhanging Oxford, and they gave such warning as they could. Let that be remembered to their credit. Let that incline us to think more kindly of them. In their lives, we know, they were infamous, some of them—'nihil non commiserunt stupri, saevitiae, impietatis'. But are they too little punished after all? Here, in Oxford, exposed eternally and inexorably to heat and frost, to the four winds that lash them and the rains that wear them away, they are expiating in effigy the abominations of their pride and cruelty and lust. Who were lechers, they are without bodies; who were tyrants, they are crowned never but with crowns of snow; who made themselves even with the gods, they are by American visitors frequently mistaken for the Twelve Apostles. It is but a little way down the road that the two Bishops perished for their faith, and even now we do never pass the spot without a tear for them. Yet how quickly they died in the flames! To these Emperors for whom none weeps, time will give no surcease. Surely, it is a sign of some grace in them that they rejoiced not, this bright afternoon, in the evil that was to befall the city of their penance."

And who, finally, but Max, could succeed by gentle mockery in making eloquent the love which Oxford inspires, but which the lyrical or impassioned mood paints less happily?

". . . The scent of these meadows' moisture is the scent of Oxford. Even in hottest noon, one feels that the sun has not dried *them*. . . . Always there is moisture drifting across them, drifting into the Colleges. It, one suspects, must have had much to do with the evocation of what is called the Oxford spirit—that gentlest spirit, so lingering and searching, so dear to them that as youths were brought into ken of it, so exasperating to them who were not. Yes, certainly, it is this mild, miasmal air, not less than the grey beauty and gravity of the buildings, that has helped Oxford to produce, and foster eternally, her peculiar race of artist-scholars, scholar-artists. . . . Oxford, that lotus-land, saps the will-power, the power of action. But, in doing so, it clarifies the mind, makes larger the vision, gives, above all, that playful and caressing suavity of manner which comes of a conviction that nothing matters except ideas, and that not even ideas are worth dying for, inasmuch as the ghosts of them slain seem worthy of yet more piously elaborate homage than can be given to them in their hey-day. If the Colleges could be transferred to the dry and bracing top of some hill, doubtless they would be more evidently useful to the nation. But let us be glad that there is no engineer or enchanter to compass the task. *Egomet*, I would liefer have the rest of England subside into the sea than have Oxford set on a salubrious level. For there is nothing in England to be matched with what lurks in the vapours of these meadows, and in the shadows of these spires—that mysterious, inebulable spirit, spirit of Oxford. Oxford! The very sight of the word printed, or sound of it spoken, is fraught for me with the most actual magic. . . ."

An accident of history has made "Zuleika Dobson" a peculiarly moving, an almost symbolic book. It tells, as a fantasy, how all the undergraduates of Oxford (except one) killed themselves for a love that could not be returned. Three years after its publication, the Colleges and streets were emptied by the harsh destinies of war. In a mood (at first) of bright romance, a generation accepted willingly the sacrifice of life, just as when Zuleika smiled, promising everything but with nothing to give, a thousand youths plunged into the Isis calling aloud her name. But to associate with the book this accident of topicality is not to minimize it as a great art—for it is one of the characteristics of great art than it shows itself apt to occasions and to incidents other than those which presided at its birth; that what was written and conceived in one mood is tested and found valid by conditions that were never present to its author's mind. "Zuleika" is a book to be read once, at least, in every year. New things emerge from it—not always comforting. Prolonged squeezing has, in my own case, produced a faint bitterness of flavour which certainly, when the tale was new, scarce one reader can have found or suspected. But, too, the old things gain on long acquaintance. In this work of his maturity Max has put the finished excellences of his style, and has made of them the framework to support a deeply felt and moving content. The gaiety is there, and it has an added sureness; the fancy, which never deteriorates into that most hideous of modernities—"whimsey"; the verbal wit, the lovely dancing style, the sly dig which restores balance just as emotion seems dangerously high between its banks. What finer instance of this last quality than the account of Zuleika's last invasion of the Duke's privacy? He has, you will remember, seen finally the fatal, the unquestionable, extent of her heartlessness. He has, for the last time, fallen out of love with her. The pearls have made their final change of colour, and he has realized how foolish it would be to die for a wanton. But hard on his resolve to sacrifice her worthlessness rather than his own life comes the word of Fate in that inimitable telegram from Tankerton (pronounced Tacton):

> *"Deeply regret inform your Grace last night two black owls came and perched on battlements remained there through night hooting at dawn flew away none knows whither awaiting instructions.*
>
> "JELLINGS."

And then he resigns himself to his destiny, knowing that he must make the sacrifice with an empty heart. The scene develops. Enchanted, defeated, by the knowledge that Dorset no longer loves her and is therefore lovable, Zuleika goes to his rooms, flings herself at his feet, is spurned —and then:

> "He asked—'To what am I indebted for this visit?'
>
> "'Ah, say that again!' she murmured; 'your voice is music.'
>
> "He repeated the question.
>
> "'Music!' she said dreamily; and, such is the force of habit that, 'I don't,' she added, 'know anything about music really. But I know what I like.'"

Again and again in the book we are brought back thus from the dangers of romantic emotion. There is genuine feeling behind the artifice, but it has been drilled to keep within bounds, is well-bred and formal, so that always we are conscious of it filling, though never escaping from, the chosen limits. To vary the metaphor, it is like air distending but never bursting the thin envelope of a balloon.

3

This prominence of feeling, even though it may be feeling in a dress-suit, is something new in English wit. The reader, entranced by Max's verbal nimbleness, is surprised at times to find what emotional hints the books contain. Feeling here never riots in romantic luxuriance, it is kept in due subordination to the style, but it is often there—lyrical at its best, at its rare worst leaning, as in "William and Mary", in "The Golden Druggett", and in "Something Defeasible", to a gentle sentimentality which fails quite to come off as it did, on the other hand, in the early and altogether charming, because so gaily artificial. "Happy Hypocrite". At both extremes it is an emotion of affection, and it is remarkable with what success Max has created from affection a standard of critical mockery. Most of our best English wit has found its inspiration in anger, some of it, as Sterne's, in sheer sentimentality. A great deal of it is satiric in intention, savage in Swift and Wycherley, malicious in Pope, petulant in Peacock. Cut adrift from the sources of anger, it tends, as in Wilde, to rest wholly upon the achievement of surface brilliance glittering about a central emptiness, though "The Importance of Being Earnest" exists to show triumphantly to what heights of ridiculous splendour mere emptiness can climb. It is rare for affection to find its best and most constant expression in mockery. It is, perhaps, safe to say that Max is our sole master in this mood. He laughs because he loves: when he ceases to love he can no longer laugh with conviction. "I suppose," said poor Maltby, not the least pathetic of all the Seven Men, "one can't really understand what one doesn't love, and one can't make good fun without real understanding." It is a lesson that his creator took early to his literary heart, and it has served him well. Max has loved many things and many persons—William the Fourth, Beau Brummell, the 1880's, the street names of London, even the Swiss President—and mainly for that reason he has seen where all of them are ridiculous. But it is in caricature and parody that the rule has borne its most abundant fruit. The pictures of his contemporaries which Max has produced at intervals during his life, the brilliant criticisms in pastiche which form "A Christmas Garland", are happiest when they are inspired by liking. It may be that the reason why his caricatures have been less frequent during recent years is not that Max in Italy knew less of the figures of modern England than that he found less and less to love in the current scene. Satire is never his main intention. He preaches no lesson, "shows up" no abuses. His genius needs congenial food, and the diet of English life has, he finds, since 1912, become indigestible. Parody is a tempting trick, and too many parodists have been moved by impatience or dislike. Their originals may often be recognizable, but too seldom are they truly seen. Love of the work parodied alone opens the door to real understanding, and it is because he has loved most of the "buds" in the "Garland" that Max can parody to his heart's—and to our—content. As in his caricatures, he is never satisfied with mere exaggeration. Rather, as an artist, should he always seeks the true stylistic equivalent into which he may transmute the raw material on which he has set to work. He never stops short at aping an author's surface mannerism (or never at his best). For the time being he adopts the other's mind, setting its point of view just a shade out of the true. While we can say that so-and-so would never have written *that*, we know at the same time that, had *that* been written at all, it could never have been written by any other person. The old, half-mocking comment on Brummell stands up to the test of practice, and Max the parodist gets his effects by looking life (or literature) straight in the face out of the corners of his eyes. With unobtrusive skill he brings it about that the twist in his vision becomes also a twist in the object, though never so obviously as to spoil our pleasure in the faithfulness of the recreation. He is never satisfied merely to make good fun: it is always fair comment as well that he seeks; the summing up, in terms of pastiche, of a considered judgment. We are affected by the best of these mimicked Great much in the same way as we should be by their true voices. It is only that something odd has happened to the echo.

". . . It occurred to him as befitting Eva's remoteness, which was part of Eva's magnificence, that her voice emerged somewhat muffled by the bedclothes. She was ever, indeed, the most telephonic of her sex. In talking to Eva you always had, as it were, your lips to the receiver. If you didn't try to meet her fine eyes, it was that you simply couldn't hope to: there were too many dark, too many buzzing and bewildering and all frankly not negotiable leagues in between. Snatches of other voices seemed often to intertrude themselves in the parley; and your loyal effort not to overhear these was complicated by your fear of missing what Eva might be twittering. 'Oh, you certainly haven't, my dear, the trick of propinquity!' was a thrust she had once parried by saying that, in that case, *he* hadn't—to which his unspoken rejoinder that she had caught her tone from the peevish young woman at the Central seemed to him (if not perhaps in the last, certainly in the last but one, analysis) to lack finality. With Eva, he had found, it was always safest to 'ring off'. It was with a certain sense of his rashness in the matter, therefore, that he now, with an air of feverishly 'holding the line', said, 'Oh, as to that!'

"Had *she*, he presently asked himself, 'rung off'? It was characteristic of our friend—was, indeed, 'him all over'—that his fear of what she was going to say was as nothing to his fear of what she might be going to leave unsaid. He had, in his converse with her, been never so conscious as now of the intervening leagues; they had never so insistently beaten the drum of his ear; and he caught himself in the act of lawfully computing, with a certain statistical passion, the distance between Rome and Boston. He has never been able to decide which of these points he was psychically the nearer to when Eva, replying—'Well, one does, anyhow, leave a margin for the pretext, you know!' made him, for the first time in his life, wonder whether she were not more magnificent than even he had given credit for being. Perhaps it was to test this theory, or perhaps merely to gain time, that he now raised himself to his knees and, leaning with outstretched arm towards the foot of the bed, made as though to touch the stocking which Santa Claus had, overnight, left dangling there. His posture, as he stared obliquely at Eva, with a sort of beaming defiance, recalled to him something seen in an 'illustration'. This reminiscence, however—if such it was, save in the scarred, the poor dear old woebegone and so very beguilingly *not* refractive mirror of the moment—took a peculiar twist from Eva's behaviour. . . ."

The passage is worth quoting at length, for as parody it is perfection. The very title of the tale "The Mote in the Middle Distance" is worth many pages of literary appraisal. That the true rhythm and idiom of the "Master" have been caught is of minor importance (it has been done before): the stressing of the peculiarly Jamesian trick of taking a metaphor (here telephonic) and elaborating it in a dozen repeated touches is less common, but even that does not constitute the main part of the triumph, nor even does the choice of children (reminiscent of so many of the stories) as protagonists, nor the sly interjection about Rome and Boston which just sufficiently breaks the pattern but not to the extent that we feel the illusion spoiled. No, what makes this the best of all parodies of Henry James (with the possible exception of Max's second essay in the genre, entitled "The Guerdon") is that it heightens our appreciation not only of the parodist but of the great novelist whose leg he is engaged in pulling. Beneath the surface of the so elaborately expressed "meaning" there lurks for us the uncomfortable suspicion that there is a depth of meaning not expressed at all. We are teased intellectually in precisely the same way that we are sometimes teased by the genuine article, by passages, say, in "The Golden Bowl", in "What Maisie Knew", in "The Ambassadors". We are conscious not so much of reading Max but of reading James—with a difference. The Beerbohm and the Jacobean obliquity have combined into a harlequin criss-cross of purposes which strengthens rather than diminishes our taste (if we have it at all) for the original. In these pastiches our author never forces his effects upon us, never points and laughs. He produces the very effect of his momentary butt, stands demurely aside, and leaves to the imitation complete freedom to establish its critical task. Thus, though how differently, we come to a closer knowledge of, say, Meredith in the following piece of dialogue from "Euphemia Clashthought".

". . . Her nose was virginal, with hints of the Iron Duke at most angles. Square chin, cleft centrally, gave her throat the look of a tower with gun protrudent at top. She was dressed for church evidently, but seemed no slave to time. Her bonnet was pushed well back from her head, and she was fingering the ribbons. One saw she was a woman. She inspired deference.

" 'Forefinger for Shepherd's Crook' was what Mrs. Cryptic Sparkler had said of Sir Rebus. It shall stand at that.

" 'You have Prayer Book?' he queried. She nodded, Juno catches the connubial trick.

" 'Hymns?'

" 'Ancient and Modern.'

" 'I may share with you?'

" 'I know by heart. Parrots sing.'

" 'Philomel carols,' he bent to her.

" 'Complaints spoil a festival.'

"He waved his hand to the door. 'Lady, your father has started.'

" 'He knows the adage. Copy-books instil it.'

" 'Inexorable truth in it.'

" 'We may dodge the scythe.'

" 'To be choked with the sands?'

"She flashed a smile. 'I would not,' he said, 'that my Euphemia were late for the Absolution.'

"She cast eyes to the carpet. He caught them at the rebound.

" 'It snows,' she said, swimming to the window.

" 'A flake, no more. The season claims it.'

" 'I have thin boots.'

" 'Another pair?'

" 'My maid buttons. She is at church.'

" 'My fingers?'

" 'Ten on each.'

" 'Five,' he corrected.

" 'Buttons.'

" 'I beg your pardon.'

"She saw opportunity. She swam to the bell-rope and grasped it for a tinkle. The action spread feminine curves to her lover's eyes. He was a man.

"Obsequiousness loomed in the doorway. Its mistress flashed an order for port

—two glasses. Sir Rebus sprang a pair of eyebrows on her. Suspicion slid down the banisters of his mind, trailing a blue ribbon. Inebriates were one of his hobbies. For an instant she was sunset.

" 'Medicinal,' she murmured.

" 'Forgive me, Madam. A glass certainly, 'Twill warm us for worshipping.' . . ."

Nothing overdone. Nothing merely facetious. The mastery is complete. The effect is Meredith's. There is the true baroque luxuriance, the terrific adornment of what, one suspects, may turn out to be no more than a country cottage or suburban villa. Only admiration could make such laughter. Indeed, we can go right through "A Christmas Garland" constructing for ourselves a sure hierarchy of the author's literary preferences. Where he loves an author his joking is superbly brilliant. Impatience or dislike limits his power. His "rendering" of Kipling, of Conrad, or Hardy, is clever enough, but it is no more. He never achieves with them the critical compression, never shows *all* of them as he does with James, with Meredith, with George Moore, with Chesterton. Small wonder that James himself said, after reading the "Mote", that he would not dare to write a line for six months!

4

It is no unusual thing for a worker in one medium to try his hand at manipulating another. Often, as Browning noted, there is something special, something dedicate, about the unwonted activity. When, according to him, Rafael made a century of sonnets or Dante once prepared to paint an angel, it was for private and sentimental reasons of their own. Others there have been, Morris, for example, who moved easily across many fields of art, almost, though never quite, a master in each. One finds oneself awarding "marks". But never with Max. That he both draws and writes is matter of common knowledge. That there is nothing to choose between them is due to the fact that he has made of pen and pencil weapons for his purpose of equal temper. The same wit vitalizes all he touches. Nimbleness of line, sensitiveness of observation, dislike of crude exaggeration, scrupulous choice, are as evident in his caricatures as in his essays. It is no accident that the "legend" is, as a rule, part and parcel of his cartoons, nor does the fact diminish their graphic value. The point to be made when he draws a scene or a person invites the accompanying comment; the words are given stress and accent by the design. The picture demands the description; the verbal perfection conjures up the thing seen. Like every true artist he is at pains to create his own peculiar world, and we, the lucky ones, are asked to view it. Only when anger (as on the occasions of his rare political attempts) blurs the ironic vision is achievement less than perfect. His talent needs to be hatched by warmth: excessive heat cracks the egg.

In his first published volume he included a youthfully mannered and deliberately nostalgic history of the year 1880. It was the period immediately preceding that of his own maturity, and because he himself is representative of the epoch in which many of us were children, we feel for his world much the same emotion as he felt—or said he felt—for the hey-day of the Jersey Lily, of the Aesthetes, of the Gaiety stage-door. He has spent the last thirty years in delicately, humorously and truthfully annotating his contemporaries. He has dealt always with what he knows intimately and appreciates deeply. He may laugh at Enoch Soames, but he feels for him: he may point a wicked finger at people and places, at books and plays, but there is rarely in his mockery a hint of malice or a thought of priggishness. No pompous volumes of reminiscence, no exhaustive survey of documents, can ever do for the period lying between 1895 and 1930 what Max has done with his essays, parodies and inventions. An accurate and exhaustive account of it would, in very truth, need "a far less brilliant pen" than his. His art has caught the topical and left it permanent. His hansoms jingle in eternity. His cultivation of an *enfance terrible* has resulted in a deathless youth. By concentrating his attention on the seemingly little things he has become great, because there is never littleness in his view of them. From the days when he wrote of "Dandies" and of "The Pervasion of Rouge", and bowed himself elegantly from the stage the better to take three decades of encores, he has always known precisely what it is that he wants to do and has done it superbly. Indeed, he has made his grateful admirers feel that it is among the few things worth doing at all.

GEORGE BERNARD SHAW

HAROLD HOBSON

WHAT EMERSON ASSERTED, BERNARD SHAW HAS PROVED. BRUSHING ASIDE the timidity of Lord Chesterfield, who advised wise men to live as much within their wit as their income, Emerson declared boldly wit's omnipotence. It levels all distinctions, he said, and makes its own welcome. It annihilates all opposition; against it, "no dignity, no learning, no force of character can make any stand".

Managed by the supple wrist of Mr. Shaw it has proved a rapier that can pierce any defence, even the sullen resistance of the British public to everything that savours of coherent thought. It has enabled him to combine a reputation greater than was enjoyed by Shakespeare at any time during his career, or for a century after his death, with a popularity equal to that of Nat Gould or Edgar Wallace. To achieve either popularity or reputation separately is perhaps no great matter; for the one it is frequently sufficient to be unintelligent, for the other unintelligible. But to unite them both is a rarer thing; not often does the discovery of a coterie become the idol of a continent without loss of caste. To do that a man needs to have all his wits about him. When in that fully-armed condition, Mr. Shaw is surrounded by a very remarkable bodyguard indeed.

Mr. Shaw has written half a century of plays. At least, that is what he himself calls them, though some of the famous actors who have donned the motley on his behalf have a more finely accurate sense of classification. The principal role in "In Good King Charles's Golden Days" was created by Ernest Thesiger, who at the end of the first performance made a speech. In it he referred with singular felicity to the entertainment that had just taken place as "Mr. Shaw's fiftieth conversation piece".

In addition to these fifty conversation pieces, and the prefaces for which they are largely the excuse, Mr. Shaw has produced a mass of writing on an infinite variety of subjects in a vast variety of forms which would suffice as the life work of any normally industrious man. He has expounded the true meaning of Ibsen and the significance of Wagner; he has written five novels and some short stories; he has provided Intelligent Women with a Guide to Socialism; he has written the most stimulating, the most unfair, and the best dramatic criticism of his age; he has proved himself a pamphleteer of the first order; he has published essays in metaphysics; he even, soon after he arrived in London from Dublin at the age of 20, composed an advertisement for a patent medicine, for which he received £5. It might perhaps be said that this is what he has been doing throughout his long and illustrious life—writing advertisements for patent medicines for the body politic—but usually at higher rates of pay.

It is, however, the plays and their prefaces that form the central fortress of Mr. Shaw's achievement: or rather, the cutting edge of his sword, for the language of attack is always more congenial than that of defence to his alert and thrusting personality. These plays fall into four main groups. There are those like "Major Barbara", "Mrs. Warren's Profession", "The Doctor's Dilemma", "Getting Married", "Heartbreak House", and "Widowers' Houses", in which he discusses problems of social organization. In a second, and early group—"Arms and the Man", "The Devil's Disciple", and "You Never Can Tell"—he reveals his purely personal bias against romantic conventions by writing of soldiers who think chocolate to be more important than firearms, and of young people who make love in terms of chemical formulae; in a third group—"St. Joan", "The Apple Cart", "On the Rocks", "In Good King Charles's Golden Days" and "Too True to be Good"—he discusses aspects of that question of leadership and government with which he has become increasingly preoccupied as the years have gone by. Finally, in "Man and Superman" and "Back to Methuselah" he advances a metaphysical philosophy by which men can, in a double sense, achieve salvation in time—that is, within the confines of material existence, and before the Life Force disgustedly sweeps them into oblivion. Mr. Shaw has also written one or two plays—like "Candida" and "Pygmalion" —which cannot easily be simplified into terms of abstract discussion. By some, these—especially "Candida"—are thought to be his best work.

Whatever opinion may be upon that point, the world success of Mr. Shaw as a dramatist has been very great. In 1894 his "Arms and the Man" was produced at the Avenue (now the Playhouse) Theatre, to the accompaniment of much applause. Between the 21st of April and the 7th of July, when it was withdrawn, it drew to the box-office the sum of £1777 5*s*. 6*d*., an average of £23 2*s*. 5*d*. a performance. This made no one's fortune, but it registered a great advance upon any of Mr. Shaw's previous financial achievements, the very sea-mark of his utmost sail being hitherto the five pounds he had been paid for his patent medicine advertisement. Since then the popularity of Shaw as a dramatist has steadily increased, till his plays are now more widely produced than anyone's but Shakespeare's. He is one of the biggest draws in New York. He is the mainstay of theatre festivals. He has had premières in as unlikely a place as Warsaw. He is a name to conjure with in Germany. He is always being played, somewhere or other, in the provinces. The result is, as he himself says, that he "passes for a millionaire". For the last forty-five years he has known no anxiety about money, except such anxieties as arise from possessing it. All this is highly satisfactory to Mr. Shaw, to Mr. Shaw's bank manager, and even to the general public, whom it suggests to be capable of responding in an appreciative fashion to the unconventionalities of genius.

2

It has been suggested that Mr. Shaw's plays can, in the majority of cases, be reduced to some formula of abstract discussion. With reasonable qualifications, this is true. What one most clearly recalls of most of Shaw's plays is the ideas to which they give expression, not the characters of the people exhibiting those ideas, still less the action in which those ideas crystallize, or, more often, fail to crystallize. After reading "Major Barbara", let us say, or even after seeing it upon the stage, few people retain a vivid impression of Cusins, Undershaft, Lady Britomart, and the rest of the persons of the drama. One cannot isolate and define them in the memory by anything comparable with the sharpness of impact of, for example, the subservience of Mr. Collins, the hypocrisy of Mr. Pecksniff, the dignity of the Bedesman, the catch phrases of Sherlock Holmes, the gloom of Mrs. Gummidge, the luxuriance of sorrow of Richard II, or the optimism of Mark Tapley. These characters of Scott and Dickens and Shakespeare and even of Conan Doyle have life of their own. They are not the puppets of their plots. They could step out of the covers of the particular books in which they appear and be perfectly at home in another story, and in other surroundings. Mark Tapley would fall to comforting Mrs. Gummidge, with a will. Into his tapestry of misery Richard would wholeheartedly weave the figure of Mrs. Gummidge's "old 'un". Mr. Collins would find the boot polish of Sir Arthur Wardour as palatable upon the tongue as that of Lady Catherine. The same transposition cannot be effected with the characters of Mr. Shaw. Cusins, Undershaft and their companions have no life or personality apart from their intellectual life: and this in turn depends upon the particular nexus of ideas in which they are caught up. The strength of Mr. Shaw is not to be found in characterization. It is not into this that he puts the full force of his arm. One would imagine that with people, with the little idiosyncrasies of individuality, he is somewhat bored.

Here, the resources of language begin to fail. Many, probably most, of Mr. Shaw's characters, regarded as beings of flesh and blood rather than as luminous intelligences operating at full blast, are unsatisfactory. They do not arouse Mr. Shaw's interest. But to say that he does not put his heart into them is meaningless. Mr. Shaw does not put his heart into anything. He has little use for that very imperfect organ. He prefers to use his brain. Yet to say that he does not put his brain into these people would be untrue: for that is precisely what he does. One of his troubles as a dramatist is that he is constantly putting his brain into his characters, and letting it get them involved in interminable and brilliant discussions about subjects that are of vast interest to Mr. Shaw as citizen, philosopher, and mystic, but which have only the most tenuous relation to the dramatic situation with which they are supposed to be concerned.

On one account at least Mr. Shaw would find heaven a great improvement upon earth, for questions of marriage and giving in marriage fill him with acutest boredom. His is an unromantic soul. He once told a girl about a friend of his who fell in love with a young woman wealthier than himself. She refused to marry him because of his poverty. And did he die? inquired the girl eagerly. Yes, replied Shaw: fifty years later. It is not surprising therefore that Shaw is not much interested in whether the Greek professor Cusins marries the Salvationist Barbara or not. The note of passion is not one that he is concerned to strike—at any rate, not in connection with physical love. He will transport no audience with visions of a Romeo and Juliet. He will work them into no ecstasy or agony, except in "Candida" or "Pygmalion", over any merely personal relationships. But when he comes to discuss any social or political or religious problem, then his brain whips itself into a white- hot fury, of intellectual activity. When he comes to the real crux of "Major Barbara"—which, as often happens with Mr. Shaw, is to be found in the preface rather than in the play—when he falls to discussing the paramount duty of avoiding poverty, then indeed the giant arises in his strength and expends the full power of his tremendous arm. "Money," says Shaw, "is the most important thing in the world. It represents health, strength, honour, generosity, and beauty as undeniably as the want of it represents illness, weakness, disgrace, meanness, and ugliness. . . . The crying need of the nations is not for better morals, cheaper bread, temperance, liberty, culture, redemption of fallen sisters and erring brothers, nor the grace, love and fellowship of the Trinity, but simply for enough money. And the evil to be attacked is not sin, suffering, greed, priesthood, kingcraft, demagogy, monopoly, ignorance, drink, war, pestilence nor any other of the scapegoats which reformers sacrifice, but simply poverty." That is the sort of thing which really interests Shaw.

In far the greater part of Shaw's work this weakness of characterization when competing with the superior attraction of social, political, and religious ideas is abundantly apparent. Shaw either disdains or is unable to invent freely those concrete incidents which epitomize men's characters. When he does invent them, he gives the impression of despising them by throwing them into the past, and making them the basis of reminiscent conversation instead of present action, as in his treatment of the incident in which St. John Hotchkiss, in "Getting Married", refuses to lead his regiment to the charge because the success of the operation would mean the promotion of his superior officer, a man who eats rice pudding with a spoon.

In spite of his deficiency in the invention of character-revealing incident, no dramatist is more skilful than Mr. Shaw in keeping the stage in a constant flow of movement, even if this movement is dramatically pointless and realistically absurd. In the first act of "In Good King Charles's Golden Days", set in the austere precincts of Trinity, in the study of Sir Isaac Newton, Charles, George Fox, and a bevy of ladies change their seats with a persistent regularity worthy of a game of General Post, with no other purpose or excuse than to break up the long stretch of essentially undramatic dialogue. In the second act the Duke of York and Sir Isaac engage in an all-in wrestling match for precisely the same reason. So do King Magnus and Orinthia in the Interlude in "The Apple Cart". When a conversation has gone on long enough in Mr. Shaw's opinion, he will introduce a burglar, as in "Heartbreak House", or an aviator, as in "Misalliance", or send someone into a trance, as in "Getting Married", or bring on a lady of mystical tendencies, as in "On the Rocks", or in some other way produce a violent change in the atmosphere of his play.

These things, however, are concessions to the groundlings. They do not really engage Mr. Shaw's interest. He takes no pleasure in fitting them into the pattern of a plot. He would be an ingenious soul who could say, off-hand, what part the scuffle of Orinthia and King Magnus plays or who could estimate the effect upon the development of the plot of the fight between Newton and the Duke of York. The fact is that in "In Good King Charles's Golden Days" there is no plot at all. No story of any kind whatever is unfolded. There is an abundance of argument: as to the true nature of fidelity, the essence of good government, the nature of the universe, the number of times that the sun has stood still: but no story. The Greeks may have thought that the story was the main part of a play: but Mr. Shaw disagrees. There is practically no plot whatever in "Too True To Be Good", or in "Getting Married", or in "Misalliance", or in "Heartbreak House". Occasionally he gives his audience a straightforward story, as in "The Apple Cart", where the definite dramatic question is posed whether King Magnus shall or shall not accept the ultimatum presented to him by his rebellious and restive Cabinet. But even here the central point of the play is not the King's personal problem, but the discussions as to the nature of kingship and of democracy.

The conclusion that emerged from consideration of Shaw's treatment of characterization is confirmed. His concern is with social, political, and religious ideas: and it is not his method to exhibit these either through development of character or through development of plot.

3

Yet there is one character upon whom Mr. Shaw has lavished all his art: one story which he has told with all the skill at his disposal. But this character does not appear in any of his plays: or, alternatively, it appears in all the characters in all his plays. It is himself; it is G.B.S.

This G.B.S. is a unique union between Mephistopheles and saint: a revolutionary and a reactionary: a flouter of conventions: a wit of the highest order: tremendous in controversy: irresistible in brilliance. He is a master of paradox, as paradox is also a master of him. He is an instructor of intelligent women in everything that intelligent women do not need to know. He presents himself as an economist, a statesman, and a prophet. The story of this extraordinary phenomenon, his triumphs and his unrivalled abilities, Mr. Shaw has been telling, with unabated zest, for close on fifty years.

This G.B.S. began in a comparatively lowly way. Born in Dublin, in 1856, he found himself a member of the class of genteel poor. There was a baronet somewhere in the family, though his whereabouts seem in retrospect rather vague. His father had an income that ran into three figures, though at the time its whereabouts seemed to be even vaguer than the baronet's. The young G.B.S. was sent to the Wesleyan Connexional School, now Wesley College, where he received his first intimation of the irrationality of the universe when he discovered that most of the pupils belonged to the Church of England. G.B.S. was perpetually at the bottom of his class. This confirmed his impression that the universe was an unreasonable place.

After spending some time in a land agent's office, G.B.S. broke loose. In 1876 he packed "a carpet bag; boarded the North Wall boat: and left the train next morning at Euston", where he heard a porter cry, in an accent quite strange to him, "Ensm' faw weel?" This, he says, "I rightly interpreted as 'Hansom or four-wheel?' I was afraid to say hansom, because I had never been in one, and was not sure that I should know how to get in. So I solemnly drove in a growler through streets whose names Dickens had made familiar to me, London being at its spring best, which is its very best, to Victoria Grove, where the driver accepted four shillings as a reasonable fare for the journey."

It was to be a long time before he could again afford an extravagance upon this scale. Nevertheless, he clung to the habiliments of gentility, and at the lowest point of his fortunes did not part from his evening clothes. Thus dressed, he was one night walking down Sloane Street, when a man stopped him "with an eloquent appeal for help", ending with the statement that he had not a penny in the world. To which G.B.S. replied, with perfect sincerity, "Neither have I." In any case, G.B.S. has never believed in indiscriminate charity, "the most mischievous sort of pruriency". When a street musician held out his cap to him in the Strand in his days as a music critic, he hurried by, muttering, "Press".

Working with furious energy at novels which no one would publish, he needed money himself. Fortunately he had his parents. "I did not throw myself into the struggle for life", he observes cheerfully: "I threw my mother into it. I was not a staff for my father's old age: I hung on to his coat tails."

I have endeavoured to show that as a creator of dramatic character, or as a teller of stories, Shaw would never have attained a hundredth part either of his popularity or his reputation: for in these directions his talents are something less than out of the common. But with the extravagant and fantastic G.B.S. we begin to draw near to one part of a reasonable explanation of the great position that Shaw holds in the contemporary world of letters. G.B.S. has taken hold of the public's imagination as firmly as Sherlock Holmes, so much so that people to whom his home in Whitehall Court or at Ayot St. Lawrence is as unknown as the other side of the moon quite blandly invent stories about him that pass with no justification whatever into the accepted canon of Shavian anecdotes.

It is said, for example, that in his days as a dramatic critic he once penetrated into the stalls of a theatre in a Norfolk jacket. The attendant, accustomed to the rigid seemliness of evening dress, protested at Mr. Shaw's coat. "Very well," he said, "if it is my coat you object to, that can soon be remedied." Whereupon he took his coat off, and saw the performance in his shirt-sleeves. This anecdote is unique in that it is the only one that is recorded ever to have aroused Mr. Shaw to anger.

The legendary G.B.S., too, is the hero of the episode of Isadora Duncan. The famous dancer is said to have suggested to G.B.S. the desirability, from the point of view of eugenics, of their collaborating in parenthood, for any child would be remarkable that combined his brains with her face. To which G.B.S. is reputed to have answered that he entirely agreed, but to have urged caution on the ground that the contemplated offspring might have his face and her brains.

But G.B.S. holds his position in the public imagination mainly to a misunderstanding. It is firmly believed by the majority of the British people that G.B.S. passes himself off as superior to Shakespeare. Most members of the public do not think any the worse of him for that. With acute memories of their boredom at studying "Love's Labour's Lost" for the School Certificate they even feel that this effort to humiliate Shakespeare gives them vicariously a bit of their own back. Nevertheless, the impression is a mistake, though a pardonable mistake.

Already it will have become clear that G.B.S. is one of the most exuberantly light-hearted of men. A certain recklessness of speech is his unmistakable sign-manual. At a performance given by an Italian string quartet, his companion remarked approvingly, "These men have been playing together for twelve years." "Surely," replied Shaw, "we have been here longer than that?" When a prominent Free Trader, later an M.P., had finished speaking to the Fabian Society, Shaw got up and observed, "We have come to the end of the intolerable boredom inflicted on us. It is incredible that anyone should have prepared this crude alphabet of the subject, above all, for the Fabian Society." It is hardly surprising that, when a lady asked Rodin whether G.B.S. spoke French well, Rodin replied: "M. Shaw ne parle pas bien: mais il s'exprime avec une telle violence qu'il s'impose."

G.B.S. has dealt with Shakespeare with the same untrammelled violence. "King Lear", he says, is an "obscene libel". It contains the "most appalling blasphemy that despair ever uttered". It "is a blasphemous libel", and probably "a seditious libel" as well. Shakespeare has no understanding of historical atmosphere; he was incapable of inventing an original play; he had no philosophy. He never once entered "that region in which Michael Angelo, Beethoven, Goethe, and the antique Athenian stage poets are great". "Cymbeline" is for the most part stagey trash of the lowest melodramatic order, in parts abominably written, throughout intellectually vulgar, and, judged in point of thought by modern intellectual standards, vulgar, foolish, offensive, indecent, and exasperating beyond all tolerance. There are moments when one asks despairingly why our stage should ever have been cursed with this 'immortal' pilferer of other men's stories and ideas, with his monstrous rhetorical fustian, his unbearable platitudes, his pretentious reduction of the subtlest problems of life to commonplaces against which a Polytechnic debating club would revolt, his incredible unsuggestiveness, his sententious combination of ready reflection with complete intellectual sterility, and his consequent incapacity for getting out of the depth of even the most ignorant audience, except when he solemnly says something so transcendently platitudinous that his more humble-minded hearers cannot bring themselves to believe that so great a man meant to talk like their grandmothers. With the single exception of Homer, there is no eminent writer, not even Sir Walter Scott, whom I despise so entirely as I despise Shakespeare when I measure my mind against his." No, cries G.B.S. sorrowfully, "to read 'Cymbeline' and to think of Goethe, of Wagner, of Ibsen, is, for me, to imperil the habit of studied moderation of statement which years of public responsibility as a journalist have made almost second nature to me".

But even "Cymbeline" is not as demoralizing as "Antony and Cleopatra", which is "intolerable to the true Puritan". The early part of the play, it is admitted handsomely, gives "a faithful picture of the soldier broken down by debauchery", but in the end Shakespeare "strains all his huge command of rhetoric and stage pathos" to provide a sham nobility. "Woe to the poet who stoops to such folly! The lot of the man who sees life truly and thinks about it romantically is Despair." That is why Thackeray moans out the words of the Preacher, Vanity of vanities, all is vanity, and Shakespeare mutters, "Out, out, brief candle." Yet there is a difference between intellectual honesty and dishonesty even in pessimism. Needless to say, this is a circumstance which does not do Shakespeare any good. Hogarth, Swift, and Strindberg may claim the benefit of it: they force you to face the facts of existence, and the conclusions to be drawn from them, if their standards be accepted. So, announces G.B.S., "I respect these resolute tragi-comedians. . . . But when your Shakespeares and Thackerays huddle up the matter at the end by killing somebody and covering your eyes with the undertaker's handkerchief, duly onioned with some pathetic phrase, as The flight of angels sing thee to thy rest, or Adsum, or the like, I have no respect for them at all: such maudlin tricks may impose on tea-drunkards, not on me."

The unwary reader, however, should not brood over these things too gloomily. They do not in the least mean that G.B.S. can see no merit in Shakespeare. Like all artists, this G.B.S. delights in the exercise of his craft, and when he gets into the middle of a fine swinging sentence he has no intention of allowing its sweep to be hampered by fiddling considerations of accuracy.

The fact of the matter is that G.B.S. reads Shakespeare "without shame or stint". He regards him as a born dramatist, for, finishing his life with "an incorrigible divine levity, an inexhaustible joy that derided sorrow", he was able to see the stuff of comedy in his own misfortunes. "Twelfth Night" is one of the crown jewels of poetry. Above all, G.B.S. does not present himself as a better playwright than Shakespeare. "In fact," he says, "—do not be surprised at my modesty—I do not profess to write better plays." Plays have already been written which reach the summit of their art, and therefore cannot be surpassed. "Peer Gynt" is one of them, and so is that obscene, blasphemous, and perhaps seditious, libel, "King Lear". Shakespeare "has outlasted thousands of abler thinkers, and will outlast a thousand more". His gift for telling a story, his enormous power over language, his humour, his sense of idiosyncratic character, and his inexaustible vital energy are qualities that, in G.B.S.'s opinion, preserve him effectively from the dark iniquity of oblivion. A certain Osman Edwards once read a paper to the Playgoers' Club, in London, on "The Superiority of Shaw to Shakespeare". He tried to prove that the advantage lay with Shaw in critical sense of life, in depth of thought, and in skill of stage technique. At this point G.B.S. rose, and begged to say a few words "in favour of his famous rival".

4

That this G.B.S. is a genuine creation, and not a mere untouched transcription of Mr. Shaw's natural personality, is easily proved. The most immediately striking characteristic of G.B.S. is his assurance; he is a fellow who is never at a loss, never disconcerted, never out of countenance. He does not know what nerves are. Mr. Shaw's psychological make-up is the direct opposite of this. When he came to London from Dublin he joined the Zetetical Debating Society, and resolved to speak at every meeting. The decision was taken only at a great cost. Whilst the previous speaker was on his legs, Shaw's heart beat "as painfully as a recruit's going under fire for the first time". His hand shook so that he could not read a word of his notes. G.B.S. is the man that Shaw would like to be, far more than the man he naturally is. He is the salesman whom Shaw has created to sell his ideas, as the theatre is the place where he has chosen to set up shop, instead of the pulpit or the House of Commons, which from some points of view might have been more suitable selections. A figure that has captured the public's at first protesting, and later reverent imagination, he ensures instant consideration for the wares which Shaw has to display, and therefore is a considerable factor in his success.

These wares are ideas, and they have been greatly praised, chiefly upon wrong grounds. Holbrook Jackson and A. R. Orage, of the *New Age*, when they first met each other in the early days of the century browsing round a second-hand bookshop in that centre of enlightenment which goes by the name of Leeds, recognized Shaw as a leader of thought, a philosopher. "We were unanimous," declares Jackson, "in our belief that only in the vitalized action advocated by him was there any hope for the redemption of a social system which had become a chaos and a desolation." This does at once too much and too little justice to Shaw. Too much because of its implication that Shaw is a great original thinker; too little because it ignores the extraordinary literary skill with which his ideas are presented.

It would not be difficult to find elsewhere than in his own brain the origin of most of the social, economic, political, and philosophic causes which Shaw has championed since he first challenged the world as a playwright. Shaw himself makes no secret of them. Creative evolution he has borrowed from Lamarck. His ideas of the relations between parents and children are to be found in Samuel Butler. His panacea of universal equality of pay was suggested by Ruskin. The conception of the Superman comes from Germany. His ideas concerning the curvilinear nature of the universe derive from Einstein. His notion of the strong man ruling without interference from democracy has been a commonplace of dictatorship for thousands of years.

It is easy enough to see how the legend of Shaw's originality as a thinker arose. It is because in the first place he presented these thoughts to an audience to whom as such they were entirely unfamiliar; that is to a theatrical audience. Shaw flung his work into a theatre which was dominated by the personality of great actors. These actors frankly liked bad plays, plays which had in them so little of the stuff of genuine thought that they could be pulled about to any extent to exploit the actor's own personal vision of life. This was the tradition of the English stage which existed from the days of Garrick to the days of Irving. Even when such actors got hold of a good play they promptly made it into a bad one: they played "Lear" with a happy ending.

In return they gave something which can plausibly be maintained to be the finest thing within the theatre's compass—they gave great acting, if the records are to be trusted, that could sear the memory and illuminate the soul. What they did not give was ideas, for their *forte* was emotion. They did not give ideas because their management of affairs was such that the theatre provided so little scope for authors with original ideas that authors with original ideas did not work for it.

Into this world of the stalest theatrical convention burst the astonishing phenomenon of Shaw, a man who not only had acquainted himself with the most advanced thought of his time, but was bent upon introducing this thought into the theatre. It is hardly surprising that this joyous new wine rushed to the heads of audiences to whom it had never been given before, and persuaded them it was of finer vintage than it could actually claim to be. This, then, is another source of Shaw's great reputation: he has transformed the theatre, making it a home of intellectual as well as emotional experience. But the driving force of his ideas alone would not have been sufficient to accomplish this transformation. At least equally essential is the skill of his expression.

The merits of Mr. Shaw's serious style are widely appreciated. He has in the past poured much scorn over what he used to call the operatic method of playwriting, in which the dramatist—Shakespeare was the usual offender in this direction—provided his actors with big speeches calling for the bravura that a prima donna lavishes upon an aria. But in his later work Mr. Shaw has taken to writing this sort of speech himself. In "Back to Methuselah" he brought all the resources of his eloquence, all his feeling for the balance of a phrase, all the mastery of his unrivalled lucidity to the long speech with which Lilith, looking forward into an immeasurable future at the as yet undreamed-of achievements of mankind, concludes the play. There is no mistaking the compelling rhythm of lines like these: "And because these infants that call themselves ancients are reaching out towards that, I will have patience with them still; though I know well that when they attain it they shall become one with me and supersede me and Lilith will be only a legend and a lay that has lost its meaning. Of Life only is there no end; and though of its million starry mansions many are empty and many still unbuilt, and though its vast domain is as yet unbearably desert, my seed shall one day fill it and master its matter to its uttermost confines."

In his subsequent work audiences have been accustomed to expect a similar piling up of eloquence in some elaborate speech. Generally they have not been disappointed. In "Saint Joan" they had the speech of the Inquisitor, a speech that is said to be longer than the entire part of Ophelia. In "The Apple Cart" there was the long speech of King Magnus in the first act in which the King explains to his disgruntled Cabinet that "politics, once the centre of attraction for ability, public spirit, and ambition, has . . . become the refuge of a few fanciers of public speaking and party intrigue". Even in the disappointing "Too True To Be Good" there is the enormous oration at the end with which the parson-thief disperses everybody both on the stage and in the audience. Actors say that these long speeches are easy to remember and recite: through them runs a rhythm that prevents their being a burden on the memory. If from the literary point of view a fault is to be found with them it is that they have singularly little magic, that especial quality which transports "the imagination clean into another country, that drenches a word, a phrase, with the light that never shone even on the Hesperides, the Spice Islands, or Cathay".

There is, however, another observation to be made. They appeal to the audience, not only on the score of beauty, but on that of thought. Yet the conditions of the playhouse, of the inexorable sweep forward of the play, make it impossible for them to be received with adequate exercise of judgment by the audience. In "In Good King Charles's Golden Day", the artist Kneller—anachronistically borrowing from Hogarth—declares that "the right line, the line of beauty is a curve". Turning to Newton, who is greatly perturbed, he asserts: "The path of the world curves, as you yourself have shown; and as it whirls on its way it would leave your apple behind if the apple fell in a straight line. Motion in a curve is the law of nature: and the law of nature is the law of God. Go out into your garden and throw a stone straight if you can. Shoot an arrow from a bow, a bullet from a pistol, a cannon ball from the mightiest cannon the King can lend you, and though you had the strength of Hercules, and gunpowder more powerful than the steam which hurls the stones from Etna in eruption, yet cannot you make your arrow or your bullet fly straight to its mark." Thereupon Newton bursts out; "Sir, if what this man believes be true, then not only is the path of the cannon ball curved, but space is curved; time is curved; the universe is curved." "Of course it is," says Kneller. "Why not?" "Why not!" exclaims Newton. "Only my life's work turned to waste, vanity, folly. This comes of admitting strangers to break into my holy solitude with their diabolical suggestions."

This is excellent dialogue, the speeches of Kneller magnificent rhetoric. But as a contribution towards making the stage intellectual it has one serious defect. This defect is simply that no audience in the world could, at the pace of an ordinary stage performance, follow and check the arguments Mr. Shaw here puts forward. This is a handicap from which nearly all Mr. Shaw's serious stage writing suffers, an inherent handicap that prevents the theatre from attaining its highest function by appeals to the intellect.

But it is not the brilliant effrontery of G.B.S., nor the reputation of Mr. Shaw as a thinker (somewhat undeserved), nor the eloquence of his serious style, that is the main factor in his success. The principal factor is his wit. What draws people irresistibly to the theatres where his works are performed is the well-known circumstance that though he talks about such abstruse matters as the economic reorganization of mankind, or even our complete supersession by an entirely new race of beings hardly more subject to human weakness than is Mr. Shaw himself, yet he convulses his audiences in laughter more uproarious than is provoked by any farce. He is totally unscrupulous in the methods he will employ to accomplish this feat. As we have seen, he does not disdain the actual physical incidents of farce, such as scuffles and fights; nor does he avoid any joke simply because it is obvious and cheap. Because he is adept at the rapier, he is perfectly willing to use on occasion the first blunt instrument that happens to hand: a noted practitioner on the violin, he does not scorn the penny whistle. He delights in the elementary misunderstanding of a simple word, and the travesty of a well-known quotation. When his ignorant and voluble politician Burge is introduced to a distinguished biologist in the second part of "Back to Methuselah", he causes him, in the wildest spirit of caricature, to exclaim: "How I wish I could have devoted myself to biology! I have always been interested in rocks and strata and volcanoes and so forth: they throw such a light on the age of the earth. (With conviction.) There is nothing like biology. 'The cloud-capped towers, the solemn binnacles, the gorgeous temples, the great globe itself; yea, all that it inherit shall dissolve, and, like this influential pageant faded, leave not a rack behind.' That's biology, you know: good, sound biology."

Mr. Shaw can never, in fact, resist a verbal joke. When Lesbia, after the lengthy discussions of marriage in "Getting Married", at the end of it all draws a deep breath, and exclaims thankfully, "To think that after all the dangers of the morning I am still unmarried! still independent! still my own mistress! still a glorious strong-minded old maid of old England!" her blundering suitor, the General, breaks in, "Do you find any real happiness in being your own mistress? Would it not be more generous—would you not be happier as someone else's mistress?" It might be thought that a wit as fertile as Mr. Shaw could afford to sacrifice a jest like this. But he can do more. Just as it is only millionaires who can afford to be careful over halfpennies, so Mr. Shaw can afford not to sacrifice it.

The essence of wit, it has been claimed, lies in the disturbance of complacency by the introduction of some unpalatable, even if partial, truth. Mr. Shaw has an absolute mastery over every variety of shock tactics. No man is so skilful as he at taking the audience by surprise. He can be under its guard and deliver a blow in the twinkling of an eye. Collins, the greengrocer, discusses marriage with the bishop's wife. To his own wife, he says, marriage came "natural". "She's what you might call a regular old hen. Always wants to have her family within sight of her. Wouldn't go to bed unless she knew they was all safe at home and the door locked, and the lights out. Always wants her luggage in the carriage with her. Always goes and makes the engine-driver promise to be careful. She's a born wife and mother, ma'am. That's why my children all ran away from home."

He can shock blandly, or brutally; blandly, as when, describing the

General, he says that he "is a well set up man . . . with large, brave nostrils, an iron mouth . . . and much natural simplicity and dignity of character", but "ignorant, stupid, and prejudiced, having been carefully trained to be so", adding, however, that "he would be no worse a man than Collins, had he enjoyed Collins's social opportunities"; brutally, as when, in "Man and Superman", Don Juan declares: "The Life Force respects marriage only because marriage is a contrivance of its own to secure the greatest number of children and the closest care of them. For honour, chastity, and all the rest of your moral figments it cares not a rap. Marriage is the most licentious of human institutions . . . that is the secret of its popularity."

The disturbance of complacency is one of the two cardinal features of Mr. Shaw's wit. Loose, conventional, lazy thinking upon any subject is abhorrent to him, so that it is not merely aristocratic or bourgeois institutions which come within the scope of his criticism. Trade Unions equally with the training of a gentleman are objects of his satire. Boanerges, the working-man Cabinet Minister of "The Apple Cart", asserts confidently that the workers will never throw him over. "No king on earth," he tells Magnus, "is as safe in his job as a Trade Union official. There is only one thing that can get him sacked; and that is drink. Not even that, as long as he doesn't actually fall down. I talk democracy to these men and women. I tell them that they have the vote, and that theirs is the kingdom and the power and the glory. I say to them, 'You are supreme: exercise your power.' They say, 'That's right! tell us what to do'; and I tell them. I say, 'Exercise your vote intelligently by voting for me.' And they do. That's democracy; and a splendid thing it is, too, for putting the right men in the right place."

The second cardinal feature of Mr. Shaw's wit is its good-nature. It has been agreed down the ages that ill-will is a fundamental part of wit. In the midst of the fountain of wit, says Lucretius, something bitter arises, which poisons every flower. This ill-nature is entirely absent from Shaw. The very exuberance of his condemnation, as in the instances of Shakespeare and the Fabian lecturer, is only the overflow of extravagant high spirits. He satirizes marriage; but he does not hate it, like Strindberg. He ridicules theories of medicine in "The Doctor's Dilemma"; but he does not hate them, as Chesterton, for example, hated them in the figure of Dr. Warner in "Manalive". He finds men and women and their associations and activities absurd and foolish and inefficient, but he neither despises them nor would rejoice in their final failure. He makes wit as good-humoured as humour.

"SAKI"

JOHN GORE

WIT HAS BEEN OFTEN AND VARIOUSLY DEFINED. FOR AN ATTRIBUTE WHICH is not commonly bestowed on human beings, it has received a great deal of attention in this respect, and still lacks the *mot juste* in definition. I shall not attempt it. I shall say no more than this: if the definition "the power of giving intellectual pleasure by unexpected combining or contrast of previously unconnected ideas or expressions" satisfies one accepted aspect of wit, "Saki" was a witty writer.

In the mid-Edwardian Age, when there still was time to spare to playing with words and other trifles, and time to appreciate the finer points of the game, I was an undergraduate at Oxford. Under the dreaming spires there was playtime in plenty; on shaven lawns, on silver river, in grey quadrangles and panelled rooms, in coverts and on ploughlands, in teeming streets and romantic wynds, we contrived easily and pleasantly enough to "lose and neglect the fleeting hours of time".

Among the nocturnal joys, which ministered to our appetites for pleasure, were regular variety entertainments arranged and carried out by gifted amateurs, for the most part fellow undergraduates. These were held in College Halls and usually followed the terminal dinners of the famous Wine Clubs. Drinking (like eating) among undergraduates was even then on the decline, and we came to the feast of wit stimulated very little by a wine-induced flow of soul. We revelled, not drank deep. Either we were very, very young and light of heart, or else the feast of wit was prepared by a *cordon bleu*. I believe that both conditions were present. We accorded to the performers a noisy and often premature enthusiasm for their fireworks which might fairly have suggested to older men or strangers that there were many drunken men in the audience.

Palmam qui meruit ferat. It is part of my argument that "Saki's" wit and not an "empty glass" contributed a lion's share to the success of these evenings. Four youths were the key-men in the cast of our variety entertainments. Their names were Harry Tennant, Jack Gilliat, Christopher Stone and Ball Mercer. Two of them have since made their names sufficiently well known in the world of entertainment. The fourth-named relied for his effects on the writings of "Saki", which at that time were delighting readers of the old *Westminster Gazette*. Mercer learned many of these sketches by heart—the "Reginald" series—and delivered them inimitably, and before long, we, his audience, learned them by heart from his performance and were only too ready to anticipate his coming rocket before the last had burst in a salvo of bright stars.

Who was this "Saki"? I do not think we knew or cared to know. We thought of him as a contemporary, one Reginald, somewhat (as we should say today) of a "lounge-lizard", a boy who cared too nuch for his personal appearance, who believed that "after all an apricot tie would have gone better with the lilac waistcoat". A rather unwholesome boy, we thought, with a taste for sweet liqueurs and Persian art, one who played no games, could not "hit a haystack" and said disrespectful things about big-game hunters and Blimps. But we never questioned his wit, if we questioned his morals. Above all, we were in no doubt at all that he was a mere boy. And a mere boy he has remained in my memory, and will for ever remain. On mature consideration, I conclude that "Saki's" wit (unlike Pope's, unlike Sir Max Beerbohm's later flights) was undergraduate's wit, and that he was a literary Peter Pan. Because he and his wit never grew up, his writings have not marched beside me past the milestones of life. Although he wrote many books, and most of them sparkled, it is always to his first "Reginald" that I return with the uncritical and unquestioning loyalty we most of us pay to books read out to us in childhood and endeared to us by the remembered voice that introduced their delights.

In point of fact, "Saki" in 1905 was, in undergraduate eyes, a man of middle age, thirty-five years old; and I think in our ignorance we had largely misconceived his character. Hector Hugh Munro was born in Burma in 1870. He had Scots blood in his veins from spear and distaff sides. He came of a military family and himself proved true to type. His father was a professional soldier stationed in Burma at the time of the child's birth. Hector Munro had an elder brother, and a sister whose biographical notes supply the bulk of the details here given concerning his life and work. Their mother died soon after Hector's birth. and their father, who was much abroad on foreign service, handed over the children to the care of his mother and two sisters, who lived near Barnstaple. The memories of childhood tend to exaggerate the size of everything, from gardens to sins. If Miss Munro's memories are to be relied on, their two aunts (Aunt Augusta and Aunt "Tom") were gorgons. Probably they were no worse than many other middle-aged, middle-class maiden ladies of a recognized type in the Victorian age; that is to say, narrow, ignorant, self-willed, quarrelsome, jealous, domineering, stuffy females, ill-qualified to bring up imaginative children of delicate constitution and dicky lungs; but not lacking in redeeming features. Be that as it may, their handling of the trust was to have a very damaging effect on the good name of the Aunt class a generation later. "Saki" aimed some of his earliest and most pointed shafts at Aunts when he began to write for a living, and the commodity of Aunts slumped badly and had not made up the decline when the Great War broke out. Hear him on Aunts in relation to Christmas presents:

> "There is, for instance, the female relative in the country who 'knows a tie is always useful' and sends you some spotted horror which you could only wear in secret or in Tottenham Court Road. . . . Then there are Aunts, always a difficult class. . . . The trouble is that one never catches them really young enough. By the time one has educated them to an appreciation of the fact that one does not wear red woollen mittens in the West End, they die or quarrel with the family or do something equally inconsiderate. That is why the supply of trained aunts is always so precarious."

No doubt it is annoying to a luxurious young man to receive, in lieu of the hoped-for liqueur glasses, or the payment of outstanding bills, or "something quite sweet in the way of jewelry" (for, unlike the good woman in the Bible, "Saki" was not above rubies")—a pair of mittens; yet even that dingy token-payment indicates in the donor-aunt a heart composed of something softer than granite, and a nature not all serpents, flint and vitriol.

But to return to the 1870's. There was adequate money available to give the children the ordinary luxuries of their kind, which did not include those which money does not buy, fresh air and light, exercise and sympathy with childhood's needs and aspirations. The children survived it and lived lives apart, lives coloured by imagination. Once every four years their father came home on leave, and then they would spend happy months together sightseeing in European countries; and occasionally a human uncle gave them a pleasanter idea of older folk. They developed innate talents, literary, dramatic and artistic. Like (but long after) Max Beerbohm, "Saki" worked out a happy satirical vein which relied for its effect on lively sketches with a pithy descriptive legend. (An admirable and early example depicts a family of chawbacons of infinite mental vacuity singing a hymn in a pew of the village church. It is headed "Missionary Sunday" and beneath:

> "Oh we, whose lives are lighted
> With wisdom from on High.")

In due course Hector went to a private school at Exmouth, and at fifteen years of age passed on to Bedford Grammar School. But he showed no marked application, and in 1893 took up an appointment which his father had secured him in the Military Police in Burma. He was happy enough there, for he was fond of riding, but malaria laid him low and in little more than a year he was forced to give up the post. He regained his health in England, hunting when he could and trying his wings in literature, and in 1896 "F.C.G." (F. Carruthers Gould) launched him in London in journalism. He began to write his "Alice in Westminster", which Gould illustrated and the public gobbled. Then he began to publish his sketches in book form and to make his name known—that is to say, his pen-name, which was taken from the cup-bearer in the Rubáiyát.*

The *Morning Post*, *Bystander* and *Daily Express* next sought his services, and the publication of "Reginald", his "Westminster" sketches, gave him a great reputation as a witty writer. "Reginald in Russia" followed. "Saki" knew something about Russia. Indeed, his one serious book, "The Rise of the Russian Empire", was well received by knowledgeable critics, and "Saki" spent some years as a war correspondent for the *Morning Post* in the Balkans and in Russia. Before the war broke out, he had published several other books (which no one else could conceivably have been accused of writing), books which delighted the intelligent among the *jeunesse dorée* and conserved, if they did not enhance, the reputation won by "Reginald". Among these were "The Unbearable Bassington", "The Chronicles of Clovis", "Beasts and Super-Beasts", "The Toys of Peace" and—prelude to the war—"When William Came". This last earned a pat on the back from that much-tried and despairing prophet, Lord Roberts. "Saki" was forty-four when the war broke out. He had made his niche in literature, a snug and secure place. But he joined up at once and served in France in the 22nd Royal Fusiliers. Refusing a commission, he worked his way up to the rank of lance-sergeant, a brave, humane, cheerful soldier, neither aloof nor intellectually superior, and he was killed near Beaumont Hamel in November 1916. No doubt at all, we undergraduates at Oxford in 1905 grossly misinterpreted his character from his writings.

Yet, if Reginald and Clovis and the rest of his greenery-yallery youths were not "Saki," who the devil were they? If they were the creations pure and simple (or not so pure and simple) of a sergeant in the Fusiliers, a son of a typical family of soldiers, then they were creations of a kind rare

---

* "And when . . . O Saki, you shall pass
Among the guests star-scattered on the Grass,
And in your joyous errand reach the spot
When I made One—turn down an empty Glass."

in literary fiction. His sister declared that he never showed the softer side of his sympathetic nature in his books. His readers may reply that he seldom revealed the sterner stuff of the Sergeant of the Line. That he was a warm-hearted friend, a helper, a good comrade, we take as truth. He remains a literary mystery, like the commodity he dealt in. Wit is brilliant and hard as a diamond, cynical as an undergraduate, elusive as a butterfly or as the shadow of an alder leaf in a breeze; not to be classified nor defined. And the character of "Saki" has escaped my net. But his pleasant voices, his Persian nightingales, still sing in the groves of memory, in the gardens of dead yesterday. Nevertheless, those who survive his day and most admire the sparkling writings of "Saki" will be the first to admit that Sergeant Hector Munro of the 22nd Royal Fusiliers was infinitely the bigger man.

2

That the bulk of the writings of "Saki" could have belonged to no age but the Edwardian none who reads them today would deny. It was pre-eminently an age (among the classes in which he lived and for whom he wrote) of luxury and ease, of pride in achievement, and of unrestrained appetite for exploiting the wider avenues of thought and action opened out by scientific invention. These things were enjoyed with a sense of security and permanence as false as foolish. There was time and to spare for the arts of peace, among which playing with words is always a favourite. But "Saki" reveals that if he was in the stream, he was not entirely propelled by it. His attitude to the Edwardian age was critical. He enjoyed its many amenities and luxuries, while he lashed at its follies, its blindness and its vulgarities. His attitude to the South African War was by no means complacent. He was perhaps in advance of his time, for he clearly held the view which, common enough today, was usually whispered by a minority at the beginning of the century. Reginald decides to write a peace-poem:

> "It begins with the usual ornithological emotion:
>
> 'When the widgeon, westward winging,
> Heard the folk Vereeniginging,
> Heard the shouting and the singing——' "

Later he turns his Muse "on London, the City of Dreadful Nocturnes":

> "And the sleeper, eye unlidding,
> Heard a voice for ever bidding
> Much farewell to Dolly Gray;
> Turning weary on his truckle-
> Bed he heard the honeysuckle
> Lauded in apiarian lay."

The poem ends with "quite a decorative bit of moral admonition":

> "Cease, War, thy bubbling madness that the wine shares,
> And bid thy legions turn their swords to mine shares."

The couplet adequately summarizes the modern view of that war and age.

Nor was "Saki" blind to the shrewd commercialism and snobbishness of his day:

"Which reminds me of the man I read of in some sacred book who was given a choice of what he most desired. And because he didn't ask for titles and honours and dignities, but only for immense wealth, these other things came to him also."

"I am sure you didn't read about him in any sacred book."

"Yes, I fancy you will find him in Debrett."

Or again:

"The Beauwhistles weren't born in the purple, you know, but they are getting there on the instalment system—so much down, and the rest when you feel like it. They have kind hearts and never forget birthdays. He . . . is something in the City where the patriotism comes from; and she—oh well, her frocks come from Paris, but she wears them with a strong English accent. So public-spirited of her. . . ."

But, despite a mature condemnation of the follies of his age, "Saki" is justly labelled a Peter Pan of literature. His wit is the essence of undergraduate wit. As he said, "to have reached thirty is to have failed in life". He revelled in shocking muscular Christians, retired Colonels, and dyed-in-the wool sportsmen:

"Like every woman who has ever preached repentance to unregenerate youth, she dwelt on the sin of an empty life, which always seems so much more scandalous in the country, where people rise early to see if a new strawberry has happened during the night."

They had ragged him at a shooting-party because he could not hit a haystack, so he got up early to shoot, and bring into the house, one of the peacocks.

"I know it was dawn, because there were lark noises in the sky and the grass looked as if it had been left out all night."

"There was a fellow I stayed with once in Warwickshire who farmed his own land, but was otherwise quite steady,"

Youthful indeed was his penchant for mocking at virtue:

"She is so desperately anxious to do the wrong thing correctly. Not that it really matters nowadays, as I told her: I know some perfectly virtuous people who are received everywhere."

One of Reginald's acquaintances—the Warwickshire farmer indeed who proved less "steady"—suddenly jumped his traces and

"eloped with a lion-tamer's widow and set up as a golf instructor somewhere on the Persian Gulf; dreadfully immoral, of course, because he was only an indifferent player, but still, it showed imagination. His wife was really to be pitied because he was the only person in the house who understood how to manage the cook's temper and now she has to put D.V. on her dinner invitations. Still, that's better than a domestic scandal; a woman who leaves her cook never wholly recovers her position in Society."

One more example must suffice to indicate "Saki's" *published* attitude to the roses and rapture of virtue:

"There have always been men who have gone about despairing of the Future, and when the Future arrives it says nice, superior things about their having acted according to their lights. It is dreadful to think that other people's grandchildren may one day rise up and call one amiable. There are moments when one sympathizes with Herod."

"Saki" was fond of hunting, but it did not deter him from ridiculing that religion through the mouth of his Clovis, and slashing its high priests and its vestals,

"those florid girls that go so well with autumn scenery or Christmas decorations in church"

and even in ill health look

"about as pale as a beetroot that has suddenly heard bad news."

He was not less severe and acute in his dealings with intellectual snobs:

"Thither came the intensely musical and the almost intensely musical, who are very many, and in still greater numbers the merely musical who know how Tschaikowsky's name is pronounced and can recognize several of Chopin's Nocturnes if you give them due warning; these eat in the nervous, detached manner of the roebuck feeding in the open, and keep anxious ears cocked towards the orchestra for the first hint of a recognisable melody."

And the "modern", executive woman was not spared:

"There's Marion Mulciber, who would think she could play bridge, just as she would think she could ride down a hill on a bicycle; on that occasion she went into a hospital, now she's gone into a Sisterhood—lost all she had, you know, and gave the rest to Heaven. Still, you can't call it a sudden calamity; that occurred when poor dear Marion was born. The doctors said at the time that she couldn't live more than a fortnight, and she's been trying ever since to see if she could. Women are so opinionated."

It is unfair to a writer of "Saki's" type merely to extract gems from his clusters and to withhold even one completed design. His sketches were much more than half a dozen pearls strung on a necklace of beads. If sometimes the reader is conscious that he is working up towards an epigrammatic firework, it is not usually so. The design of a sketch was often itself a jewel. It is hard to make choice among so many examples of his art, but perhaps the awful story of "The Woman Who Told The Truth" will serve as well as another:

There was once [said Reginald] a woman who told the truth. Not all at once, of course, but the habit grew upon her gradually, like lichen on an apparently healthy tree. She had no children—otherwise it might have been different. It began with little things, for no particular reason except that her life was a rather empty one, and it is so easy to slip into the habit of telling the truth in little matters. And then it became difficult to draw the line at more important things, until at last she took to telling the truth about her age; she said she was forty-two and five months—by that time, you see, she was veracious even to months. It may have been pleasing to the angels, but her elder sister was not gratified. On the Woman's birthday, instead of the opera-tickets which she had hoped for, her sister gave her a view of Jerusalem from the Mount of Olives, which is not quite the same thing. The revenge of an elder sister may be long in coming, but, like a South-Eastern express, it arrives in its own good time.

The friends of the Woman tried to dissuade her from over-indulgence in the practice, but she said she was wedded to the truth; whereupon it was remarked that it was scarcely logical to be so much together in public. (No really provident woman lunches regularly with her husband if she wishes to burst upon him as a revelation at dinner. He must have time to forget; an afternoon is not enough.) And after a while her friends began to thin out in patches. Her passion for the truth was not compatible with a large visiting-list. For instance, the told Miriam Klopstock *exactly* how she looked at the Ilexes' ball. Certainly Miriam had asked for her candid opinion, but the Woman prayed in church every Sunday for peace in our time, and it was not consistent.

It was unfortunate, everyone agreed, that she had no family; with a child or two in the house, there is an unconscious check upon too free an indulgence in the truth. Children are given us to discourage our better emotions. That is why the stage, with all its efforts, can never be as artificial as life; even in an Ibsen drama one must reveal to the audience things that one would suppress before the children or servants.

Fate may have ordained the truth-telling from the commencement and should justly bear some of the blame; but in having no children the Woman was guilty, at least, of contributory negligence.

Little by little she felt she was becoming a slave to what had once been merely an idle propensity and one day she knew. Every woman tells ninety per cent of the truth to her dressmaker; the other ten per cent is the irreducible minimum of deception beyond which no self-respecting client trespasses. Madame Draga's establishment was a meeting-ground for naked truths and over-dressed fictions, and it was here, the Woman felt, that she might make a final effort to recall the artless mendacity of past days. Madame herself was in an inspiring mood, with the air of a sphinx who knew all things and preferred to forget most of them. As a War Minister she might have been celebrated, but she was content to be merely rich.

"If I take it in here, and—Miss Howard, one moment if you please—and there, and round like this—so—I really think you will find it quite easy."

The Woman hesitated; it seemed to require such a small effort simply to acquiesce in Madame's views. But habit had become too strong.

"I'm afraid," she faltered, "it's just the least little bit in the world too——"

And by that least little bit she measured the deeps and eternities of her thraldom to fact. Madame was not best pleased at being contradicted on a professional matter, and when Madame lost her temper, you usually found it afterwards in the bill.

And at last the dreadful thing came, as the Woman had foreseen all along that it must; it was one of those paltry little truths with which she harried her waking hours. On a raw Wednesday morning, in a few ill-chosen words, she told the cook that she drank. She remembered the scene afterwards as vividly as though it had been painted in her mind by Abbey. The cook was a good cook, as cooks go; and as cooks go she went.

Miriam Klopstock came to lunch the next day. Women and elephants never forget an injury.

There is a real difficulty in dealing with "Saki's" "Unbearable Bassington". If one half of the praise which Maurice Baring bestowed on it (in his introduction in the Collected Works), be justly bestowed, it is too good a book to misuse and misinterpret here with a choice example of wit or a four-line excerpt to illustrate style. The Collected Edition came soon enough after "Saki's" gallant death for his literary merits to be assessed through the rose-coloured spectacles of love or admiration for his personality. It does "Saki" no service to compare him with Meredith or even Maupassant, and it is the partiality of friendship which asks: "Have we any book in which the joy and pain of life are so intimately blended as in the "Unbearable Bassington?" That is the exaggerated praise—excusable perhaps in the circumstances—at which Max Beerbohm poked fun in his "Maltby and Braxton". Mr. Baring and Mr. Rothay Reynolds may have been happier in the hours of their second readings of "Bassington" than I was. Mr. Baring—a shrewd critic—is not blind to "Saki's" faults, his mere verbalism, his sacrifice of sincerity to brilliancy of phrase. But, though his eyes are open to "Saki's" faults, he does not admit the handicap. The tinsel *is* tarnished and has dulled the fabric. To the mind of 1940 "The Unbearable Bassington" may well seem "The Unreadable Bassington". The phase will pass. The book, in a hard and heartless setting, reveals flashes of rare insight, at least into the depths of human misery and futility, and some of its epigrams are the essential truth and wisdom of humanity; but it is not of the stuff of which classics are compounded. It is fairest and wisest to leave it severely alone in choosing selections from "Saki"—in 1940.

Always, in truth, one returns for quotation to "Reginald" from "Saki's" other books, partly no doubt because its form is more suitable for quotation than are some of his more continuously constructed works. There are other reasons, too. As has been said already, *on revient toujours à son premier amour*. "Reginald" impinged on my consciousness in my own youth and the tiara of clustered brilliants which sparkles on his brow still gives the effect of diamonds, not of paste. Clovis and the rest of the precious young men are but Reginald dressed in the fashions of succeeding years, and their fireworks are the same make of rocket and Catherine-wheel, let off with an occasional damp squib. We grow old; the years pass in everlasting anxiety and hardship, and, while we marvel and cast back longing looks at that false-golden age of security and ease, we yet contemplate it not without shame; as of time wasted and great opportunities missed, of years spent in playing, which were offered to mankind as a god-sent breathing-space for planning and rebuilding. The jewels and fancy dresses of that dead carnival are tawdry and tarnished; the fresh, bitter night winds have banished from the banquet-hall the fumes of wine and smoke and with them the carnival spirit of the feast. "Yon rising Moon that looks for us again. . . ." for ever looks in vain. Now her light is hid and "Saki", like her, has passed down the sky to that place which awaits all mortals, witty and wise or ponderous and foolish. His joyful errand is run. Just as spoken wit belongs to its hour and to its context, which can never again be recaptured as a setting for its ephemeral brilliance, so "Saki" belongs to his age and to the spirit of his age, and that, too, is difficult to savour again, if savour it we would. Turn down an empty glass. . . .

But if that be a justifiably sad farewell to "Saki", it is no fit good-bye to Hector Munro. By his friends he was loved as the kindliest of companions and—finest proof of kindliness—as one "who was utterly incapable of boring a fellow-creature—man or dog or woman or cat or child of any age"; one "who felt the keen sense of honour and strength of purpose and stark simplicity which were his essential qualities".

3

"Saki's" political writings reveal him as a man of good sense, shrewdness, strong patriotism and high ideals. In the spring of 1914 he was writing "Potted Parliament" in the *Outlook*, and some of his aphorisms in that commentary reveal one or other of these qualities:

"An army moves at the rate of its slowest unit; it is the fate of a Coalition to move at the rate of its most headlong section."

"One of the most exasperating features of the House of Commons is its resemblance to an overcrowded kitchen range. Pots that are at boiling-point have to be set aside to simmer while others take their place."

And on the eve of the Four Years' War, he wrote:

"And this is how —— [one of our dailies] writes of our possible and desirable action at this crisis:

"'If we remained neutral we should be, from the commercial point of view, in precisely the same position as the United States. We should be able to trade with all the belligerents . . . we should be able to capture the bulk of their trade in neutral markets.'

"There seems to be some confusion of mind in these circles of political thought between a nation of shopkeepers and a nation of shoplifters. If these men are on the side of the angels, may I always have a smell of brimstone about me."

No need here to turn down an empty glass. His glass is not empty, it brims over with full-bodied stuff, the stuff that Englishmen drink today, as they drank it yesterday and will drink it tomorrow, however highly it be taxed. It is here and now that we may bid him *au revoir*, with little fear that the smell of brimstone is about him.

MARY RUSSELL MITFORD

JAMES AGATE

FOR MY SUBJECT I HAVE CHOSEN A WITTY WOMAN, AND THIS DESPITE MY conviction that a woman should not possess wit, and that if she does she should keep very quiet about it! Wit I hold to be unfeminine; any woman possessing wit lacks femininity; therefore no witty woman can be a true woman. I snap my fingers at any logician who faults this!

There is a famous passage in Montague's "Dramatic Values" in which that great critic animadverts against what he ironically calls the Wholesome Play. Here is his objection to such plays: "They abound in a kind of half-made women, obtrusively weaker vessels, 'hither all dewy from a convent fetched', and often as breathless and monosyllabic with aghast innocence as if they had run all the way—'sweet clinging natures', like a well-knitted sock, and about as fit as a sock for true marriage and comradeship; a type the elaboration of which is really so much sensual savagery, going back as it does towards the relation of some Mogul or Khalifa to scared, half-grown slave-girls, if not to the relation of buck elk to the timorous doe of sentimental convention."

The operative word here is, of course, "sock", and it is my view that a man who is truly married is or should be knitted to a sock. And who has ever heard of a witty sock, with the one possible exception of Jane Welsh Carlyle? Who, excepting Jane, while losing no tittle of her wit, was true comforter to her husband? Dreadful, for example, must have been the plight of Orlando after that wedding in Arden. Dreadful, too, the state of Benedick after he left the church. And most dreadful of all that of Mirabell. Yet have there ever been in art or nature more exquisitely witty creatures than Rosalind, Beatrice, and Millamant? And have there ever been more annoying creatures than Meredith's sparkling galaxy? Clara Middleton is well enough in a book, I dare say. But who wants to live with a woman who cannot don a nightgown without giving vent to an epigram, or doff it without uttering two?

Wit may, however, be granted to unmarried ladies as a concession on condition that they utter it only on paper. Had my chosen subject been a married woman, she would not have been my choice. Had she merely spoken her wit she would have been passed over. But since Mary Russell Mitford was everything a woman ought to be except beautiful and married, I sing her here!

Let it be first of all said that she did not find writing an easy matter. Listen to her nine years before the appearance of her famous book, "Our Village":

"I have been teased by booksellers and managers, and infinitely more by papa, for a novel and a play; but, alas! —far worse off than the worthy citizen of Molière, who had spoken prose all his life without knowing it—I have been obliged to refuse because I could only write in rhyme. My prose—when I take pains, is stiffer than Kemble's acting, or an old maid's person, or Pope's letters, or a maypole—when I do not, it is the indescribable farrago which has at this moment the honour of saluting your eyes.

"This is really very provoking, because I once—ages ago—wrote four or five chapters of a novel, which were tolerably lively and entertaining, and would have passed very well in the herd, had they not been so dreadfully deficient in polish and elegance. They had no more grace than a dancing bear; so I threw them into the fire forthwith, and have never since advanced out of the leading-strings of metre. Now it so happens that of all other qualities this unattainable one of elegance is that which I most admire and would rather possess than any other in the whole catalogue of literary merits. I would give a whole pound of fancy (and fancy weighs light) for one ounce of polish (and polish weighs heavy). To be tall, pale, thin, to have dark eyes, and write gracefully in prose is my ambition; and when I am tall, and pale, and thin, and have dark eyes, then, and not till then, will my prose be graceful."

2

Now let me come to the facts of Miss Mitford's life. Round about 1785 a Dr. George Mitford married an heiress. Dr. Mitford had an Edinburgh medical degree which served him little, and his wife was the daughter of a Dr. Russell, rector, vicar, and country magistrate who, dying, left his daughter some land and the sum of £28,000 in what Lady Bracknell would call the Funds. Now Dr. Mitford was by nature a gambler, and like all gamblers he looked on life through rose-coloured spectacles. Of a naturally ruddy complexion, he is said on his death-bed at the age of eighty-two to have looked pink and cheerful. And there can be no doubt whatever that he was possessed of the invaluable and indefinable attribute of charm: "He breathed his last without a struggle or a sigh . . . almost with his own beautiful colour, the exquisite vermilion for which he was so famous, on his sweet, serene countenance."

Mary was born in 1787, and her claims on the world's attention are four—"Our Village", her letters, her wit, and the model care with which she looked after her father, a man who was at least as good an original for Dickens's Harold Skimpole as was Leigh Hunt: "Some men want legs of beef and mutton for breakfast; I don't. Give me my peach, my cup of coffee, and my claret; I am content. I don't want them for themselves, but they remind me of the sun. There's nothing solar about legs of beef and mutton. Mere animal satisfaction!" Thus Skimpole, but it might equally well be Dr. Mitford. Here he is again, on the subject of privation: "Yes, this is the bird's cage. This is where the bird lives and sings. They pluck his feathers now and then, and clip his wings; but he sings, he sings!" So Dr. Mitford sang.

It was entirely due to his daughter's care that the old boy could sing and be happy in his cage. Having run through his wife's fortune he found himself compelled to take refuge from creditors within the rules of the King's Bench. This happened in 1795, the year in which the miracle happened. This was the taking of the child Mary to the lottery office when she made that choice which resulted in a prize of £20,000. At once the Doctor took a new red brick house in Reading, set up life again with his phaeton, his horses, and his dogs, for whose upkeep he looked to his skill at whist. Not content with these things, he purchased a farm, pulled down the Elizabethan dwelling-place, and created Bertram House, named after the castle of his Northumbrian ancestors, of whom he was inordinately proud. But while Dr. Mitford's skill at whist showed no falling-off, his general luck did, and from about 1805 onwards we find him beginning to depend and rely on the earnings of his daughter's pen. In 1820 ruin once more began to stare him in the face, which stared back as pinkly as ever! The family had to move to Three Mile Cross, "not," writes Mary, "to a cottage, but to a series of closets, the largest of which may be about eight feet square, which they call parlours and kitchens and pantries; some of them minus a corner, which has been unnaturally filched for a chimney; others deficient in half a side, which has been truncated by the shelving roof: a garden about the size of a good drawing-room, with an arbour which is a complete sentry-box of privet. On one side a public house, on the other a village shop, and right opposite a cobbler's stall."

Her mother, described as a cheerful and managing sort and who appears to have managed everything but her husband, died in 1830. The Doctor himself passed away in 1842. Mary herself lived until 1855. In 1837 she had been granted a pension of £100 a year, and later her father's debts were paid by a public subscription, among the list of subscribers being the Queen (privately), Mrs. Browning, Thomas Moore and Serjeant Talfourd.

3

Miss Mitford's best characteristic is perhaps her cheerfulness. In her case as in that of Dr. Johnson's friend this quality will keep breaking in. In the midst of her worst worries, on the occasion of the enforced removal to Three Mile Cross, she writes to her painter-friend, Sir William Elford:

"Notwithstanding all this, the cabin, as Bobadil says, is convenient. It is within reach of my dear old walks; the banks where I find my violets; the meadows full of cowslips; and the woods where the wood-sorrel blows. We are beginning to get settled and comfortable, and resuming our usual habits. Papa has already had the satisfaction of setting the neighbourhood to rights by committing a disorderly person, who was the pest of the Cross, to Bridewell. Mamma has furnished up an old dairy and made it into a not incommodious store room. I have lost my only key, and stuffed the garden with flowers. My little dog Molly, after a good deal of staring and squeaking and running about (she seemed conscious of some degradation from the change), has at last pitched upon a chair to lie on when I turn her out of my lap; and the great white cat, who was likewise very eloquent and out of his wits, has given this very evening most satisfactory proofs of finding himself at home, by resuming his ancient predatory habits and stealing all the milk for our tea. (N.B.—We were forced to go without.) Moreover, it is an excellent lesson in condensation—one which we all wanted.

Sir John Squire does not hesitate to describe "Our Village" as a classic. He says of the sketches in it: "They are not all about one village, or indeed any village: she drew on her memory for scenes and characters of all kinds and from all periods of her early life. But mostly she stayed round Reading, dwelling upon familiar rustic people, places, and seasons. She is equally felicitious painting portraits (not least of people with humours), describing domestic backgrounds, and taking country walks in all weathers. He who should wish to recover the 'interiors' of the period, the furniture, china, and fabrics in whatever rank of house, can find more in her than in any novelist; she is as faithful and full with the 'low life' of labourers and publicans, keepers, poachers, and milkmaids, as George Morland himself; to read her is to live in her village."

But not a word here about the writer's wit, that quality in her which gives me such delight! Far and away the best essay in her book, in my view, is that entitled "A County Cricket Match". Where an unwitty person would be content to say that the villagers had been forced to stop playing cricket on the Sabbath, Miss Mitford has this: "An unnatural coalition between a high-church curate and an evangelical gentleman farmer drove our lads from the Sunday-evening practice." Then consider this charming account of the defection from the team of the redoubtable blacksmith, James Brown:

"Brown was sent to Coventry; and when I first heard of his delinquency, I thought the punishment only too mild for the crime. But I have since learned the secret history of the offence (if we could know the secret histories of all offences, how much better the world would seem than it does now!), and really my wrath is much abated. It was a piece of gallantry, of devotion to the sex, or rather a chivalrous obedience to one chosen fair. I must tell my readers the story. Mary Allen, the prettiest girl of M——, had, it seems, revenged upon our blacksmith the numberless inconstancies of which he stood accused. He was in love over head and ears, but the nymph was cruel. She said no, and no, and no, and poor Brown, three times rejected, at last resolved to leave the place, partly in despair, and partly in that hope which often mingles strangely with a lover's despair, the hope that when he was gone he should be missed. He came home to his brother's accordingly; but for five weeks he heard nothing from or of the inexorable Mary, and was glad to beguile his own 'vexing thoughts' by endeavouring to create in his mind an artificial and fictitious interest in our cricket match—all unimportant as such a trifle must have seemed to a man in love. Poor James, however, is a social and warm-hearted person, not likely to resist a contagious sympathy. As the time for the play advanced, the interest which he had at first affected became genuine and sincere: and he was really, when he left the ground on Sunday night, almost as enthusiastically as absorbed in the event of the next day as Joel Brent himself. He little foresaw the new and delightful interest which awaited him at home, where, on the moment of his arrival, his sister-in-law and confidante presented him with a billet from the lady of his heart. It had, with the usual delay of letters sent by private hands in that rank of life, loitered on the road, in a degree inconceivable to those who are accustomed to the punctual speed of the post, and had taken ten days for its twelve miles' journey. Have my readers any wish to see this *billet-doux?* I can show them (but in strict confidence) a literal copy. It was addressed,

'For mistur jem browne
'blaxmith by
S——.'

The inside ran thus:'Mistur browne this is to Inform yew that oure parish plays bramley men next monday is a week, i think we shall lose without yew, from your humbell servant to command

'MARY ALLEN.'

Was there ever a prettier relenting? a summons more flattering, more delicate, more irresistible? The precious epistle was undated; but, having ascertained who brought it, and found, by cross-examining the messenger, that the Monday in question was the very next day, we were not surprised to find that *mistur browne* forgot his engagement to us, forgot all about Mary and Mary's letter, and set off at four o'clock next morning to walk twelve miles, and play for her parish, and in her sight. Really we must not send James Brown to Coventry—must we?"

"Was ever a summons more flattering, more delicate, more irresistible?" Or, we may ask, less true? We find Mary writing to Sir William Elford: "You, as a great landscape painter, know that in painting a favourite scene you do a little embellish, and can't help it; you avail yourself of happy accidents of atmosphere, and if anything be ugly, you strike it out, or if anything be wanting, you put it in." I have no doubt whatever that Mary Allen's letter was put in!

And now, reader, prepare for one of the prettiest strokes of the Mitford pen! This is a sentence in the same essay:

"But, alas! I have been so long settling my preliminaries that I have left myself no room for the detail of our victory, and must squeeze the account of our grand achievements into as little compass as Cowley, when he crammed the names of eleven of his mistresses into the narrow space of four eight-syllable lines."

This enchants me, since here Mitford dares even more than admit to herself the fact of male libertinage; she risks being known to her village as a person consenting to such knowledge! Think you, reader, that Cowley had *exactly* eleven mistresses? I suspect not. Mitford, as a great little writer, knew that she must here "a little embellish". She knew also that a cricket team is made up of eleven players, and that eleven must be the number of Cowley's mistresses, whether in truth it was less or more.

And now I would ask my reader to compare this wit of yesterday with one of the greatest wits of today, Mr. Osbert Sitwell. *She* writes this:

"*They* began the warfare—these boastful men of B——. And what think you, gentle reader, was the amount of their innings? These challengers—the famous eleven—how many did they get? Think! imagine! guess! You cannot? Well! they got twenty-two, or rather, they got twenty; for two of theirs were short notches, and would never have been allowed, only that, seeing what they were made of, we and our umpires were not particular. They should have had twenty more, if they had chosen to claim them. Oh, how well we fielded! and how well we bowled! Our good play had quite as much to do with their miserable failure as their bad. Samuel Long is a slow bowler, George Simmons a fast one, and the change from Long's lobbing to Simmons's fast balls posed them completely. Poor simpletons!

they were always wrong, expecting the slow for the quick, and the quick for the slow. Well, we went in. And what were our innings? Guess again!—guess! A hundred and sixty-nine! In spite of soaking showers, and wretched ground, where the ball would not run a yard, we headed them by a hundred and forty-seven; and then they gave in, as well they might. William Grey pressed them much to try another innings. 'There was so much chance', as he courteously observed, 'in cricket, that, advantageous as our position seemed, we might, very possibly, be overtaken. The B—— had better try.' But they were beaten sulky, and would not move—to my great disappointment; I wanted to prolong the pleasure of success. What a glorious sensation it is to be for five hours together winning—winning—winning! always feeling what a whist-player feels when he takes up four honours, seven trumps! Who would think that a little bit of leather and two pieces of wood had such a delightful and delighting power?"

He writes:

"At first the game was very silent, except for the drawing-room conversation of bat and ball; this wooden small-talk would proceed for some time, and then, suddenly, one of the talkers would snub the other, and away would run the fat white mice over the flat green baize. The banana-vendor was silent (why couldn't she have kept quiet before?) and weird women-enthusiasts, possibly the wives of the cricketers—epicene, tweed-clad figures, crowned with large straw-hats, wearing sensible-brown shoes with flapping and fantastic leather tongues lolling out of them, and, exhibiting, tucked into their coats, men's ties, blazoned in dreadful stripes that held for them some hidden significance—leant forward, watching with a flushed and strained inanity, or occasionally allowed it to be seen by a smile, glance, or exclamation, that they had duly followed some esoteric subtlety of form or style. The men were even less emotional. They sat there rigidly, smoking, occasionally tapping their pipes as a woodpecker taps its beak, against the wooden rail in front of them. One wondered if this was their way of communicating with their mates, some form of expression superseded in mankind by speech. But their round, clear eyes held in them no meaning that they could possibly wish to convey to anyone. Now and again there might be a flutter of excitement at some peculiarly imbecile sally, such as when a batsman allowed himself to be caught out, or the umpire decreed, in another case, the mystic 'l.b.w.'. Even the wooden contingent in the deck-chairs would then vibrate for a moment, while in the stands behind them there would be a seething of hats and handkerchiefs; but these outbursts were rare."

I know not whether Miss Mitford or Mr. Sitwell is the better wit; I know which is the better Englishman!

Her style must be said to have been at its best when she took least pains with it. When she is most easy at her desk she will, for example, describe a dull country-house as being like an "inhabited desert island", or a dandy six feet tall with huge shoulders and a pinched-in waist as "a wasp in a solar microscope, or a Brobdingnagian hour-glass, only I don't think the hour-glass would be small enough in the waist." Her imagination did not stop here, but went soaring after the adequate image. Not the Portsmouth Block-houses, nor the new Mint, she declared, gave her so high an idea of the power of machinery as "that perfection of mechanism by which those ribs are enclosed in those stays". The last sentence might have been Jane Austen's, and, indeed, it is of extraordinary interest to have Mary's picture of her great rival as she was in her youth:

"Mamma says that Miss Austen was the prettiest, silliest, most affected, husband-hunting butterfly she ever remembers; and a friend of mine, who visits her now, says that she has stiffened into the most perpendicular, precise, taciturn piece of single-blessedness that ever existed, and that, till *Pride and Prejudice* showed what a precious gem was hidden in that unbending case, she was no more regarded in society than a poker or a fire-screen. . . . She is still a poker—but a poker of whom everyone is afraid."

4

Much of the charm of the Mitford Letters comes from such pronouncements upon contemporary writers. It is a shock to find that she did not like Jane's Elizabeth Bennet, whom she described as too pert and too worldly a heroine to be loved of such a man as Darcy. Not like that character of whom Robert Louis Stevenson said that she had but to speak and he was at her knees! We find our authoress in full blast upon the subject of the fashionable Anna Seward, always an abominable and now a discredited poetess. Here she is in Mary's judgment: "The Venus and Muse of a provincial city; the one-eyed monarch of the blind at Lichfield, who thought nobody could see elsewhere; the pedantic coquette, and cold-hearted sensibility-monger: in a word, the female Dr. Darwin." Of Scott our letter-writer has much to say. "Waverley", whose authorship was still in dispute, cannot be the work of Dugald Stewart, whom Horace Walpole had acclaimed as a stylist. "Waverley", that half-French, half-English, half-Scotch, half-Gaelic, half-Latin, half-Italian hotch-potch, that "movable Babel", must be Scott: "There is not in the whole book one single page of pure and vernacular English, one single period of which you forget the sense in admiration of the sound." Later judgment has had nothing more to add. But it does not, like Mary, place Fenimore Cooper on Sir Walter's level.

Wordsworth in 1814 had passed his heyday, and his glory had not been reborn. Our Mary likes him little, perhaps because she had little taste for the monumental: "There is nothing heard of in London but Epics—ponderous Epics. Mr. Wordsworth has one, and Mr. Eustace is about to fatigue the world with another." And again: "I have been trying to admire Mr. Wordsworth's poetry. I do not mean by 'admire' merely to like and applaud those fine passages which all the world must like, but to admire *en masse*—all, every page, every line, every word, every comma; to admire nothing else, and to admire all day long. . . . Mr. Wordsworth not only exacts an entire relinquishment of all other tastes besides taste for his poetry, but if an unlucky votary chances to say, 'Of all your beautiful passages I most admire so-and-so,' he knocks him down by saying: 'Sir, I have a thousand passages more beautiful than that. Sir, you know nothing of the matter.' One's conscience may be pretty well absolved for not admiring this man; he admires himself enough for all the world put together."

Browning catches it hot. Those few things which are clear are weak as water; those on which his reputation rests are just riddles. Mary is told by Carlyle's admirers that "The French Revolution" is his greatest work. She concedes that it may be, but is convinced that nobody who did not know the story would gain the slightest idea of it from Mr. Carlyle's three volumes. And that, our critic says acidly, is not her idea of a history. The great man's prose, she adds, needs translating into English before it can be enjoyed—a remark which Wilde prigged to use again about Meredith! Emerson "would have been a greater writer and thinker if Carlyle had not fallen in his way." Nor does the greatest of all English novelists, one Charles, stand this severe contemporary test: "Look at the great novelists of the day, Dickens and Thackeray (although it is some injustice to Thackeray to class them together, for he can write good English when he chooses and produce a striking and consistent character); but look at their books, so thoroughly false and unhealthy in different ways; Thackeray's so world-stained and so cynical, Dickens's so meretricious in sentiment and so full of caricature. Compare them with Scott and Miss Austen, and then say if they can live. Neither of them can produce an intelligent, right-minded, straightforward woman, such as one sees every day; and a love story from Thackeray could hardly fail to be an abomination." But Mary did like Pickwick, whom she compared to the creations of Hogarth and Shakespeare. And this was praise from a critic who deemd Fielding's "Tom Jones" to be vastly overrated!

Reverting to Wordsworth, who appears to have been a bee in this busy bonnet: "When I was telling you some of Mr. Wordsworth's absurdities, did I tell you that he never dined? I have just had a letter from Mrs. Hofland, who has been with her husband to the Lakes, and spent some days at a Mr. Marshall's, for whom Mr. H. was painting a picture—but Mrs. Hofland shall speak for herself:—'On my return from Mr. M.'s to our Ullswater cottage, I encountered a friend who condoled with me on the dullness of my visit. "Dull! It was delightful." "The long *triste* dinners, the breakfasts, the suppers, the luncheons!" "To be sure fourteen people must eat, but these said dinners were anything but dull, I assure you. Why do you call them so?" "Because Mr. and Mrs. Wordsworth were staying there, and were so overcome by those shocking meals, that they were forced to come away. The Wordsworths never dine, you know; they hate such doings; when they are hungry they go to the cupboard and eat." ' "

5

At one period of her life Mary Mitford wrote plays—rombustious melodramas full of dukes and desperadoes. Macready once produced a tragedy by her entitled "Julian" which failed. Her views on the stage, however, were entirely and characteristically sensible:

> "By-the-way, when we were abusing Kemble, I wonder (only I believe that I was a little *dashed*) I did not tell you that I have a theory respecting play-writing and play-acting which Shakespeare certainly, and I think Garrick, contrived to realize. It does appear to me that no man can be a perfect tragedian who is not likewise a good actor in the higher branch of comedy. A statesman not at the council board, and a hero when the battle is safely ended, would, as it seems to me, talk and walk much in the same way with other people. Even a tyrant does not always rave, nor a lover always whine. A king may order his horse without a start, and a misanthrope talk of the weather without a groan. Now, Messrs. Kemble and Co. never do converse—they always declaim, and that not in the very best manner; so that between long pauses and unnatural cadences, the audience have nothing for it but to fall asleep and dream of Shakespeare."

And she had her own independent view, too, about Edmund Kean:

> "Well, I went to see Mr. Kean, and was thoroughly disgusted. This monarch of the stage is a little insignificant man, slightly deformed, strongly ungraceful, seldom pleasing the eye, still seldomer satisfying the ear—with a voice between grunting

and croaking, a perpetual hoarseness which suffocates his words, and a vulgarity of manner which his admirers are pleased to call nature—the nature of Teniers it may be, but not that of Rafaelle. I am quite sure that in any character where he can possibly raise his voice above conversation pitch—where there is anything like strong writing that he can contrive to rant, or anything resembling passion for him to tear to rags—his acting will always be, if not actually insupportable, yet unequal, disappointing, and destructive of all illusion. It is extremely dangerous to avow this heresy. Belles and beaux, who know as much of the drama as my Marmion, praise him in one word—'He electrifies me!' Clever men like him much, and praise him much more, because he is not Kemble, whom I dislike as much as they do; and then, for the *coup de grâce*, up starts some elderly gentleman and knocks you down at once with—'Madam, I have seen Garrick, and since the days of Garrick I never saw'—and so forth."

About a certain Mr. Thomas Hope and his resemblance to Byron:

"Did you, my dear friend, ever happen to read Mr. Thomas Hope's book about furniture? Or do you happen to recollect (which will do just as well) the famous quizzing the said book met with in the *Edinburgh Review?* The book itself seemed to me, when I saw it in a fine presentation copy, all scarlet and gold, to be a grand piece of furniture itself, and one as little made to be read as a chair or a table. Well, this Mr. Thomas Hope has, they say, written 'Anastasius'. The *New Monthly Magazine* says so; but that's rather an argument against the fact, inasmuch as the *New Monthly Magazine* does certainly, assertion for assertion, tell more lies than truths; but Lady Madalina Palmer says so on good authority; so that this incredible fact must be believed. Perhaps I am talking Greek to you all this time, and you have not read 'Anastasius'. Well then, it's a book which, but for this testimony, I should from internal evidence have attributed at once to that prince of wickedness and poetry, Lord Byron. It's altogether Grecian; is not that like Lord Byron? It's exceedingly sceptical; is not that like Lord Byron? It complains of a jealous wife; is not that like Lord Byron? It is full of fine and gloomy poetry (in prose), which is of the very same style with Lord Byron's. It is still fuller of the light derisive mockery—the tossing about of all good feeling, so gibing and so Voltaireish, which no one could or would do but Lord Byron. It is a most uncomfortable book—is not that like Lord Byron? And lastly, it is all full of the sneering, misanthropic wretched author; is not that Lord Byron?"

About Mme D'Arblay:

"I do not think very highly of Madame D'Arblay's books. The style is so strutting. She does so stalk about on Dr. Johnson's old stilts. What she says wants too much translating into common English, and when translated would seem so commonplace, that I have always felt strongly tempted to read all the serious parts with my fingers' ends."

And again:

"As to the little Burney, I don't like her at all, and that's the truth. A girl of the world—a woman of the world, for she was twenty-seven or thereabout—thought clearly and evidently of nothing on this earth but herself and 'Evelina'.

The letter following this in the Brimley Johnson collection begins: "Mine Own Love—I have had a wandering poetess here today." This is addressed—and I write it with a thrill—"To Miss Barrett, Wimpole Street."

About William Chambers, the Edinburgh publisher:

"He came to pay me a visit, and has assisted us by a good deal of information and advice, such as getting parishes to agree and interchange their libraries. He says that the obstacles to all education in England and Scotland are the clergy.

I am quite of that mind from my own experience, but I did not expect to hear him say so. He is a very superior person. He has persuaded Miss Edgeworth to write a book for young people—remarkable considering her age, for she must be turned of eighty, but still one that justifies my theory of not writing too long, inasmuch as it reads just like an imitation of her own better works. It is called 'Orlandino', and is a story of a lad reformed from drinking by a younger lad."

About dancing:

"What, indeed, should I do at a dance with my dumpling of a person tumbling about like a cricket-ball on uneven ground, or a bowl rolling among nine-pins—casting off with the grace of a frisky Yorkshire cow, or going down the middle with the majesty of an overloaded hay-waggon passing through a narrow lane? What should I do at a ball?"

About the Alps she has this: "Great authors are great people—but I believe they are best seen at a distance. The Alps are only fit for the background of a picture, and not always for that."

And here is a characteristic sally: "You can't conceive what a thief I am in my heart. I went to Lord Rivers's the other day to see his stud, and I was seized with a prodigious inclination to steal near a hundred greyhounds."

That is what I like about the Mitford wit—it's quietness. She would put a whole roomful of Max's Mrs. Cryptic-Sparklers to silence with a cold douche of plain common sense. No woman's thoughts were ever less out of the way; and none that I know of has turned her thought more entertainingly. Her wit must have been a great compensation for her physical plainness, for as she herself confesses in a letter quoted above, she was a dumpling to the view. Mary is to me one of the great letter-writers, far closer to my heart than your wan Dorothy Osbornes and wordy Wortley Montagus. Here is a complete example, written to her father:

To Dr. Mitford, New Slaughter's Coffee House.

August 8, 1811.

Mamma says the great art of letter-writing is to construct an epistle without one possible subject. And truly, if such be the fact, no two people have a better opportunity of improving in this way than those who have the honour of sending you a sheet full of nothings. Indeed, my dearest love, upon a careful revision of our letters I do not suppose that upon an average they would be found to contain one piece of intelligence a week; unless, indeed, you may call it news to hear that our ci-devant *dairymaid Harriet, who has now the honour of assisting in Mrs. Curtis's seminary for young ladies, is reported to have consented, at the request of her admirer, William, to leave her place at Michaelmas in order to share his fate and Mrs. Adam's cottage. God help them, poor fools; what will become of them! Two such dawdles never existed.*

Marmion is more beautiful than ever. He will certainly win the cup at Ilsley this year. I hope you mean to run him, my pet. He has an hereditary claim to it.

Fanny Rowden cannot mean to assert that all who have breathed the air of 22 *Hans Place must be female Solomons! If she does, Heaven help her! Don Quixote, when he took the fair nymph of the inn for the daughter of the Governor of the Castle, did not make a greater mistake. I am very anxious to see the 'Triumphs of Religion'. Miss Cope has reaped a golden harvest; but I am much mistaken if 'Suicide' be equally successful. Those sort of begging experiments never answer above once.*

Mammy and all the pets desire their love. They are all well.

Ever and ever,
Most fondly and faithfully your own,
Mary Russell Mitford.

Brimley Johnson has left us a reassuring account of her last days: "She enjoyed the sweets of popularity, and a pilgrimage to Three Mile Cross had become something of an institution. If 'within one week a young friend had asked her to edit her poems, another to write up and present her Tragedy, a third person (whom she had never seen) to read an MS. novel'; on the other hand, 'very few ever went away disappointed from the narrow, comfortless presence-chamber of the grey-haired lady, who beamed upon her guests from that wonderful wall of a forehead, and welcomed them so cordially with a most admirable voice'." . . . He tells us that there was now "a very pathetic expression about her mouth and in her large, slowly moving, sad, grey eyes, though they lighted up every now and then with a glancing gleam of the drollest humour".

Her end shows a certain resemblance to that of another great Englishwoman. She had moved to a charming cottage at Swallowfield, after which came a time when she was wheeled about in a bathchair until on January 10th, 1855, in her sixty-eighth year, she passed away "so peacefully that she hardly knew which moment was her last". At that very hour the Crimean War was raging. Or you might put it that in full Crimean War Miss Florence Nightingale was raging—Miss Nightingale who also was to end her days in a bathchair, and whose last recorded utterance was: "Too kind—too kind!" Mary Russell Mitford had been too kind to her father, and it is pleasant to know that in the end the world was kind to her.

WITS' END